The Radical Acceptance

of Everything

Living a Focusing Life

by Ann Weiser Cornell

and featuring Barbara McGavin

 CALLUNA PRESS

CALLUNA PRESS
2625 Alcatraz Ave., #202
Berkeley, CA 94705-2702
USA
510-666-9948

Cover image: Kim Sohee
Design and layout: Barbara McGavin

ISBN 0-9721058-3-2

For my beloved first family

Audra H. Weiser 1919-2002
David W. Weiser 1921-1988
Mark D. Weiser 1952-1999
Mona W. Holmes 1953-1999

radically unconditional love

and for my nieces and nephews who fill my life with
delight

Nicole, Josh, Corinne, and Christopher

ALSO BY ANN WEISER CORNELL

The Power of Focusing:
A Practical Guide to Emotional Self-Healing

ALSO BY ANN WEISER CORNELL
& BARBARA MCGAVIN

The Focusing Student's and Companion's Manual,
Parts One and Two

Contents

✳ newly written for this book
○ co-authored with Barbara McGavin
❖ by Barbara McGavin

Introduction

This book is a collection of nineteen of my articles that have been previously published (but usually in places that are hard to access today), four new articles I wrote especially for this book, and one very special article by Barbara McGavin. I began learning the Focusing process in 1972, and I began writing about it around 1983. Why is *this* the right time, after 22 years, to publish a collection of these articles? And how am I hoping people will use this book?

Kierkegaard said that we live our lives forward but we understand them backward. As I hold this book in my hands, I have a sense of the life and work that I have been creating over the last thirty-some years. There are themes that emerge, and I can begin to say what some of them are:

(1) An inner process of *radical acceptance* – being in a state of *Presence* – is an astonishingly facilitative environment for emotional healing.

(2) There are processes that enhance an *inner relationship* between an "I" in Presence and a "something" which needs Presence.

(3) Many of these facilitative processes are *linguistic;* they have to do with a *facilitative use of language.*

(4) Not everything that needs our attention is in our awareness; some aspects have been *exiled* and need to be invited back again. (So *radical acceptance of everything* includes acceptance of aspects not in awareness.)

(5) The experience of helping another person find the *inner relationship* of Focusing (also called "felt sensing") is subtle, rewarding, humbling, and endlessly fascinating.

(6) People can be amazingly facilitative for each other, by not much more than being there and saying some of the other person's words back. This is the gift of *Focusing partnership.*

(7) My own ongoing journey as a healing, awakening person is intimately connected to (can't be separated from) what I can give to or be for others.

As I sit with this list of seven themes, I feel an uneasy sense. The list sounds rather dry and abstract compared with how delicious and rich it has felt to live this work. *And* I can feel how the list is incomplete... but I know that if I tried to add to it, it would still be incomplete. Holding the book, with the 24 articles and their introductions, feels more complete.

In choosing the articles for this book I had three criteria. They needed to be (1) influential, (2) relevant today, and (3) my personal favorites. After I had chosen nineteen articles that met those criteria, I realized that some major areas of my work were missing, so I wrote four more articles to fill those gaps. Finally, I decided to include an article by Barbara McGavin (with her permission) because it had changed my life so profoundly and has formed the basis of all of my work since I read it. In addition, five of the other articles published here were co-authored with Barbara McGavin, and many of those not officially co-authored with her are drawn from our collaborative work, especially in the Treasure Maps to the Soul section.

How might this book be used? I am imagining four kinds of readers – though of course one person might fit more than one category.

First, I am hoping that you will be drawn to this book if you are involved in your own emotional healing, pursuing some of the issues I'm engaged with here: releasing action blocks, transforming self-criticism, reclaiming exiled parts of your self. This includes everyone who is touched by the words "radical acceptance of everything" and who feels an inner sense of "wanting more of that."

Second, I'm hoping for an audience of people who want to go deeper into the remarkable Focusing *(felt-sensing)* process developed by my teacher, Eugene Gendlin. Almost all of my articles were written originally for Focusing "insiders," people who knew what the Focusing process was and were able to do it. Many of the articles were published in *The Focusing Connection* newsletter, which is published for people using Focusing in their lives.

I am hoping that this book of articles will be accessible to people interested in Focusing but new to it. I have done my best to clarify what may be unclear, in the introductions to the articles, as well as including some articles at the start of the book that introduce the process. But if you find yourself wanting to experience Focusing yourself (not always easy from a book!), the very best way is to have a one-to-one Focusing session with a Focusing teacher. I've included a Resources section in the back to help you connect with the worldwide Focusing community.

The third kind of reader I envision would be Focusing teachers like myself. We teach Focusing in one-to-one sessions and in workshops, or perhaps we are therapists, life coaches, spiritual counselors, bodyworkers, etc., who bring Focusing into our sessions. Near the end of the book is a section "For Focusing Teachers" where I've put some of the newest articles, because this is an area that remains at the leading edge of my work. I welcome a dialogue about how we can be facilitative to the wonderful variety of people we encounter, while still remaining true to ourselves.

And finally, I have in mind an academic kind of reader, who is interested in the contribution these articles might make to the ongoing understanding of psychological process, emotional healing, and facilitative language. That is a large enterprise; I'm happy to make these articles more accessible so that these ideas too can be refined and improved in the mill of those discussions.

What is Focusing? It's a process of awareness, a learned process and also a natural one, that involves sensing inwardly, in the body, the whole way it feels in there about situations in one's life. The uneasy feeling in the pit of the stomach, for example, that tells one that something is funny, not right, in the room one has just walked into... We are familiar with that kind of sensation, but we often don't know, until learning the Focusing process, how every situation can give a "felt sense" like that, or how those felt senses can open up, reveal intricate information, and release, relax, shift.

Focusing was identified, named, and developed as a taught process by Dr. Eugene Gendlin. It is based on research he and colleagues did in the late 50s and early 60s, and also based on his groundbreaking work in philosophy. His book, *Focusing*, appeared in 1978, and since its appearance people from all over the world have sought him out for workshops and training, many becoming Trainers (Focusing Professionals) in turn. The Focusing process now has a presence in over 25 countries, with the largest communities in the US, Canada, Germany, Japan, the Netherlands, the UK, and Argentina. Gendlin's nonprofit Focusing Institute, based in New York, helps connect people with Focusing teachers and therapists using Focusing, and has an online bookstore that includes books, audio tapes, CDs, and videotapes. Their immensely helpful web site is www.focusing.org.

Focusing has a history, and so do I.

I first met Focusing in 1972, when I was a 22-year-old grad student in Linguistics at the University of Chicago. The story of my own evolution can also be found in the pages of this book: how Focusing was difficult for me at first, how I became a Focusing teacher almost by accident, how and why my teaching of Focusing evolved and transformed from the ways I had been taught. You'll find my prejudices and my passions on every page, and I hope the glimpses into the personal side of my story will be entertaining and help you connect personally to the concepts and methods presented here.

I need to say a word about the contribution of Barbara McGavin to this book. You will find her woven all the way through it. Few people are gifted with the privilege of true collaboration. Barbara and I have worked together so closely for so many years that the question who came up with which ideas is essentially meaningless (though I've long suspected that the most brilliant ones are hers). My gratitude and appreciation for her are far beyond my ability to express.

Other people to thank: Neil Friedman, whose excellent collection of articles, *Focusing: Selected Essays,* is an admired model for this one;

My first Focusing teachers, Elfie Hinterkopf and Les Brunswick; my first Focusing partners, Danny Massad, Jane Batt, and Judy Wyatt; Reva Bernstein, my first longtime Focusing partner, and Bonnie Davenport, my second, all for their endless patience with me;

Bebe Simon, the true mother of Inner Relationship Focusing ("Maybe you could ask it where it would like to go");

Rob Foxcroft, who eternally returns to the essence of Focusing, sensitively guards the right of people to take responsibility for each other, and never lets us forget the philosophy behind it all;

Ed McMahon and Peter Campbell, for their enormously valuable emphasis on Caring Feeling Presence;

Margaret Warner, for inviting me into her family therapy sessions as a cotherapist in 1980, for writing with me, and for her own remarkable gifts as therapist and theoretician – and friend;

Joan Lavender, for starting with the periphery of the body that day in Chicago in the early 80s, and for all those great conversations since;

Jay Cornell, for the metaphor of the shy animal at the edge of the woods, and for insisting I put my photo in that first brochure;

Dave Young, for making the distinction between visual images and body-based images, and then making sure that I got it;

Kevin McEvenue, genius at Presence, for sharing the mutual spark in 1989 that led to "Living with Focusing," and for saying "when a part of us feels that it is loved, it awakens to its own healing";

Elena Frezza, beautiful wise woman, for following that impulse in 1989 that led to Focusing flourishing in Argentina and a lifelong friendship;

Mieko Osawa, connoisseur and world traveler, for inviting me to Japan and for thoughtful translations of my work, but most of all for taking her time;

Christine Langeveld and Erna de Bruijn, for inciting me to create evernew workshop topics, for introducing me to the delights of the North Sea, and for having the most peaceful garden on earth;

Jane Bell, for being my Focusing partner through some of the most mysterious parts of my process, and for being a shining, brave, brilliant example of how to live a manifesting life;

Wilja Westerhof, for friendship, feedback, and believing in me;

Robin Winn, for challenging me to do sessions and teach workshops from the lower part of my body (although that's not how she said it!);

Kohlim Jaeger, whose passion for excellence and astonishing range of abilities make me the luckiest employer in the world;

Kathryn Bader, graphic designer extraordinaire, for coming through in the final stretches;

Helene Brenner and Larry Letich for love, brilliance, friendship, and for making me a lifetime member in the Happy Outcomes Club, and Joy and Maya Brenner-Letich for being such fine examples of happy outcomes themselves;

Beatrice Raue-Konietzny, for angelic friendship;

Gisela Uhl and Rob Parker, brave co-travelers in the realms of *A Process Model;*

Carole Ervine, whose steady Focusing partnership during the Cumbrae week in 2004 prepared me for an extremely productive writing weekend in Glasgow, and all the Cumbrae week philosophers, for unforgettable embodied intellectual stimulation and friendship;

Sharon Zamkovitz, excellent Focusing teacher, for showing me how to drive a U-Haul and talk like a truck driver and for showing up (time after time) when I needed it the most;

Judy Schavrien, for believing in me and standing by me always; and

Gene Gendlin, *sine qua non.*

Finally, eternal gratitude to my wise and indomitable daughter, Mika Berman, who never lets me get away with not listening to her, and to my irrepressible partner, Joseph McBride, author of fifteen books and counting, to whom we owe the fact that most of the commas in this book are in the right places, and who is still trying to get me to write *The Sexual Secrets of the Focusing Masters.* Sorry, Joe, maybe next time.

Berkeley, California
May 2005

The Radical
Acceptance of
Everything

*We'll begin our journey into this territory with some
articles introducing Focusing, including the story of my
own first involvement with it, followed by some articles
introducing some of the other important concepts in this
book, including identification, exile, and Presence.*

*The original article "The Radical Acceptance of
Everything" is joined here by its sequel, written ten years
later. We learn that "radical acceptance" of whatever
comes in an inner process is rather different from accepting every outer circumstance, yet it sets up a unique precondition for positive change.*

*An article written for this book, never before pub-
lished, "Facilitating Presence," shows in practical terms
how to invite a form of radical acceptance, called
"Presence," at those times when it is most needed.*

*And finally, we offer Barbara McGavin's life-
changing article about offering radical acceptance to a
part that wants to die.*

What is Focusing?

Co-authored with Barbara McGavin
From The Focusing Student's and Companion's Manual, *2002*

The core of Focusing is a natural human process of sensing within and resonating the symbols that emerge with your inner felt experience.

When was the last time you sat down and let yourself become quiet, and then brought a listening, getting-to-know-what's-there type of awareness to your own inner self? If you're like most people in modern developed countries, such moments are rare. It seems our lives are moving faster and faster, with less and less time to listen to the whispers within.

Focusing is a radical departure from the usual ways we operate in our culture. When you learn Focusing, you learn to be with your own sensations and feelings, and you discover that they have communications for you. You learn to turn toward what you are feeling with interested curiosity, rather than being caught up in feelings and acting out of them. You find out how to include and accept all sorts of inner experiences, with no need to take sides in an inner war that labels some parts of you as "bad."

At first, it will be easier to practice Focusing by setting aside a special time to do it, ideally with a friend, as we will show you. But after you learn Focusing you will be able to do it sitting, standing, walking, driving... You will be able to live your life from a Focusing place, in a Focusing way. You will be able to know, from moment to moment, whether what you are doing is coming out of your truest sense of yourself, and how that feels.

Focusing is used in many areas: with personal problems, combined with art, writing, movement, health care, psychotherapy, with children, stress management, in relationships, education, developing new ideas in philosophy, art, architecture... The list goes on and on. Focusing can be everywhere in your life, at work, as you do your shopping, talk with your children or partner, read a book, go for a walk in the woods, write a poem.

In our culture we are used to associating intelligence with the brain. Learning and practicing Focusing will bring you in touch with a larger intelligence inside you, an intelligence that is body-based and that can sense what needs your attention – that you can trust and follow.

In these pages we will show you what we consider a "simple" form of Focusing. Even so, it has many stages and may seem rather complex. We invite you to remember that Focusing itself is simple – far simpler than the words that can be said about it. The stages we teach are like training wheels: they are there to help you until you don't need them anymore. As you practice Focusing, more and more you will find yourself setting down the book, setting down the cards, and just following your body's sense with interested attention. That's Focusing.

Introduction to
Three Key Aspects of Focusing

This article is excerpted from the audiotape called "Introduction to Focusing" (available from www.focusingresources.com), which I created as a way for people to get further acquainted with Focusing. I envisioned it as something I could hand to my students, as something they could hand to their families and friends, and as an alternative to offering introductory talks about Focusing. I must have done a pretty good job distilling the essence of Focusing, because this excerpt was chosen by the Focusing Institute to appear on its website, and in countless International Conference packets, in the years since it was written.

Since some of you are still wondering what Focusing is, this is a good spot for it in this book.

Three Key Aspects of Focusing

Appeared in The Focusing Connection, *March 1998*

There are three key qualities or aspects which set Focusing apart from any other method of inner awareness and personal growth. The first is something called the "felt sense." The second is a special quality of engaged, accepting inner attention. And the third is a radical philosophy of what facilitates change. Let's take these one by one.

The Focusing process involves coming into the body and finding there a special kind of body sensation called a "felt sense." Eugene Gendlin was the first person to name and point to a felt sense, even though human beings have been having felt senses as long as they've been human. A felt sense, to put it simply, is a body sensation that has meaning. You've certainly been aware of a felt sense at some time in your life, and possibly you feel them often.

Imagine being on the phone with someone you love who is far away, and you really miss that person, and you just found out in this phone call that you're not going to be seeing them soon. You get off the phone, and you feel a heaviness in your chest, perhaps around the heart area. Or let's say you're sitting in a room full of people and each person is going to take a turn to speak, and as the turn comes closer and closer to you, you feel a tightness in your stomach, like a spring winding tighter and tighter. Or let's say you're taking a walk on a beautiful fresh morning, just after a rain, and you come over a hill, and there in the air in front of you is a perfect rainbow, both sides touching the ground, and as you stand there and gaze at it you feel your chest welling up with an expansive, flowing, warm feeling. These are all felt senses.

If you're operating purely with emotions, then fear is fear. It's just fear, no more. But if you're operating on the felt sense level, you can sense that *this* fear, the one you're feeling right now, is different from the fear you felt yesterday. Maybe yesterday's fear was like a cold rock in the stomach, and today's fear is like a pulling back, withdrawing. As you stay with today's fear, you start to sense something like a shy creature pulled back into a cave. You get the feeling that if you sit with it long enough, you might even find out the real reason that it is so scared. A felt sense is often subtle, and as you pay attention to it you discover that it is intricate. It has more to it. We have a vocabulary of emotions that we feel over and over again, but every felt sense is different. You can, however, start with an emotion, and then feel the felt sense of it, as you are feeling it in your body right now.

Felt sensing is not something that other methods teach. There is no one else, outside of Focusing, who is talking about this dimension of experience which is not emotion and not thought, which is subtle yet concretely felt, absolutely physically real. Felt sensing is one of the things that makes it Focusing.

The second key aspect of Focusing is a *special quality of engaged accepting inner attention.*

In the Focusing process, after you are aware of the felt sense, you then bring to it a special quality of attention. One way I like to say this is, you *sit down to get to know it better.* I like to call this quality "interested curiosity." By bringing this interested curiosity into a relationship with the felt sense, you are open to sensing that which is there but not yet in words. This process of sensing takes time – it is not instant. So ideally there is a willingness to take that time, to wait, at the edge of not-yet-knowing what this is, patient, accepting, curious, and open. Slowly, you sense more. This can be a bit like coming into a darkened room and sitting, and as your eyes get used to the lower light, you sense more there than you had before. You could also have come into that room and then rushed away again, not caring to sense anything there. It is the caring to, the interest, the wanting to get to know it, that brings the further knowing.

There is not a trying to change anything. There is no doing something *to* anything. In this sense, this process is very *accepting.* We accept that this felt sense is here, just as it is, right now. We are interested in *how* it is. We want to know it, just as it is.

Yet there is something more than just accepting. In this *interested curious* inner attention, there is also a confident expectation that this felt sense will change in its own way, that it will do something that Gene Gendlin calls "making steps." What is "making steps"?

The inner world is never static. When you bring awareness to it, it unfolds, moves, becomes its next step.

A woman is Focusing, let's say, on a heavy feeling in her chest which she feels is connected with a relationship with a friend. The Focuser recently left her job, and she has just discovered that the friend is applying for the position. She has been telling herself that this is not important, but the feeling of something wrong has persisted. Now she sits down to Focus.

She brings awareness into the throat-chest-stomach area of her body and she soon discovers this heavy feeling which has been around all week. She says hello to it. She describes it freshly: "heavy... also tight... especially in the stomach and chest." Then she sits with it to get to know it better. She is interested and curious. Notice how this interested and curious is the opposite of the telling herself that this is not important which she had been doing before. She waits, with this engaged accepting attention.

She can feel that this part of her is angry. "How could she? How could she do that?" it says about her friend. Ordinarily she would be tempted to tell herself that being angry is inappropriate, but this is Focusing, so she just says to this place, "I hear you," and keeps waiting. Interested and curious for the "more" that is there.

In a minute she begins to sense that this part of her is also sad. "Sad" surprises her; she didn't expect sad. She asks, "Oh, what gets you sad?" In response, she senses that it is something about being invalidated. She waits, there is more. Oh, something about not being believed! When she gets that, *something about not being believed,* a rush of memories comes, all the times she told her friend how difficult her boss was to work for. "It's as if she didn't believe me!" is the feeling.

Now our Focuser is feeling relief in her body. This has been a *step*. The emergence of sad after the anger was also a step. The Focusing process is a series of steps of change, in which each one brings fresh insight, and a fresh body relief, an *aha!* Is this the end? She could certainly stop here. But if she wanted to continue, she would go back to the "something about not being believed" feeling and again bring to it interested curiosity. It might be that there's something special for her about not being believed, something linked to her own history, which again brings relief when it is heard and understood.

Focusing brings insight and relief, but that's not all it brings. It also brings new behavior. In the case of this woman, we can easily imagine that her way of being with her friend will now be more open, more appropriately trusting. It may also be that other areas of her life were bound up with this "not being believed" feeling, and they too will shift after this process. This new behavior happens naturally, easily, without having to be done by will power or effort. And this brings us to the third special quality of Focusing.

The third key quality or aspect which sets Focusing apart from any other method of inner awareness and personal growth is *a radical philosophy of what facilitates change.*

How do we change? How do we *not* change? If you are like many of the people who are drawn to Focusing, you probably feel *stuck* or *blocked* in one or more areas of your life. There is *something* about you, or your circumstances, or your feelings and reactions to things, that you would like to change. That is very natural. But let us now contrast two ways of approaching this wish to change.

One way assumes that to have something change, you must make it change. You must do something to it. We can call this the Doing/Fixing way.

The other way, which we can call the Being/Allowing way, assumes that change and flow is the natural course of things, and when something seems not to change, what it needs is attention and awareness, with an attitude of allowing it to be as it is, yet open to its next steps.

Our everyday lives are deeply permeated with the Doing/Fixing assumption. When you tell a friend about a problem, how often is her response to give you advice on fixing the problem? Many of our modern therapy methods carry this assumption as well. Cognitive therapy, for example, asks you to change your self-talk. Hypnotherapy often brings in new images and beliefs to replace the old. So the Being/Allowing philosophy, embodied in Focusing, is a radical philosophy. It *turns around* our usual expectations and ways of viewing the world. It's as if I were to say to you that this chair you are sitting on would like to become an elephant, and if you will just give it interested attention it will begin to transform. What a wild idea! Yet that is how wild it sounds, to some deeply ingrained part of ourselves, when we are told that a fear that we have might transform into something which is not at all fear, if it is given interested attention.

When people who are involved in Focusing talk about the "wisdom of the body," this is what they mean: that the felt sense "knows" what it needs to become next, as surely as a baby knows it needs warmth and comfort and food. As surely as a radish seed knows it will grow into a radish. We never have to tell the felt sense what to become; we never have to make it change. We just need to provide the conditions which allow it to change, like a good gardener providing light and soil and water, but not telling the radish to become a cucumber.

How I Met Focusing

Appeared in The Focusing Connection, *March 2004*

It's hard to write about those times, because I can say, "I was confused" – and I was, very confused – but then it sounds as if I knew I was confused, and I didn't. As I look back, it's like seeing a woman with thought-balloons all around her head. They would tell her what was going on for her if she would only read them – but she doesn't. They float around with her, unread and unchanging, and as I look back, I can see them. She doesn't even know they're there.

So I sat in that room, on the day that would change my life forever – it was the library of the University Church but it had nothing to do with the church, or the university. I was 22 years old, a graduate student in Linguistics at the University of Chicago, reasonably brilliant when it came to ideas and theories and a total, absolute moron when it came to feelings.

I sat in that room feeling all sorts of things and not knowing I was feeling them. The man in the front of the room looked almost absurdly relaxed – mellow, as we said then. For one thing, he was sitting on a table. I had known some very laid-back university professors, and some of them had leaned on tables as if they would have liked to sit on them, but no one before had ever actually sat on one, cross-legged, bonelessly relaxed, talking to us as if we were friends his own age sitting in his living room, instead of fifty people crammed into the space, fifty people of all ages and colors and social conditions but mostly students, like me, straining to hear, wanting to understand what this guy was saying to us. I had been told by two different friends that this was the place to be, this was What Was Happening on Sunday night in this university neighborhood of Chicago, and I was there.

The unread thought-balloons said: I'm nervous. I wonder if people will like me. I hope I can get this right. I hope I can get this right really quickly so that people admire me for how good I am. I feel strange, I don't fit here, I don't fit anywhere, my body feels too big, I have to figure out the way to be here, I have to figure out what will make other people comfortable and do that, so they'll let me stay.

His name was Eugene Gendlin but everyone called him "Gene," even his own graduate students, no "Mister," no "Doctor" or "Professor." He told us we belonged here, that that was the first rule of this space: "If you're here, you belong here." That felt good because this was a meeting organized by and for psychology students; if there had been rules about who didn't belong, they probably would have excluded me.

Earlier, an energetic woman with a blond pony-tail had told us some of the history of these Sunday night meetings. It was 1972; twenty-nine months earlier, nearly a decade of student unrest and popular protest of the U.S.'s ill-fated war in Vietnam had been capped by the tragic killing of four students at Kent State, and two at Jackson State. A wave of college closings had followed. A group of psychology students at the University of Chicago had felt the call to do something, to participate, to be part of the solution, to be on the bus. But simply marching or striking or sitting had felt too anonymous. They wanted to do something that they were uniquely suited to do. They decided they would start a crisis hotline, a place where people could phone up and find a listener, and more – people could also find a place to sleep ("crash"), maybe some work, maybe some low-cost medical care.

They had asked one of their professors, Gene Gendlin, to give training in listening skills for those operating the hotline. They started meeting with him on Sunday nights to learn and practice Listening and "Focusing," a self-awareness skill he had developed. The Sunday night meetings became a community in themselves. When people called on the hotline, and complained of being lonely, they were invited over for Sunday night. There was no distinction between those who came to help and those who came to be helped. It was assumed that we all needed to be listened to, and we all could listen. By the time I showed up, it had been going for over a year, and far more people were coming for the Sunday night training and "community" than for the hotline.

It was called "Changes," after the catch-phrase "goin' through changes."

I've told my own Focusing students that it was hard for me to learn Focusing at first. They don't know the half of it. Week after week I tried – and failed. I just couldn't get it. I was jealous of these people, these others, with their tears and their anger and their rotten childhoods. It felt like they had the meat of our work, the feelings, and I had none. I remembered my childhood as ordinary-OK, pretty good most of the time, with a cheerful mother and a father who took us out on enthusiastic trips like to see the first Sputnik go overhead – no deaths, no beatings, no divorces, nothing very bad. I didn't feel sad. I never felt angry. The worst that I felt was sort of large, awkward, out of place, embarrassed – and I wasn't sure that counted. Even that was so easy to ignore that I doubted I was really feeling it. Maybe I was making it up so I'd have something at least to focus on, when the others were talking about their anger at their fathers and their rage at their mothers.

That first night, a Sunday early in October in 1972, Gene led us through an exercise. I wasn't the only beginner there that night, but to me it looked like everyone else in the room was closing their eyes like old hands, hunkering down in their places, looking like everyone but me knew exactly what they were doing. Gene said, "Now go to the place where you have feelings," and I didn't have a clue what he was talking about. He could have been talking about flying to the moon.

I have a vivid memory of trying to feel something, trying to find the inner feelings that he was talking about. I saw my insides like a calm pool, nothing happening. I wanted so much for there to be something, but there wasn't. At the same time, when I look back, there are all those unread thought-balloons, all those inner events that were happening but weren't noticed, didn't count. Can I do this? Will I ever be able to do this? Is there something wrong with me? Will Danny want to focus with me? Do I belong? Will I be accepted? Am I OK?

The inner life of feeling is not such a difficult thing to be in touch with. Training in not-feeling has to begin early, and be very thorough. In the sixteen years of my childhood, I saw my mother angry once, and scared once. Neither time did she acknowledge her feelings – those were simply the only times I remember seeing them on her face and in her body. I couldn't have said, "Mom, are you angry?" Feelings were unspeakable, more unspeakable than bathroom words, sex words. Don't feel, don't notice, don't talk about it.

What isn't noticed or spoken about becomes unreal. Dad's drinking, his mood swings, his depression – they were never noticed or spoken about, so they didn't exist. At age 22, trying to learn to focus, trying to remember my childhood, I literally did not remember the way Dad would lash out with criticism and sarcasm when he felt bad about himself. It was as if there was a family story, a "party line," and the party line was that we were "Fine." We were a happy family, we enjoyed doing things together, we loved each other. End of story.

Dad wasn't self-absorbed, depressed, critical and sarcastic, so I had no feelings in response. How could I? How can you have feelings about something that isn't happening?

When I was sixteen years old, my family was in the midst of a painfully difficult and upsetting situation – which no one was talking about. For nine years, Dad had been the Dean of Faculty of a small midwestern college, gathering a brilliant group of fine teachers, luring them from around the country with promises of unprecedented academic freedom. Now Dad and the faculty he had gathered were in a power struggle with the President and the faculty *he* had gathered, and it looked like Dad was losing. Dad had accepted a temporary appointment at Cornell University, a thousand miles away. Half the faculty, our dear friends and support circle, were leaving. Mom didn't know what she was going to do with a house and three children. Our life was crashing down around our ears. No one was talking about it.

In the midst of that, I sat my mother down at the kitchen table and told her that I was going to spend the summer in California, living with my boyfriend. In effect, I was telling her that I was having sex with my boyfriend. Tears of fear and helpless anger came into her eyes. "Don't you know," she said in a choked voice, "that fornication is illegal?"

Finally I got sick and tired of seeing all the people around me have deep and powerful Focusing sessions, and getting nothing myself. I was determined, bound and determined, that this next session was going to be a deep one.

The custom was to meet in pairs during the week, to practice the skills we were learning on Sunday nights. This was called "Focusing partnership." I had three or four Focusing partners, and one of them was Danny. When I was Listening and it was Danny's turn to focus, he had wonderfully interesting sessions about his anger at his father for forbidding him to go to art school. I was terribly envious of those sessions. It was on the way over to Danny's student apartment for a partnership exchange that I found myself filled with determination: "By God, I'm going to have a deep session, too!"

I lay down on the floor, something we usually didn't do – the custom was to focus sitting – and Danny sat near me, quiet and attentive. I closed my eyes and I felt myself going deep. I had a vague idea that I was going to focus on those feelings of being too big, awkward, out of place in social situations. There was a swirling sensation, and then there was a memory.

I never fit in, and I never understood why not. It was constant pain, all through my school days, from third grade through eighth. I wasn't accepted, I wasn't liked, and being sensitive and smart I knew it. I received every message that said, "You're weird, we don't like you," and I took it deep inside myself, like poison, like knives.

That was the memory that came to me, lying on Danny's floor in that Chicago apartment, and for the first time I let myself feel the yearning to belong, to be accepted, the loneliness, the feeling of knowing in my bones that I was odd, weird, unliked. The pain of being jeered at, peered at, mocked. For the first time, all of that could be felt, known. It existed. Until it existed, it couldn't be changed.

The feeling of being excluded and yearning to belong reminded me of something, something older for which there was no memory, just a feeling quality in my body. I fell into it, let it lead me. It was like… It was like… The only way of describing what it was like was this: it was like standing in the doorway of my parents' bedroom, in that apartment where we lived when I was four to six… loitering in the doorway, wanting to go in, but not feeling welcome. Inside the bedroom my mother was standing, holding a baby… my baby brother. They were there, the most-desirable Center of the Universe, and I was outside, in the cold, dead reaches of space, a nothing, yearning to be brought into existence with a look, a touch…

And then something did happen. I went up to my mother, I said to her, "Pick me up, too."

And my mother said, "I can't pick you up, you're too big."

And maybe it wasn't until that moment that I got it, how I always felt too big in social situations where I wasn't sure I belonged. Maybe until that moment "too big" had been one of those unread thought-balloons: there, but not to be known. It was amazing. It was a revelation. I had had a deep session!

Sometime later, I told my mother about that session, that memory, and asked her if something like that might have happened. She said yes, it might well have. If her arms were full of baby, and her four-year-old was asking to be picked up, rather than saying, "I love you," or "Oh, honey, I wish I could," she might well have said, "You're too big."

"We thought we had to be logical with you," she explained.

I wrote this in 1998, during a time of emotional turmoil and painful confusion. In a way, the article itself is a Focusing session, and so I place it here, near the beginning of this volume, as an illustration of what we are talking about. When I published the article in 2003, I took out the more personal details. For this book, I have decided to put them back in, because the process makes more sense, and may be easier to connect to, if you know some of the story behind the session.

This article contains and illustrates the most important message that I want to communicate in this book: that freedom, empowerment, and change can happen when we are able to *be with* all the aspects and sides of ourselves. The move from *identification (merging)* to *Presence* is what this article (and this book) is all about – how important, how crucial this is, and how this move enables a release that previously felt impossible.

This article tells the story of a time when I felt confused, mired, stuck in a sort of romantic obsession with a man who was neither suitable nor available. Through the process I show in this article, I was able to turn toward the parts of me that felt confused and stuck, get interested in them, and feel the *wanting for me* held deep within them. This is tapping the life energy which is held even in our most painful parts. That this life energy exists, even in the most painful parts, and how we can reach it, are also key parts of the message of this book.

As a postscript, about a year after this session I met Joe McBride, now my life partner, with whom my quality of connection is as deep as I would wish. I believe it was Focusing sessions like this one that allowed me to be more fully present in all my relationships, including the one with Joe.

*with editing and additional material by Barbara McGavin
Appeared June 2003 in the "Treasure Maps to the Soul" email newsletter*

"I am in pain, and I am trying not to be."

As I write those words, I feel a flare of hope. My hope comes from that tiny word "and." So often I am in pain – emotional pain if not physical as well – and lost in it, or lost in the struggle to escape it, without awareness of either. But when I know that I am in pain *and* I am trying not to be, I am in a new place, which is more than the pain and the longing to escape it.

I am in pain – *and* I am trying not to be. I know it will help to see these two aspects as parts of me, so I rephrase it: Something in me is in pain – ah, yes, that is a big part of me! – and something in me is trying so hard not to be in pain. Ah, yes. Now they are both more strongly here, and more clearly separate – from each other, and from me.

Now that I can see both these two as parts of me, I know that neither one should win – indeed, neither one *can* win. So I can begin to step away from the seemingly eternal War between them, each one pulling to take over the central position in my consciousness. I can remember that the truth is in both, somehow, and I won't be able to get to that place until I have acknowledged each one.

Something in me is in pain, and I can say to it, "Hello, I feel how much pain you're in." There is a sigh of relief from somewhere inside me when that is heard.

Something in me is trying not to be in pain, putting on such a determined effort, trying to cheer me up, distract me, lecture me on facing "reality" and "moving on" – whatever tricks it knows, it is trying. So I say to it as well, "Hello, I feel you trying for me not to be in pain." Another sigh of relief.

These two acknowledgments put me more in contact with both parts, rather than causing one to eclipse the other, and it feels as if there is now more space around both.

Without ignoring the other, I turn toward the one that is in pain. I feel into it. I can feel its tendrils going down into my past, my life stories, my struggles to be more whole. I can feel the "what it's about" details, and I can also feel that it's more than that.

What it's about this time is a love affair that never really started, and how much I think about this man now, much more than he thinks of me. An obsession, part of me (the other part) wants to call it.

(The pattern of two sides pulling in opposite directions, for example one in pain and one trying not to be, is universal. This is the essence of the work that Barbara McGavin and I are bringing into the world, called "Treasure Maps to the Soul" — that this experience of being in an inner "war" is a place of power, *the* starting place for transformation.)

It doesn't feel that way. It feels stuck, mired, hopeless. How can I get anywhere with two such strong parts pulling me in opposite directions? I hear a whisper inside me that the way to happiness and freedom is just to let go of the old pain and move on. I find my head nodding, but I don't really feel any better, deep down. Then I recognize that this is the voice of the second side, trying its hardest to make the pain go away. I am still in the War. But at least I know it.

There is more. Recognizing that there are two sides pulling against each other is only the beginning. But it is an essential beginning. Without this, the rest of the process cannot even start.

So often we are lost in this War, stuck in it, without awareness. Before going further I want to emphasize this: there is no way forward until we are aware of the War. Not being aware of the War, we are just as much *in* the War, pulled one way and the other, at its mercy — but with no road to change.

The Road to Change

I start with the pain about my not-quite love affair. What will change this? What will release it? What will allow me to move to a new place with this?

We must start with a paradox, one that will feel perhaps frustrating at first: the only way to change is not to change. Or, to put it more helpfully: the only way to change is not to *try* to change. I need to approach my pain from a place of not needing it to change, not trying to make it change. Of course, this makes sense. The pain must be allowed to be fully here, have its full life, be fully heard. Only then could it change. If at the same time I'm trying to make it change, how can I hear it as it is? I can't.

But I *do* want it to change. Must I pretend I don't?

Ah, but here is where the idea of "sides of me" comes in again. Remember: something in me is in pain, and something in me is trying not to be. *And* there is more to me than either of these. When I can acknowledge both, then I am in a new place, a larger place, that is not in either side. This is the place where change can happen. We call it Presence.

So I am in pain. Something in me is in pain. I am acknowledging this place in me, angry, sad, outraged, despairing. And I am acknowledging something in me that doesn't want to be in pain, that really really wants that pain to go away. And both are here.

I am being with both. I am sensing that both are here. The pain place is in my belly, dark and cloudy. The not-wanting-to-be-in-pain is higher, a feeling around my shoulders of wanting to lift off, get up and away. Both are here.

I am waiting with both, taking time. In time, I know, one of them will need to be first.

It's the not-wanting-to-be-in-pain that is insisting, pulling my awareness to it. All right. I check with the pain place. "Yes," it mutely offers, "go ahead. I'll still be here when it's my turn." I know it will.

The Not-Wanting-to-Be-in-Pain

I sense it around my shoulders and chest, a kind of pulling upward, like it's saying, "Come on! Come on! We don't have to feel bad! That's old stuff!"

I acknowledge it. "Yes, I really sense you there." And I sense for its mood, its emotion. At first this isn't easy, almost as if it wants to claim it doesn't have an emotion, it's just doing its job. But when I sense under that, to its mood or tone, I can feel an anxiety around its edges. There's an urgency to this pulling up. It's anxious. It's worried about something.

"Maybe you're worried about something," I check with it. There's a sense of yes, it agrees with that. It is worried, concerned. It's concerned about me, what I will get into, what will happen to me.

I invite it to let me know what it's worried about, what it's not wanting to have happen to me. And I can feel that it doesn't want me to get stuck in feeling bad. I let it know I hear that. I can feel *in my body* that it doesn't want me to get stuck in feeling bad. Yes, of course.

There is more, I can tell. The pulling up is as insistent as ever. I invite it to let me know what it's not wanting me to go through, if I get stuck in feeling bad. Sensing... Ah. It's something about... a memory comes, the summer after college, loving that man who didn't love me. How awful that felt. It doesn't want me to go through *that* again.

I let it know I really hear it. And I know it feels heard, because the pulling has stopped. There's a resting there now. There has been a shift. It's ready for me to hear the other side.

The Pain Tells Its Story

I can feel it in my body, restless, antsy, defiant. I sense for its emotion. It is angry. No. Not right now. It has been angry at other times, but right now it is baffled. How could our connection feel so good, it says, and now he doesn't want to be with me? I'm letting it know I hear how baffled it is.

It says that's not quite right. Yes, it's baffled, but that's not the question.

It's this: *How could God/the Universe let me experience a connection that felt as good as that, and not let it continue?* I am the Listener. I say to it, *You really want to understand how God and the Universe could let something happen that felt so good, and not want it to continue.*

There is an inner stillness now. It's like the stillness of water. There's a sense of depth, something deeper, and I am waiting with infinite patience, waiting to feel what is deeper.

"What am I supposed to do with this wanting?" I hear it saying.

"Ah," I say to it. "You feel *such* a big wanting. And you're feeling you need to do something with it."

Yes. There is a wanting there. And that is a shift. What was restless and antsy and defiant is now filled with quite a different quality: this wanting. Understand: it doesn't feel any *better*. But it feels in some way deeper, truer. And I realize that in some way it *does* feel better. *It's clear that it's not him I'm wanting, not that person, but the quality of connection that I had with him, for that short while.* Yes. And of course it doesn't know any likelier way to get it than to hope for reconciliation with him, so of course it feels "obsessed" with him. But if it knew a way to have that some other way, it would want the other way. It really is the quality of connection that it wants.

And I can feel how this feels different now, in my whole body. Quite different – the whole thing has shifted.

Now, I am not in pain.

I've been astonished and touched by the number of people who have responded, over the years, to the title of this article. "The Radical Acceptance of
Everything" does have a lovely ring to it. The reactions have been overwhelmingly positive – other than a few who have misunderstood it to mean that one
should accept everything in the outer world: war, rape, Fox News, etc.

Let me be clear right now: I am writing about Inner Relationship
Focusing, and so I am talking about a radical acceptance of all that arises in the
inner world, not all that one encounters in the outer. (Whether one can or wishes to accept the circumstances of the outer world is another matter, not what
I'm writing about – though perhaps the two are related.)

And then there is the concept of "acceptance." There are two connotations
of this word in common use, and they struggle with each other. One of them
says, in effect, "OK, this is here right now." The other one says, "OK, this is
here, and it always will be – and I should be happy about that, or at least not
upset." There is an element of resignation to the latter stance, a sort of giving
up on anything ever changing. It would be this meaning that someone is using
when they say, "I can't change it, so I just have to accept it." This isn't the
acceptance I mean. I mean the acceptance that says, "It is so, right now," the
acceptance that is the opposite of denial.

My old friend Bebe Simon, a Focusing teacher who is tireless in champi-
oning autonomy, says that we can't make ourselves accept anything, and of
course she is right. We can, however, notice whether we accept it.

When I wrote this article, it wasn't even about the acceptance of *everything* in
the inner world. That came later. The impetus for writing this article was the
realization that my teaching and practice of Focusing were coming to be
increasingly different from what I had been taught, and that there was something that those differences all had in common: in each case, the new way could
be described as a kind of acceptance of how things are, in the Focusing process
here and now, rather than requiring things to be some other way.

(1) I was taught that felt senses (meaningful body sensations) had to come
in the trunk area of the body, between the throat and the lower abdomen. If a
sensation wasn't in that area, we were told it wasn't a felt sense. A headache, for

example, or a pain in the back or the legs, was not a felt sense and could not be worked with except indirectly. The Focuser needed to get a sense "of" that sensation, in the middle trunk area of the body, with phrases like, "Can you bring that in here [pointing to stomach]?" or "Can you get a sense in here [trunk area] about that?"

(2) Similarly, I was taught that physical symptoms were not, and could not be, felt senses. Again, we needed to get a felt sense "of" the physical symptom, and that needed to be in the trunk area. So a headache had two problems in being accepted as a felt sense: It was outside of the middle trunk area, and it was possibly a physically-caused symptom. We were taught methods for "going around" physical pain, assuming it would not change. ("Even if the pain is like a boulder in the middle of a field, you can still walk around it.")

(3) I was taught that the inner critic was an intractable "superego" that would never be kinder than it first appeared, and should be treated "disrespectfully" so that one wouldn't stay stuck as its victim. Gene Gendlin would wave his hand off to his right, as if waving someone away, and say dismissively, "Come back when you have something new to say." We always laughed.

(4) I was taught Clearing a Space. Actually, when I first learned Focusing, in 1972, I was not taught Clearing a Space, because it wasn't part of Standard Focusing Procedure back then. But by 1980, when I joined Gene Gendlin in teaching the workshops that people started demanding after his book *Focusing* came out, Clearing a Space had become the first step of Focusing, and the one on which we spent the longest. To do Focusing, you had to first move out (e.g. as if onto a shelf in front of you) each "thing" you were feeling. Often there were problems in doing this, so we developed elaborate ways to help (e.g. "If it's too heavy to lift, maybe you could roll it out" or "Maybe you could fasten little balloons to it and float it out").

After I moved to California in 1983 and began teaching Focusing on my own, it slowly dawned on me that all of these four teachings were wrong; that is, the statements that one *could not* do Focusing unless… were simply untrue. Focusing could and did happen, beautifully and successfully, outside the box of these strictures.

This realization happened slowly, because I tend to be slow to change, and to do my best to follow what I've been taught. Sometimes fellow Focusing teachers, my friends, would come to me with reports of breaking the "rules" and getting great results. And sometimes the revelation came when I was sitting with one of my own Focusing clients.

(1) I suspect it was one of my own clients who taught me that felt senses don't have to come in the middle area. I was probably sitting with someone, trying to show them how to do Focusing (that is, I was *guiding* them

through it), when they had a vivid and obviously meaningful sensation outside the middle area. Perhaps it was "a tightness in the back of my neck as I think of my daughter," or "a sad throbbing in my knee." Guiding someone through Focusing is an intuitive process, and one may try moves based on one's sense of the person one is with, and what that person needs, that one may never have been taught. Whatever it was, I went with it, and it worked. After that, the rule that a felt sense *couldn't* form in the back of the neck, or the knee, had no sway with me. The proof of the pudding is in the eating.

(2) Joe Tein, a Focusing teacher who now lives on Bainbridge Island, WA, told me how, with miraculous results, he had broken the rule that Focusing couldn't be done with physical pain and symptoms. Joe's story of the man whose pain went away was published in *The Focusing Connection.* Since then a number of people have reported amazing results treating symptoms as felt senses; including recently Bev Stevenson, "A Remarkable Focusing Session with Pain from Severe Physical Damage," and Barbara McGavin, "The Sentient Body: Focusing on the Physical."

(3) Urged by my friend the Focusing teacher Ilehlia LeIndra, I began to consider being compassionate to the critic. She was not the first or the last to urge more kindness toward this harsh voice, but she gets credit for being the clearest advocate, to me, of the position I now hold: that what is called "The Critic" is simply a part of us like any other that needs compassionate treatment in order to feel safe enough to open. (See the introduction to the article "Radical Gentleness" in this volume for a longer story of how I made this change, including some of the other people who were there before me.)

(4) Other Focusing teachers may have made Clearing a Space optional before I did, but my clearest memory is sitting across from one of my own clients and realizing that he didn't need to set his experiences out in order to do Focusing, so why was I making him do it? I was in California, trying to grow my own practice as a Focusing teacher, and I needed to show people in one session how Focusing could be useful to them, or they wouldn't be coming back. If I had only an hour with this person, why make him spend half of it, or more, setting things out, if he was already able to be with whatever presented itself? Dropping Clearing a Space from the canon was practically an economic necessity!

All of these areas are challenges to (or changes in) what could be called Standard Focusing Procedure. I'd like to say a word here about teaching in the same way that one was taught.

In all teaching, there are conservative tendencies – "Our teachers probably know something, or they wouldn't be our teachers. Let's teach the same way we were taught until we're absolutely sure that something needs to be changed" – and radicalizing tendencies – "This way of teaching doesn't work as well as we'd like. Let's change it and see what happens." This is natural. Over time, the result will inevitably be change. As a living, changing teacher meets living, changing students, it's natural that the teacher will change his or her teaching methods. Teaching methods are not sacrosanct. With regard to Focusing, the teaching methods are not what Focusing *is*.

The misunderstanding that arose was that Focusing *was* the six steps that Gendlin developed for teaching it. I even heard people say, when asked for a definition of Focusing, "Focusing is this process that has six steps..." And I couldn't help feeling, whenever I heard that definition, that something was being lost and the questioner was being shortchanged. To define a process by the way it is taught is to lose the essence of the process, something that is beyond any particular method of teaching it. Gendlin himself, who developed the "Six-Step" teaching method, often said, "The steps are not Focusing, they are just a rope across the territory. When you know the territory, you no longer need the rope." But too many people, for my taste, had made his steps sacrosanct.

The story of how I changed my Focusing teaching methods away from what I had been taught has many facets. "The Radical Acceptance of Everything" tells one part of this story. You will also find parts of it in "Radical Gentleness" and "Relationship = Distance + Connection," and especially the article "The Origins and Development of Inner Relationship Focusing." It is a story that is about my own growth as a person, my journey into trusting my own truth and the feedback of my own senses, and my willingness to step out and live the truth I was seeing. This is something we all need to do. I expect it of my own students. When Gene Gendlin saw me in 1998, after I had been developing my own way of teaching for seven years, he gave me a big smile, an enormous hug, and said ,"Keep going!"

The Radical Acceptance of Everything

Appeared in The Focusing Connection, *November 1994*

When we do Focusing as traditionally taught, it is as if we are inhabiting two worlds. In one world, we have absolute trust for the body and the body's process. In the other world, we treat some experiences as acceptable and others as unacceptable, needing to be set aside or excluded in order for the process to continue. In this second world the Inner Critic is treated as an interruption, as are thoughts. Felt senses may only come in the trunk area of the body, and chronic physical symptoms are not considered to be felt senses.

For the past several years I have been aware that my experience goes counter to this traditional teaching. For example, I have found that felt senses may come outside the "classic" Focusing area of throat, chest, belly. I have found that compassion for the critic may be more useful than setting the critic aside. But recently there has been a new synthesis in my practice of Focusing, both in myself and as a teacher. Many seemingly disparate threads have revealed themselves to be, really, one cloth. The name that I would give to this new understanding is "the radical acceptance of everything."

What if we approach the teaching and practice of Focusing with a fresh and open mind? What if we let go of the various strategies and techniques we have been taught, and simply begin with three essential statements?

(1) Focusing is spending time with something that is not yet clear, something that has more to it than can be put into words at first.

(2) There is a bodily process that is more than the physical body as narrowly defined.

(3) The bodily process is trustworthy.

If you are someone who believes that Focusing can be defined by any number of steps ("Focusing is a ___ step process") or that Clearing a Space is a necessary part of every Focusing process, then you probably won't be willing to follow me along this road. I propose we start by agreeing that there is an essence to Focusing that is beyond steps, and beyond any particular step, except perhaps the step of Being with What's There.

So if we start with the essence of Focusing as captured in those three statements, and clear everything else away, what follows? Let's see.

Felt Senses Outside the Trunk Area

I was taught to guide a person's awareness into the trunk – throat, chest, and belly – and if they felt something outside that area, to ask them to notice what they felt in the trunk about that. For example, "You might notice if you're feeling something in your throat, chest, stomach area that goes with that ache in your jaw." And of course there are other ways of phrasing this. But the traditional wisdom was either (1) felt senses come only in the trunk, or, more kindly, (2) felt senses may come elsewhere, but when felt in the trunk they communicate with the focuser more easily.

When Leonardo da Vinci was a boy, he was told that a nail placed in a tree would grow taller every year as the tree grew. Everyone knew that this was so. He tried it, and he found that it was not so; trees in fact grow from the top, and a nail placed at a certain height will never grow higher.

When I tried treated senses in the periphery of the body as if they were felt senses, both with myself and with others, they behaved like felt senses. They "made steps," opened, revealed meaning, and attending to them eventually resulted in felt shifts.

If the bodily process is trustworthy, then perhaps it offers felt senses precisely in the area of the body where it most wants them to be felt. To make the sense move first, before it can be attended to, feels not respectful of the body's wisdom.

Physical Symptoms as Felt Senses

I was taught that physical symptoms cannot be felt senses, and that if a person had a physical symptom, they might be able to feel their feeling about having it, but that was the most that Focusing could do. Then I started hearing about people who didn't follow "the rules" and who got amazing results from treating physical symptoms as felt senses. I published two of these accounts in this newsletter: Joe Tein's "Focusing with Pain" and Shirley Marten's "And Then the Pain Went Away."

Then in 1990 I had a chance to try this myself. It was the night before I was to start teaching a five-day workshop at the Omega Institute with Kevin McEvenue, and he had joined me to trade Focusing. I was depressed because I had a sore throat, a familiar symptom which always led to a cold, and I didn't want to have a cold. I told this to Kevin and he, another non-rule-follower, said cheerfully, "Let's focus on it!" When treated as a felt sense, the sore throat yielded meaning, something about how I was putting pressure on myself to be an "expert." By the next morning, the sore throat was gone, and I felt fine. No cold.

Last month in England I tried this again, on a cold that had already been going for twenty-four hours. There were four or five symptoms, and I picked the most prominent, the feeling of rawness in my lungs. After I had heard its inner meaning, having to do with having taken on someone else's feelings, I had one of the most amazing experiences of my life – I felt the symptom leave my body in the space of about thirty seconds. Interestingly, the cold remained, with all the other symptoms continuing and running their courses. I do wonder what would have happened if I'd had the time to focus on each one in turn!

However, I have found in my work with myself and clients that treating a physical symptom as a felt sense doesn't always lead to an alleviation of the symptom, and that it doesn't matter. I have one client who has a chronic condition of dry eyes. She often starts her sessions with awareness of her eyes, and receives meaning from that awareness. This is a rich area for her, even though the symptom has not yet changed. I'm convinced that even a broken leg would have a felt sense "quality" or "aspect" if attended to in this way, and would yield meaning, even though we wouldn't expect the leg to knit instantly.

We seem to have an ingrained assumption that experiences are *either* physical or emotional, but not both. I believe this assumption arises from the tragic legacy of the mind-body split. If we see with fresh eyes, why couldn't something be both physical *and* emotional? Why couldn't it yield emotional meaning through Focusing, even though it has also been accurately physically diagnosed?

Thoughts and Other "Distractions"

For many years, I treated thoughts as intrusions on the Focusing process. When a focuser would say to me, "My mind is coming in," I would say, "Maybe you could thank your mind for its help and ask it to step aside for now." If a focuser said, "I'm getting distracted," I would say, "Maybe you could let that distraction go and come back to your body."

But then a new and radical possibility began to come into my awareness. What if there *are* no distractions? What if each thing that comes is somehow a part of the process, and can be welcomed as such?

I watched a student guide working with a new person in a training seminar. The focuser reported that he felt nothing in his body. The student worked diligently to enable him to feel something. At one point the focuser reported, "Thoughts about my work are coming into my head." In accordance with my teaching, the student asked the focuser to set those thoughts aside. But, watching the session, I was struck by the possibility that the thoughts might have been a part of the process. Perhaps the thoughts had been the body's way of introducing content and meaning. I wondered what would have happened if the guide had said, "Maybe you could notice how you feel in your body about those thoughts about your work."

Today when a focuser tells me they are distracted, my response is, "Maybe the distraction is relevant." If it's not, we'll soon know. But let's not throw it out *before* we check whether it might have been the body's way of bringing the next piece.

Recently I was doing a first session in a workshop setting. The focuser's felt sense was of a pressure on her abdomen, but it kept disappearing when she tried to stay with it. Finally she opened her eyes and looked at me.

"It isn't working," she said. "I keep getting distracted."

"Maybe the distraction is relevant somehow," I suggested.

"I don't think so," she said. "I had an image that a black cat walked in and sat down."

"OK," I said. "Let's let the black cat be here. Is it still here?"

She closed her eyes, checked, and nodded.

"So see if you can sense what mood it's in."

She sensed, then said, "It's scared."

"Oh, so let it know you hear that it's scared. And then see if it might want to let you know what it's scared about."

"I get an image of my mother, and a choking in my throat. Guilt. I wish I could take care of my mother better."

That was the key to the session, and when she acknowledged it, she felt relief and release.

After the session was over, the focuser told us that the black cat had been the one she'd had when she was a child, which had been killed.

An hour later, as we were about to end the session for lunch, a black cat walked into the workshop room as if it owned the place. We gasped – how did that happen? It was the final touch to a lovely session.

I'm left with renewed appreciation that anything which comes in a session is probably a part of the process, and nothing should be dismissed as a distraction until it is carefully resonated first.

The Critic

And what would happen if we extend our radical acceptance of everything to Mr. Critic as well? What if we see the inner critic not as an interruption, but as a natural part of the process?

I approached my recent series of workshops with this new possibility in mind, freshly inspired by Barbara McGavin's article in the September 1994 *Focusing Connection*. ["The 'Victim', the 'Critic' & the Inner Relationship: Focusing with the Part that Wants to Die" appears in this volume.] Previously, I had taught a three-part approach to the critic. First, ask it gently to step aside, second, if that doesn't work, ask it its positive purpose, and third, if nothing else works, ask the critic to move around in front of the focuser and have the focuser ask it, "What hurt you or worried you or scared you that you'd be talking to me like that?" It was a very elaborate set of techniques that sometimes took quite a long time.

When I began doing sessions at the Focusing Center of the Hague, I found myself treating the appearance of the inner critic in a much simpler, more organic way. When the focuser reported, "Now my critic is coming in," I would say, "Ah, yes. And maybe you could notice if there's some feeling or emotion, right there."

It's hard to describe how wildly successful this was! You would think that people would talk about the critic's anger or contempt, or report the downtrodden felt sense of the criticized part. But what actually happened was not that at all. Over and over again, by feeling and reporting the emotion that came with the critic, the focuser went right back into the very heart of the Focusing process. "It's grief," one woman reported. "There's so much fear there," said a man. In each case, being with this emotional quality led into deep process. The critic was *not* an interruption, it was simply a way that part of the process chose to express itself.

So the radical acceptance of everything brings a new possibility of trust, a feeling of greater wholeness to the Focusing process. As guides we are no longer guardians of the gate, watching to allow in some experiences and exclude others. Instead, we are holders of the open space that includes whatever wants to come. We are not afraid of what comes in the focuser. We know that there are no enemies in the inner world. We enable the focuser to form a positive relationship with what comes, a relationship of listening and acceptance or, if that isn't possible, a relationship with the part that finds it hard to accept what's there. The spirit is one of inclusion, not exclusion. The attitude is one of welcome.

The radical acceptance of everything is consistent with the spirit of Focusing, and it works. Do try it yourself, and let me know how it goes.

The Radical Acceptance of Everything, Part Two

Appeared in The Focusing Connection, *November 2004*

In 1994 I wrote an article called "The Radical Acceptance of Everything." I chose that title because I had come to realize that the ways in which my Focusing work was developing were all in the direction of accepting and including more experiences as legitimate for Focusing-type attention. Inclusion, rather than exclusion, was the watchword.

In the years since then, as Barbara McGavin and I have developed the body of work called Treasure Maps to the Soul, the phrase "Radical Acceptance of Everything" has come to mean even more than including physical symptoms, sensations outside the trunk area, distracting thoughts, etc. It has come to refer to a whole philosophy of inclusion of *aspects of self* that might otherwise be ignored, discounted, or exiled.

Last week I was guiding a man through his first Focusing session. As often happens, he was able to experience a felt sense in his body (something sad), but when I invited him to simply spend time with it, he reported, "I have a hard time doing that. I'm impatient with it."

If I hadn't been using the philosophy of Radical Acceptance of Everything, I might have attempted to persuade him to be more patient with that sad place. "See if it's OK to be more patient with that sad place." In other words: "Don't be impatient." Then his impatience, or as we would say, something in him that was impatient, would be pushed away, marginalized, judged. That's not what we want. (I will say more about why we don't want that a little further on.)

Instead, I invited him to acknowledge "something in you that's feeling impatient with that sad place" and to turn toward *that* with interested curiosity as well. Soon the part of him that was impatient began to soften, and allowed a wholehearted curious attention to go toward the sad part, which had much it wanted him to hear.

After the session was over, he remarked, "Wow, that was really radical acceptance." I smiled. Indeed it was. And why was that so important? To examine the reasons, let's look first at the essence of the Focusing process.

What Focusing enables is a process that Eugene Gendlin calls *carrying forward.* When "carrying forward" happens, something missing is filled in, something needed is supplied, something blocked is released, and the process that was wanting to happen can happen. We experience carrying forward all the time, all through our daily lives, when we walk, when we breathe, when we eat. Focusing involves carrying forward at the level of *meaning*. When there is a sensing of the whole way something feels ("felt sensing"), there can also be a sensing of the right next step. For example, a poet has a felt sense of the whole poem, not only what's already written but also the more-than-words that hasn't yet been written. Out of this sensing comes a knowing of the right next line of the poem. Focusing can be used in this way with any of the creative arts, with thinking and theory-building, with stress reduction and decision-making. Inner Relationship Focusing (and the Radical Acceptance of Everything) applies especially to Focusing with emotional healing.

In the realm of Focusing and emotional healing, something quite remarkable occurs. *The carrying forward happens when something in us is fully heard.* Almost always, all the inner place needs is to be heard, from Presence, for all that it is feeling. This may involve hearing what it is not wanting, or what it is wanting, or what it went through sometime long ago. It does not involve solving or fixing or doing.

We may think we have to *do* something, to fix what's wrong, to solve the problem. But that's not so – in fact, *doing* actually delays the carrying forward that needs to happen, because doing doesn't come from Presence, it comes from another part of us. (It's a part of us, not Presence, that has the notion that something must be done, often with a driven sense of urgency. It needs to be acknowledged, not acted from. Of course, that's another example of Radical Acceptance of Everything.)

It should be noted that we are not against action! There is action that comes from the Self in Presence, and it is flowing, effective, transformative. The problem comes when one part tries to take action to fix another part, out of fear of having the feelings that would otherwise have to be felt. That sort of action leads to polarization and resistance. What is called a "block" inside is almost always the interaction of two parts, one trying to get another one to move or change, the second one resisting.

If we identify with either of those parts, we're stuck in the polarization, stuck in the inner conflict. The other side gets pushed away, exiled. And neither one can get the attention it needs, in the way it needs, to enable its *carrying forward*.

So you're sitting there in a Focusing process. You know that the process is greatly facilitated by being patient, accepting, welcoming toward what you are sensing, so that it can tell its story, evolve, carry forward. You notice that you feel not patient but impatient, like you're wanting to push for an outcome. What do you do?

Why not change impatience into patience? Why not change criticism and judgment into acceptance? What's wrong with trying to be strong instead of weak, kind instead of cruel, confident instead of frightened? All of that sounds like a positive direction to move in – but the *how* makes all the difference. The results are *not* all that matters.

Imagine trying to solve the problem of homelessness by loading the homeless people onto buses and shipping them to another city, putting them all in jail, or even shooting them! No, the clean streets would not be worth the human cost. The same is true in the inner world. When aspects of our selves are exiled, they don't just quietly go away. They fester, become saboteurs, act as blocks, remain unchanged. And rightly so, because they should not be treated that way; they too have a contribution to make.

Gendlin writes: "We think we can make ourselves good by not allowing the feeling of our negative ways. But that just keeps them static, the same from year to year" (*Let Your Body Interpret Your Dreams*, p. 178). What is unfelt cannot evolve and change.

For most of us, encounters with other people's disapproval as we were growing up resulted in our trying to cut out aspects of ourselves. Amy's parents were frightened when she needed them. They pulled back from her expressions of need, and for Amy that felt like disapproval and abandonment. As a result, she tried not to be "needy." She tried to cut out and rid herself of any needing of her parents. But (fortunately) we can't rid ourselves of our own parts. All we can do is exile them, send them underground, far from awareness. The result is that we are less than fully ourselves – and those exiled aspects cannot have the carrying forward that they need.

And that's the problem, exactly that. *Exiled aspects cannot carry forward.* When we push away something that we feel, even with the best of intentions ("I want to be more patient with myself"), we set up a situation in which something cannot change, because it is out of awareness.

But are we not just moving the prescription to a higher level? Rather than "Be Patient," etc., are we not saying, "Be accepting"? Be Radically Accepting! All the time!

I understand that it could be heard this way, but no, it isn't the same thing at all. Because Radical Acceptance isn't a feeling that you must make yourself feel. It is a frame, and an action. The frame says that anything that isn't Presence is something that needs Presence. The action is to turn toward whatever isn't Presence, and acknowledge it. This can be done no matter what mood you're in... so it isn't a prescription for a right way to feel. It's like turning toward someone tugging at your sleeve. "Ah, I'm sensing something in me is impatient. I'm saying hello to it..."

The more we do this, the more we have the experience that we don't have to *try* to be kind, compassionate, gentle, strong, connecting, creative... because we already are. The Self in Presence has those qualities, and many more, without trying, without effort. When you turn toward what isn't Presence, what you experience, what you *are*, is Presence.

Presence has become central to Inner Relationship Focusing, as well as to the Treasure Maps to the Soul work on Focusing with difficult areas that Barbara McGavin and I are creating. If you are a Focuser, staying in Presence with what needs your attention inwardly is a key to successful Focusing in the area of personal growth and emotional healing. If you are a Focusing partner, the most facilitative thing you can do is to be in Presence yourself, and second, to support your partner in staying in Presence. If you are a Focusing therapist, your Presence to your clients, and their Presence to themselves, makes all the difference. What is Presence, why is it important, and how can we cultivate it? In order to answer these questions, I'd like to go back into my own history and show how this concept developed.

I learned how to teach Focusing from watching Gene Gendlin teach it, as I assisted him in weekend Focusing workshops from 1980 through 1983. Then I moved to California and began teaching Focusing on my own. As I interacted with my students, putting what I'd been taught into my own words and answering questions, as one does in those situations, my teaching gradually evolved. Still, I felt I was deriving everything I taught from what I had learned from Gene Gendlin.

The origin of Presence is in what has been called "The Focusing Attitude." In my teaching, I would invite people to ask inwardly, about a felt sense they were having, "Can I be friendly to this?" (Gendlin, *Focusing*, p. 81, "The Friendly Hearing": "It is important... to establish this atmosphere of a friendly hearing. Be prepared to accept for a moment whatever feelings you find inside.")

And then of course people would sometimes say, "What if I can't be friendly to that? What if I'm angry with it, or scared of it?" And I would say, as Gene always said, "Then see if you can be friendly to that!" (*Focusing*, p. 95: "Whatever gets in the way, you can focus on that for the moment, instead of the problem or difficulty you wanted to focus on.")

I loved the clarity of this: anything which can't feel friendly is something which needs friendliness. So I wasn't telling people they had to feel a certain way – accepting, or friendly – in order to focus. They could always focus. They just needed to turn to whatever was there, either to the thing that came or to whatever was in the way of being with the thing that came.

The word "friendly" was problematic, however, being just a bit too strong for the purpose. It was Bebe Simon who convinced me that "hello" was a better idea. As Bebe put it, "Hello doesn't mean I love you." Saying "hello" has just the right amount of openness, contact without devotion.

Not only was this "turning to whatever was there" clear and elegant, it struck me that it was really the heart of the process. If I can turn to whatever is in me with this quality that "hello" is the start of, including turning to whatever in me is in the way of that turning to, then I have everything. That's it. Being with, staying with whatever is here, interested, curious, allowing... that's all of it.

So I got more and more interested in this process of turning to what's in the way. And what I noticed was that no matter how people described what came first, they usually said "I feel" or "I am" about the second thing, the thing in the way of turning to the first thing.

"I don't like it."

"I'm scared of it."

"I want it to change."

And it didn't feel right to me to reflect back, "It's tight, and you want it to change," because the "tight" and the "wanting it to change" need to be next to each other, equal, both turned toward. If "I" want it to change, then who is there to turn toward the "wanting to change"? And who is there to be an unbiased listener to the "tight"? I wanted to reserve the word "I" for the one who could turn toward anything. So I started saying, "It's tight, and you're aware of a wanting-it-to-change." Or: "It's tight, and you're aware of something in you that wants it to change."

When someone says "I want it to change" instead of "Something in me wants it to change," this is *identification*. I've come to believe that identification with parts (and the accompanying dissociation from other parts) is a root cause of suffering. What I mean by "parts" in that sentence is "partial experience," "non-whole experience." Anything not compassionate – not loving, allowing, Listening, etc. – is a part. We can and should welcome it and listen to it. Identifying with it means it's less likely to get listened to, more likely to be acted out of.

The genius of Focusing has always been this "Third Way," neither identifying nor dissociating. Our Western industrial culture knows only two ways to be with experience: plunging into the center, "it's me," or denying, "it's not me." I go around the world with a tattered poster that I call "The Three Guys." The guy on the left has a red cloud around his whole body, and he says, "I am angry!" The guy on the right has a red cloud behind his back, not in his body, and he says, "I am not angry!." (I demonstrate this by clenching my teeth, tapping my foot, and growling "I am not angry!") The guy in the middle has a red cloud around his belly, labelled "something," and nearby, connected with an arrow of relationship, the word "I." He says, "I'm sensing something in me is angry." Only in the middle case will "the anger" get a hearing, have some company, be able to make steps. Because someone is there, the "I," keeping it company.

The problem of the "I" is a complex one, of course. John Welwood is a noted advocate of Focusing in the world of psychotherapy. He is also well known for bringing Tibetan Buddhist philosophy into therapy. In a chapter called "Reflection and Presence: The Dialectic of Awakening," he comes down on the side of Buddhism, declaring that Focusing "and other reflective methods" don't go far enough. Because "from the perspective of contemplative practice, the root source of human suffering is this very split between 'me' and 'my experience.' Suffering is nothing more than the observer judging, resisting, struggling with, and attempting to control experiences that are painful, scary, or threatening to it" (*Toward a Psychology of Awakening,* p. 101).

For Welwood, Focusing is essentially characterized by the experience of an observer being with what is felt. However, he assumes that that observer may have biases such as "judging, resisting, struggling with, and attempting to control." My reaction is no, that is not the observer. The observer, the "I," is that which turns toward judging, which turns toward resisting, which turns toward struggling with and attempting to control, and therefore is not that.

So I began to wonder what kind of thing would strengthen and support this Inner Relationship, where an "I" without bias is present with a "something" that needs awareness.

The first thing I looked at was what was already happening that was successful. What were people already doing, especially listeners whom I admired, which now could be seen as supporting this Inner Relationship? My advanced training in linguistics allowed me to see things in the structure of sentences that might not be immediately obvious to the people who were actually making the sentences.

And I noticed something quite wonderful and astonishing. There was a *form of responding* often found in my favorite listeners which as far as I knew nobody had ever talked about. This form of responding captured the wholeness, the "I" and the "something," the "experiencer" and the "experiencing," both. I started teaching this to my beginning Listening students, and found they leapt to advanced Listening levels.

Here's how it works: the Focuser is reporting on a present experience. The listener says it back, yet adds a few words "in front" of what the Focuser says. Those words are "you" to refer to the Focuser, and then a verb of present awareness, such as "are sensing," "are noticing," "are aware of." And then what the Focuser said. Like this:

F: "It's tight."
L: "You're noticing it's tight, there."

F: "I'm scared."
L: "You're aware that right now you're scared."

F: "This is an awfully hard thing to stay with."
L: "You're finding this an awfully hard thing to stay with."

Can you feel the difference between these responses and the "bare" responses, e.g. "It's tight," "You're scared," "This is an awfully hard thing to stay with"? For me, especially when I'm the one Focusing and the listener does this, there's a spaciousness, like a big breath. Like, "Oh, yes, *I'm* here!"

I also found that when I responded like this, and when I taught others to respond like this, the Focusers tended much more to stay out of overwhelm. This made Focusing more accessible to them. It also gave them an inner sense of spaciousness, a sense of identifying with, or being, a much larger Self than usual. Sometimes I called this the Larger Self, or the Larger "I," until Barbara McGavin brilliantly found us the word "Presence." (She actually borrowed it from John Welwood, but as we've seen, he doesn't mean quite the same thing by it.)

The other thing I found happening in my favorite listeners was a very interesting use of the word "something" to point to experiencing which could be sensed more into, as in "You're sensing *something* there that is tight." Sometimes they would also say "this place," as in "You can sense this place where you feel..."

I noticed that sometimes people described their experience as "it" or "something" or "this place," and sometimes they described it as "I," as in "I feel scared." I noticed that Listening felt best when the listener at least matched this, said "it" when the person said "it," and said "you" when the person said "I." The following, for example, felt awful to me:

F: "This place is scared."
L: "You are scared."

I asked myself, what is it about that Listening response which so outrages my sense of rightness? Because the Focuser had begun to differentiate, to feel *with* something inside, and the "something" felt "scared." When the listener said back, "You feel scared," all that fineness was lost. We were back to the lonely universe of "I" alone, "I feel scared," and no one to *be with* the scared.

So then I began to experiment a little with going in the other direction. If going from "it" or "this place" to "you" felt so awful, how would it feel to go in the other direction, from "I" to "it" or "that place"?

F: I feel scared.
L: Something in you feels scared.

Almost all of the time people liked this, and could take the next step more easily, of feeling into this "something." A very few would say, "No, *I* feel scared," and I would say "Ah, *you* feel scared." and we were back on track – on their track.

These two insights ("you're sensing" and "something in you") combined to make the form of language that Barbara McGavin and I call Presence Language. We now teach this in all our Focusing classes, and it features prominently in our *Focusing Student's and Companion's Manual.*

Facilitating Presence in the people who come to me for Focusing sessions has become second nature to me – but not so much that I ever take for granted the amazing transformations that I am witness to, the relief and freedom that people start to feel when I show them this simple and elegant way of giving support and Listening to their own difficult places.

There is a big gap between telling about a process and the actual doing of it. So I decided one of the most helpful things I could do, to show Presence in action, was to tell the stories of some recent sessions in which people came to me feeling both overwhelmed and out of touch with their emotional source, and in which being facilitated in finding Presence was helpful to them. These sessions were done on the phone, so I was able to take notes. Some details are supplied by memory and therefore may be inaccurate; the sessions have also been shortened. And of course some details have been changed to protect the privacy of the individuals. But as examples of how I work with people these stories work well, and the language and the style are an accurate reflection of what happens.

Facilitating Presence

Newly written for this book

As I travel around teaching workshops in Focusing and facilitative language, one of the questions I'm asked, especially by therapists and counselors, has to do with facilitating Focusing for people who are in a difficult relationship with their own emotional experience. They wonder if my Inner Relationship methods will work with someone who is feeling so overwhelmed or frightened by their emotional experience that they have a difficult time staying with it. I say it can... but I can see they are still wondering.

When we are working with people who feel overwhelmed by or frightened by their emotional experiences, it's tempting to use methods that contain or manipulate the overwhelming experience (e.g., "See if you can shrink that anger down to a size you can handle, and then set it farther away from you"). The problem with this type of intervention is that it reinforces the client's *identification* with the part of them that is feeling overwhelmed. (See "Relationship = Distance + Connection" in this volume for other problems and further discussion.)

In this article I would like to give two partial transcripts of clients who were experiencing emotional overwhelm in the very first session with me, and show how I used language that facilitated and supported them to find an experience of *Presence* – the ability to *be with* emotional experience without being overwhelmed by it. It is hoped that these examples will make it clearer how facilitative this work with Presence can be, and how it forms the foundation for doing further inner work. Showing the rest of the process, however, once the person is able to be in Presence with their emotional experience, is beyond the scope of this paper. For now, I hope you'll go along with me on this: a person who can be in an empathic relationship with what he or she is experiencing is well on the way to healing, though this healing may still take time and the supportive presence of another person.

These sessions were done on the telephone. The descriptions that follow are based on notes that I was able to take during the sessions.

Carrie (not her real name) emailed me in great distress. She had been experiencing increasing degrees of overwhelming fear.

"My main symptom for the past couple weeks has been to wake up with a sick dread, terror and doom. This is something really huge, and it needs care, and I feel I am making it worse by resisting it." I agreed to give her a first Focusing session on the phone that very night. As we discussed the process, I explained that Inner Relationship Focusing could offer her relief through helping her develop an increasing ability to be in *Presence*.

"Presence," I said, "is the ability to simply *be with* anything that is in your awareness." Carrie said that sounded good to her.

Even before we started the session she was near tears, her breathing and heartbeat rapid, especially when she told me that ever since she went to a workshop (for a well-known method of releasing stressful memories) she had been feeling much worse. "I tried to manipulate the images of my grandfather molesting me when I was four, but they just got stronger."

"I can hear the tears in your voice," I said. "That sounds like it's really painful to you."

"It's like there's a heavy stone sitting on my chest. I can hardly breathe."

"I can hear that you're already experiencing feelings in your body. But let me take you through a grounding process here at the start of our session, if that's OK, because I think that will make it easier for you to find Presence with what you're going through." Carrie agreed.

I guided her into body awareness through her body, first the outer area, arms and hands, legs and feet... and then the contact of her body on what she was sitting on, with special emphasis on feeling her weight supported and resting into that support. I had learned from Barbara McGavin, and then from my own experience, how important that inner experience of lower-body support is for Presence.

Slowly and with a gentle voice I invited Carrie to let her awareness come into the inner area of her body, into the whole inner area that included her throat, chest, stomach, and abdomen... and anywhere else in her body that called to her. I welcomed her to give a gentle invitation in there, like she was saying, "What wants my awareness now?" And then, when she was aware of *something*, to let me know.

"A tension in my head... And something in my back."

I waited a moment to see if she would say more, and then I said, "So you might acknowledge each of those two places, like you're saying to each one, 'Yes, I know you're there.'"

There was an intent silence. After a few moments I added, "And you might notice if your awareness is especially drawn to one of those places right now."

"It's my back," Carrie said.

"So you might take some time to describe where and how you're feeling that in your back."

"I feel it in my lower left back... It feels heavy... dull, and... black."

I had explained to her that I would be reflecting some of her words back to her, and that when I did, I hoped she would check those words with her inner experience, to sense if they were right, or if other words fit better. When I reflected back slowly, "You're sensing... something in your lower left back feeling heavy... dull... black...," she responded, "That's exactly right." Then I invited her to acknowledge that place, "Like you're saying 'Yes, I know you're there.'"

She gasped. "When I do that, I get this overwhelming sensation in my chest!"

"So you might move your awareness to something strong you're feeling in your chest, and acknowledge it as well... Maybe sensing how you would describe it..."

"I'm feeling really really afraid," she said.

Immediately I noticed that Carrie had moved from *describing* her experience to *identifying* with it. The clue was that she said "I'm feeling" instead of "*it's* feeling." Sometimes when people do this, I start by reflecting exactly what they said. But in this case I sensed that Carrie was ready for a different way to be with her felt experience.

"You're sensing *something in you*," I said, "that's really really afraid."

"Yes," she said, smoothly picking up on the Presence language I was using, "and it's also sad... and lonely..."

"Maybe you could let it know you hear how afraid it is... how sad it is... how lonely it is..."

"Wow!" said Carrie. "I'm doing that... and it says that's right and it has a lot more to tell me!" Carrie's voice sounded bright and excited for the first time.

Notice what a special moment this is. An inner experience that started out as something physically described ("overwhelming sensation") has come alive with its own point of view, its own meaning. "It says it has a lot more to tell me." By being *in relationship with* her own inner experience, Carrie has facilitated an inner *shift*. Imagine how much harder this would have been coming from the stance of "I'm feeling afraid."

What did I do to help this shift happen? I used *Presence language* in reflecting back what she said. Here is that segment again:

Carrie: "I'm feeling really really afraid."
Ann: "*You're sensing something in you* that's really really afraid."

Compare this to just saying back what she said: "You're feeling really really afraid." Isn't it likely that a direct reflection, without Presence language, would have thrown Carrie up against her own overwhelm? Then I would have had to intervene in other ways that might have taken her farther from her process itself. Repeating only the word "afraid" has the same problems. Presence language, although it takes more words to say, gives the Focuser support in finding a solid place to stand in relationship to what they're feeling, and a way to *be with* rather than *be in* their inner experiencing.

Presence is facilitated, not just once, but all through a session. A little later, when this "something" in her told her that it had a lot more to tell her, Carrie reacted from another part of her:

"I'm scared to hear it tell me more, I don't know what that might be."

Now we come to a very important point in our understanding of Presence. Again Carrie is saying that she is afraid. Earlier, when she said she was afraid, she was *identified with* this part of her in her chest. By acknowledging it instead of identifying with it, she was able to move into a different, more healing relationship with it. Now she is saying that she is afraid *of* it. But why should we believe that this "I'm afraid" is any more her whole self than the previous one? Very likely she is identified again – this time with a part of her that has a feeling *about* the feeling in her chest.

Here is what I said: "Sounds like another part of you is coming up now, something in you that's scared to hear this one tell more."

"Yes," said Carrie. "That's right." And I heard a deep breath of relief.

Ann: "Maybe you could acknowledge this *something in you* that is scared to hear this other one tell more."

Carrie: "Yes, it's OK. I can listen now."

In this case, acknowledging was all that was needed.

Ann: "And you might notice how all that is feeling now in your body."

Carrie: "I can feel that place in my back again... It's feeling tight and a little nauseous."

Ann: "You're sensing that place in your back... feeling tight... and a little nauseous...." (As I said back her words, the tone of my voice was lower and the words were more elongated, compared to ordinary conversation. It's as if I'm saying, with the tone of my voice, *Please check if this is right.*)

The next thing Carrie said was, "I should have fought back." I guessed she was talking about the molestation by her grandfather. We might guess from her words that Carrie is identified again, but she might not be; she might be in Presence but *quoting* what that part of her is saying to her. It doesn't matter, though, because my response would be the same whether she is identified or just quoting. The philosophy of Presence tells me that these words come from *something in her,* whether she is aware of that or not.

Ann: "Something in you says, 'I should have fought back.'"

Carrie: "I hate myself for not fighting back."

Now Carrie does sound identified, and I'm going to give her some help to come into Presence with the parts of her she's identified with.

She's in a complex situation here, as she was before, when she said *I'm scared to hear it tell me more.* Both of these situations exemplify the inner experience that Barbara McGavin and I call "The Feeling about the Feeling." This is when one part of us has a feeling (usually fear, impatience, or aversion) about another part of us.

Ann: "See if it would be OK to say it this way, if this would feel true, if you would say, 'I'm sensing something in me that hates me... that hates something else in me... for not fighting back.'"

Carrie repeated the words the way I had suggested them, and then said, "Yes, that's true. Something in me hates something in me... I can feel the hating in my back."

Ann: "You're sensing it feels like hating, there in your back."

Carrie: "Not exactly like hating... more like fighting. It wants to fight."

Notice this "content mutation," familiar from Focusing – as she senses directly what she had called "hating," it becomes – or perhaps it was all along – "fighting."

Ann: "You might see if it's OK to stay with that *something* in you, in your back, that feels like fighting, and listen more to what it's feeling."

Carrie: "It feels fierce. It wants to punch and hit."

Ann: "You're sensing it feels fierce. It's letting you know it wants to punch and hit. You might let it know you hear it..."

Notice how I am continuing to frame my reflections in Presence language. Not "It feels fierce" but "You're sensing it feels fierce." Not "It wants to punch and hit" but "It's letting you know it wants to punch and hit." This supports Carrie in *being with* what she is contacting. Then I give a suggestion which supports Presence and Inner Relationship: "You might let it know you hear it..." It's obvious by what she says next that Carrie follows my suggestion.

Carrie: "It's saying to me, Why have you never listened to me before?"

Ann: "Sounds like it would have wanted you to listen before. ... You might let it know you hear that, that it would have wanted you to listen like this a long time ago."

Carrie: "Yes, that's exactly right. It's telling me that there's a lot it wants me to know, that could really help me. It wanted to tell me a long time ago. This is amazing!"

And so the session continued...

At the end of the process, Carrie was feeling deeply relaxed. Her bodily-felt emotional places had been heard instead of being pushed away or identified with. Instead of getting caught up in her feelings and feeling them too intensely, she had been able to be a *compassionate witness* to her own felt experiences. Because she could be in Presence, her feelings began to feel some relief, and she had started building a trusting *inner relationship* with the places in her that, as it turned out, not only wanted to tell her about distress but also had helpful information they were waiting to give her about healing that distress.

The next day I received this email: "I want to thank you again for our session last night. When I worked with you I finally felt like change was possible, that I can move through incredibly painful things and finally find myself again. I had hope. I feel quite horrible today, as I woke up with nausea and sick terror and dread, but I wonder if we kept working if I could learn to listen to that while feeling safe, and heal it. Part of me feels worse, but part of me feels better. I am just amazed that with all the therapy, and kinds of therapy I have had for so many years, I never really felt so connected as I did last night."

One session didn't resolve her problems, but we wouldn't expect that it would. What did happen was that she "finally felt like change was possible." Presence isn't the end of the process, it's the beginning. Being able to be in relationship to emotional places rather than being identified with them is a precondition for the work of emotional healing – which still needs to be done.

My role had been to hear her, and even more, to facilitate her hearing herself. The essence of the state of Presence is that *in Presence, we are listeners.* In Presence, we can listen with interest and acceptance to whatever arises. We don't take sides, we don't try to make an outcome happen, we just listen. The result is that every part of us feels deeply heard, and the process that has been waiting to happen, can happen.

Being in Presence with "Resistance"

Carrie felt her emotional experiences intensely in her body. Another kind of experience of overwhelm is illustrated by our second example. Sometimes a person responds to emotional intensity by shying away from the experience, which can result in a process that seems reluctant to get going.

Connecting inwardly in a Focusing way can be like a dance with a shy partner. Sometimes a part of us comes forward, sometimes it holds back, hides, even disappears. This has been called "resistance," but I seriously doubt whether that kind of label is helpful. It's the same as in the world of interpersonal relationships, where labeling the character of another ("You're selfish!") can lock in polarization, while having empathy for the other can open a space for cooperation and change. Calling something "resistance" doesn't tend to open a channel for empathizing with what might be going on from its own point of view.

What would happen if we assumed that all our parts and aspects – and those of our clients – have good reasons for behaving the way they do? Perhaps if something in us is shy, it's really letting us know that it needs to feel more safe. Perhaps if something in our client keeps disappearing, it's communicating that it needs to go slower or feel more safe.

Kris (not her real name) told me in her first session that she was having a hard time coping with life. She felt that, even though she was in therapy with an excellent therapist, her depression had gotten worse: "I feel like I'm breaking down." She had told her therapist that she needed a way to get support in between their sessions, and he had referred her to me for some Focusing teaching. My job would be to guide Kris through Inner Relationship Focusing and show her a way to keep company with all of her feelings. Ultimately, I would be teaching her how to do this for herself. (Her sessions with her therapist continued concurrently.)

The following is an abridged transcript of her first session with me, on the phone. You will see that the invitations into Presence (in italics) are offered not once, but persistently. There is an attitude of steady invitation that is not forcing or intrusive but, ideally, supportive of the move into an awareness that may not be what the person is accustomed to at all. (Ellipses … indicate pauses.)

When I invited Kris to bring awareness into her body (see Carrie's session above), she reported that it was hard to feel her body. I wondered out loud what her experience of that was, and she said, "Rushing. Rushing here and there."

Ann: "Maybe you could *acknowledge* that feeling of rushing here and there."

Kris: "It doesn't sink in. I don't relax. What I get into is a judgment about it."

Ann: "So maybe you could also *acknowledge* a part of you that's judging, like you're saying to it, Yes, I know you're there."

Kris: "That sinks in a little more. I feel a dropping down, getting grounded in my body."

Ann: "And it's great to just take time to feel that."

Kris: "I notice I can't do that for very long. I start jumping out of my body again."

Ann: "So you're noticing *something in you* that feels the need to jump out of your body."

Kris: "Yes... I'm not sure where to go with that."

Ann: "Maybe you could just acknowledge something in you that's feeling the need to jump out of your body."

Kris: "I can't really find it. I'm not sure where I am."

Ann: "OK. You might want to sense that middle area of your body especially, throat, chest, stomach, belly... and just sense what wants your awareness now."

Kris: "All that's happening is... I start feeling like I'm really young. I can't acknowledge it because I'm consumed by it."

Ann: "Yeah... You start feeling like you're really young... ... Maybe noticing where in your body that's centered or where you feel it the most."

Kris: "That's really helpful. Now I have a feeling of being separate from it. I can feel my whole body, but then I can also feel this in my throat and upper chest."

Ann: "So that's great that you're feeling your whole body, and *from there*, you might take some time to *be with* what you're feeling in your throat and upper chest."

Kris: "It's really young. Like it's weak and sad."

Ann: "You're sensing it's really young. You're sensing it's weak... and sad..."

Kris: "It's curled up. Like it isn't going anywhere."

Ann: "You're sensing it's curled up. Yeah. ... And maybe you could just *be with it* as it's curled up there."

Kris: "OK."

Ann: ".....just giving it your interested curiosity... like you're sitting with it, interested in it...."

Kris: "That's the next thing I have trouble with. It doesn't seem to be changing much."

Ann: "Ah... maybe you could *acknowledge something in you* that's wanting it or expecting it to change more."

Kris: "That's right. Something in me is impatient. It's anxious."

Ann: "So just *acknowledging* that, open to more it wants you to know about itself.... And also *being with* this curled-up place, sensing how *it* feels now."

Kris: "It's just this circular movement, like a rocking feeling."

Ann: "You're sensing it now like a circular movement, like a rocking feeling.... And see if it's OK to *just be with that*."

Kris: "The anxious feeling is wanting this part to be touched, embraced. I feel anxious about being alone with it."

Ann: "*You're sensing something in you* that's anxious about being alone with it. Like something in you wants it to be touched... by someone."

Kris: "That's right."

Ann: "And maybe you could just *be with* something in you that's anxious about being alone with it. Let it know you hear how anxious it is."

Kris: "It's very anxious. Like it can't stand just seeing it there, with no one touching it."

Ann: "You might let it know you hear how *very* anxious it is."

Kris: "And the other one is still just rocking."

Ann: "And maybe it's OK to just *be with both*, one that's rocking, one that's anxious about seeing it there."

Kris: "It's like I just can't stay with it."

Ann: "And maybe you could be gentle with that, and *acknowledge* that, that something in you has a hard time staying with it."

Kris: "That's it. I just felt something relaxing when you said that."

The session went on from here in a similar vein, with me continuing to invite Kris to acknowledge and be with any experience she was having. Her ability to be in Presence with her own experiencing was slowly developing.

In Kris's first session, I did a number of things to introduce and support the experience of Presence. First, I invited her to acknowledge any experience that arose, even if (especially if) it seemed *not* to be the experience we had invited. So, when I invited her to sense into her body, and instead she found an experience of "rushing here and there," I invited her to acknowledge that. Next she reported "a judgment about it." I invited her to acknowledge that. That second acknowledging began to have an impact. She reported dropping down into her body. Since that sounded like an enjoyable feeling of greater connection with herself, I invited her to take time just to feel it. But very quickly, something in her pulled her out again. So again we acknowledged that.

The power of acknowledging comes from its neutrality and its universality. We are doing nothing to make a change. We are simply acknowledging. Anything can be acknowledged, including not-being-able-to-acknowledge.

After acknowledging, we moved to *being with* the felt experience. *Being with* is a kind of contact, keeping company without doing anything. When Kris became aware of two parts of her in conflict, I invited her to *be with* both. When it was hard for her to be with something in her inner experience, that again became something to *acknowledge*. In general, the persistent use of Presence language supports the client in becoming more and more available as a nurturing listener for her own inner experiences. For someone who didn't receive this growing up, this can be difficult and of course ultimately very rewarding.

With my Listening responses and my gentle, non-judgmental invitations, I was modeling the attitudes that I hoped Kris would begin to take toward herself. I was demonstrating "Radical Acceptance of Everything" (see that article in this volume, especially Part Two), assuming that every experience Kris was having had some good reason to be there. If she wants to jump out of her body, I say, "So you're noticing *something in you* that feels the need to jump out of your body." I may even add the words "...for some good reason." From Presence, our respect for what the parts of the person need to do is absolute. No wonder the word "resistance," with its built-in judgment, no longer seems helpful.

I hope it's clear that, even in the short time described in this transcript, Kris is coming into contact with something powerful and important in herself. A rocking part of her, and another part of her that is anxious about seeing it there, evoke in me a guess about something that happened long ago. (See "Focusing on Childhood" in this volume.) It's not for me to say what that might be, but my instincts tell me that this is a rich place for her to stay, and to dwell in with interested curiosity. It also makes sense that it might be a tough place to stay, if she easily becomes identified with the part of her that is anxious. So we accept the amount of contact that is ready to happen now. As Gendlin says, "Even a moment of feeling it in your body allows it to change."

Kris later told me, about the process she learned in her sessions with me: "Diving deep into something right away doesn't work as well for me. If there isn't that [Presence] language, it gets entrenched, and I might as well stop the session right there." She appreciated learning the power of Presence: "It's huge [i.e., positive] for me not to have to wait for my therapist. I've found something where I can be with myself and manage my emotions, and not get caught in them."

There are many ways of understanding what happens when someone is "resisting," when there is a "superego attack," when inner contact is difficult. The model that Barbara McGavin and I have developed understands all of these phenomena as parts or aspects of the self, behaving with motivations of protection (not-wanting) or attraction (wanting). We contrast identification ("partiality") with Presence, the ability to be with any part with an accepting, allowing attitude.

When Presence becomes possible, then the rest of Focusing becomes possible: the allowing spaciousness that invites the felt sense to take its next steps, to sense its own carrying forward.

The state of being in Presence is like a place to stand, to be with inner experiences of all kinds, including strong emotional experiences. When a person says s/he is feeling overwhelmed, or fears being overwhelmed, that is really a statement about the lack of Presence. The ability to be in Presence with our own emotional experience is something that can be built over time, with practice and patience, in the same way that trust is built in relationships, by behaving in a trustworthy way over time.

The "Victim," the "Critic," and the Inner Relationship – Focusing with the Part that Wants to Die

Our friendship began in 1991 when Barbara McGavin invited me to pass through England on my way to a conference in Scotland, my first time in the UK. She met me at the train in Bath, where she lived, and the tape playing on her car stereo was the theme music to my favorite cult TV show. (Angelo Badalamenti's music for David Lynch's *Twin Peaks*, for those who like to know all the details!) It turned out we liked the same kinds of books and movies too, and I found that as she showed me her favorite spots in Bath, they were just the kind of places I liked. By the end of the Focusing exchange weekend that Barbara had arranged, we were well on the way to becoming close friends.

She organized my first workshop in England one year later, at the Beacon Centre near Exeter, a three-day exploration of my Focusing innovations, called "The Inner Relationship." What I had developed so far on the Inner Relationship aspect of Focusing meshed with the direction that Barbara's Focusing practice was taking, and the two streams of our teaching and thinking soon joined into a richer and deeper flow. Within a few years we were full partners at the workshops, and Inner Relationship Focusing was ours.

The plan for late summer of 1994 was for me to teach in the Netherlands at the Focusing Center of my dear friends Erna de Bruijn and Christine Langeveld, and then go over to England for two workshops with Barbara near Exeter, followed by another workshop with Barbara in Ireland. I've written elsewhere about how life-changing this trip was, about what happened to me in Glastonbury just before these three workshops. (See "The Treasure Maps Story – So Far" in this volume.)

But even before I got on the plane for the Netherlands, something happened to profoundly change my view of Focusing with difficult places, and that was reading this article by Barbara. She sent it to me for publication in *The Focusing Connection,* so I was its first lucky reader. The possibility of being able to say to an unbearably painful part of myself that it could be the way it was forever if it needed to be – the radical generosity and grace of that statement – blew me away, and changed every session that I did, with others and with myself, from then on.

The "Victim," the "Critic" and the Inner Relationship: Focusing with the Part that Wants to Die

by Barbara McGavin
Appeared in The Focusing Connection, *September 1994*

I first remember wanting to die when I was about six. And while my attempts were doomed to failure – holding one's breath or attempting to smother oneself with a pillow doesn't work very well, and perhaps was less than whole hearted (thank god) – there was within the attempting a sense of there being no hope of real love or contact or understanding from my parents. There was a deep sense that I could not and never would be OK. And I wanted to die – it seemed the only hope of escape from something that was unbearable and would continue forever.

To survive, I stopped trying to be really me and acted more and more the way they wanted me to be. I turned away, locking my heart away, the essential me always out of reach. Throughout the years that followed, there was respite from these feelings of hopeless despair. Being involved in outer activities distracted me; they were even enjoyable in their own right. But I can sense how I was never fully connected with my riding or painting or reading or singing or piano playing. There was always a gap between the "real" me – it feels like a physical disconnection at my navel – and the me who was enjoying all these activities. I could not risk exposing myself. By really being committed to something and putting my heart into it, I risked having the heart of me destroyed. By revealing my enthusiasm for something, really caring about anything or anybody, I was vulnerable to attack. And my father was master of the art of crushing an idea or a feeling or an enthusiasm with just a look or a simple dismissive comment. I mastered my defense; if I didn't really care about anything, nothing he said could really reach me and I couldn't be destroyed. And life went grey. It has taken me years to realize that the breakdown that I had when I was fifteen, makes sense. I was not crazy or bad or inadequate. I made the only choice that I could have made and still stayed alive. I can feel the contempt my father had for me during this time. There was something wrong with me. I was not OK. Even through my seeing a child psychiatrist (who was a nice man but totally useless – writing this brings tears, as I realize that he was perhaps the first person in years who just let me be without any pressure to speak or explain myself or be different), there was this weight from my father of wanting me fixed, wanting me different, a silent critical, contemptuous, hateful push, push, push...

When I was eighteen I went to another psychiatrist. I was having nightmares and couldn't sleep, I had outbursts of rage, including more than once when I attacked my father and would happily have killed him. I still remember the extreme anger that I felt when I said that my mother was unhappy and the psychiatrist replied, "Don't you think that your mother is happy and it is you who is unhappy?" Years later I found out that only a few months earlier my mother had tried to commit suicide. I felt so unheard; even my grasp of reality was being questioned. I felt so scared that I was "going crazy," and this person was only intensifying that. And my father and mother were treating me as if I was sick, that it was all me. The sense of shit inside was so strong, and my sense that I could cope with life was so weak. Thoughts of suicide were with me almost constantly.

By the time I was 21, I was convinced that I was useless and was never going to be able to amount to anything. I was weak, crazy, incompetent, lazy; contempt was too good for me. Worms had more value. I was enrolled in a horticultural course at a local college. To get there meant traveling across town every morning (two buses and the subway). There was a railway bridge that we went over and every time we passed it I fantasized throwing myself off. Traveling the subway became more and more difficult. I hugged the wall in fear. There was such a strong feeling that if I let go even for a minute, I would find myself under the wheels of the train. The struggle between the part that wanted to die and the part that wanted to live was so intense. And the part that wanted to die was getting stronger and stronger. (Although this was not how I experienced it at the time. It just felt like it was only a matter of days before I would jump.) I am very clear that if I had not read a small notice on the board at the college that I would not be here today. It was for the counseling service, open Tuesday, Wednesday and Thursday afternoons between 2 and 4. It was 2:30 on Tuesday afternoon. A small, dark, bearded, smiling Jewish man came forward when I asked for Jan Shoicet, and my journey back to myself began.

Although the changes that happened through the therapy that I entered at that time were helpful and the thoughts of suicide receded and good feelings about being alive grew, my sense of myself as being OK at the core remained very fragile.

After the birth of my daughter, with my relationship with my husband mired in our collective psychological shit, suicide felt more and more like the only way of releasing me from what felt like unbearable pain, impossible impasse. I just didn't feel that I was strong enough to keep on enduring. So I ignored the future and concentrated on one day, one hour at a time. And slept as much as possible. And then a little book turned up. I read it and part of me prayed that what it said was true. And whole heaps of me said, "Don't get your hopes up. You've done Primal Therapy, Gestalt, Bio-energetics, Polarity Therapy, Pulsing, Psychodrama, Psychosynthesis, Assertiveness Training... and none of them has really hit the mark. All the wonderful promises of this and that have turned out to be hollow, or at least things that happen for others and not for you. You're too damaged ever to be OK. So don't hold your breath on this one either." So you can imagine my relief when something shifted, really shifted for the first time, when I did Focusing, and I found that I felt lighter, and there was real movement, and I felt more like me. And it felt real all the way through – it had happened to me too! Focusing was not just a bundle of false hopes and empty promises. It was the genuine article, the real McCoy. And here, right in here, almost right away there was this sense of a me that was OK, not my problems, not my shit.

One thing that bothered me through the years that followed was that there were still periods, even very recently, where the part of me that wanted to die was still very strong – where I would be very close to being completely immersed in feeling that my essential inadequacy was the reason that I was not able to solve some problem in my life. I would wonder: am I really not OK? Is it the Focusing process? Is it the way that I am doing it?

It may seem obvious to others that my feelings of wanting to die are directly linked to being under internal attack, but it has taken years for me to make that connection. For a long time I was really confused as to how to recognize my Critic, even after reading the many articles in *The Focusing Connection*. I didn't really hear words, my Critic didn't speak to me. After many years of Focusing, I have become aware of the signs of being under attack. It is more like recognizing the attacker's spoor. Some of the signs are: when I feel really shitty in my middle for no apparent reason; when I start to feel that I have to hide my feelings or behave differently; when I feel shame. These first three are the clearest and most reliable indicators for me; I know I am under attack for sure. Also: when I find it hard to summon up enough energy to tackle the ordinary tasks of life, when I feel that I want to withdraw from people, when I feel really critical of others, when I feel that my house is not clean enough, when I feel I am not giving my daughter enough attention, when I feel am not doing enough, when I feel I am letting the people in the British Focusing Network down because I am late with the newsletter, again! All of these are signs that now have me checking the undergrowth.

While it has always been clear that being identified with the Critic or with the feelings that the Critic brings are not helpful, just putting them to one side has also been more than unhelpful. It has kept me stuck in the past, repeating the old patterns over and over again, sometimes with close to fatal results. When I put them to one side, without their being really experienced and worked through, they just creep back and reemerge later. For years, I was really unclear about just what I needed to do to release this impasse. I tried Ann's three-step process with the Critic, I tried Gene's suggestions, I tried sensing what the Critic was trying to do for me, I tried backing up and sensing the new life. But none of them really got to it.

This next bit is the most important bit of all. These two kinds of inner experience, being identified with the Critic or with the feelings that come when under attack, are perhaps the most difficult to not wind up either dissociating from or identifying with. The way that keeps me from collapsing into the experience or running from it is the same as with anything else that comes: relationship. When I can build a relationship, I can stay there and sense it directly in my body without becoming identified. It has become very clear to me that if the parts of me that criticize and attack me and the parts that suffer from this attack are not sensed in the same way as anything else that comes, with the same kind of relationship of being with, then they will never have the opportunity to be healed. "They that are abused, hurt, violated, rejected, misunderstood, criticized, want to die" and "they that have taken on the fear, unlived, unhealed parts of my parents and the world and abuse me" will continue to act out, undermining my life and my sense of OK until I directly sense in my body the quality of how that whole thing is. I need to sense the place that has been attacked, just how it is for that part, and I need to sense the place that is attacking, just how it is for that part. They need to be heard, sensed, allowed to say just how bad it is, and just exactly how it is that bad *for them*. That is what they want from me. Then there is real movement. And real grief, and real rage, and real regret and sorrow, and fear, and lots and lots more.

It is essential that my relationship is real, that I don't pretend that I am feeling loving when part of me is hostile and rejecting. If I ask myself, "How friendly am I feeling towards what has come?", then I can sense all the complex and ambivalent feelings that come, and they can all have space. I have found that asking "Am I feeling friendly?" has an implicit skew towards feeling I should feel friendly. That doesn't seem to happen when I phrase it the first way. I have feelings around the word Survivor. My insides do not want to identify with "survivor" any more than with victim – although I was certainly abused and I survived the experiences. To call myself a Survivor feels like stepping back into the straitjacket of the past, identifying with my experiences of being a victim rather than being with them. My insides also object to capitalizing Victim and Survivor. When they become named like that they solidify into static structure-bound objects, and I stop sensing them directly.

What I can say with clarity and strength is, "I survived. I am aware of the strength and courage that I needed to find within myself to stay alive. I am aware of how hard it was to choose to live. I am aware of how sometimes it felt like cowardice not to kill myself. I am aware of how much pain and isolation I endured. I can really sense that part, and I can let it know that I can feel just how horrible it was. I can feel just how much that part wanted to die, over and over and over again." And I say to that part: "This is hard to say, because there is a part of me that would like you to feel differently, but I promise you that you can stay just the way you are for as long as you need. I will not pressure you to change, or feel differently or be different in any way. I will do my best to make a space where you can change, when and if you are ready in the way that you want to and hear what you need heard and support you in the ways that you need." When I make a promise like that to part of me, then it is easier to make that space and defend it from further attack. And, of course, the parts of me that feel hostile need hearing and defending too – they don't have to change how they feel either.

It has taken years of Focusing (I began in '83) for me to really be grounded in that experience of being the part that is OK. Through my struggles with making distance with something when I was learning Clearing a Space, I have learned to respect my body's need to have me stay with something right now. I have learned to be gentle and compassionate to what comes, to hear its fears that I might abandon it or want to fix and change and deny it. I have learned that something comes as pain when I am trying to ignore it. I have learned that if I can let it know that I hear it and that I want it to be there and to know what it is that it is longing to tell me, that it will ease and then we can just be together for as long as it needs. If I can tell it that it can be there just as it is for the rest of my life if it needs to (and, of course, mean it), then it can trust me and it can come forward, and let me know what it needs to have heard. And if I can really just hear what it needs to have heard, it changes and moves and I am no longer the same.

It has taken me the best part of twenty years to make a separation between me and the part that wants to die and the part that wants to kill me. I don't want to deny them anymore, that is really important. And I don't want to identify or be identified with them anymore either. Until now, I could not have spoken of my feelings of wanting to die openly. Only a very few people have ever known about these feelings at all. Although I understood how other people might want to commit suicide and I never felt critical of them, I felt that people would think I was weak and sick and crazy and despise me for such feelings (as my parents did). People would pity and look down on me. Or even worse, would shy away from me. They would somehow see me and treat me differently if they knew this about me. And I can sense that for some part of me this is still how it is. I can still feel that fear tightening in my stomach. I really don't want people to pity me, or to see me as psychologically fragile or damaged. I'm not. I am actually so strong now that I can be with these parts and love them just as they are for as long as they need. Writing this has helped me to clarify where I am on this journey — and to make several important steps along the way. One of the most important is to come out of the closet about all of this and still love myself. Perhaps even more important, to sense me as essentially strong and whole. Maybe I'll even find that others still see me as strong and capable and fundamentally OK and love me too. As I write this I see the faces of my dear friends all over the world, and feel your love and know that you do.

Treasure Maps
to the Soul

*Treasure Maps to the Soul is an approach which applies
Focusing to difficult life issues such as action blocks,
addictions, severe self-criticism, and depression. For over
ten years now, Barbara McGavin and I have been
developing this approach, and a brief history of this
development is told in "The Treasure Maps Story – So
Far."*

*The first article we published about the Treasure
Maps work was called "Standing It," and this article is
still a good introduction to a central aspect of the basic
approach. "The Dog Story" is a teaching tale about the
process of exile, one of the basic concepts of Treasure
Maps.*

*"Releasing Blocks to Action" and "Radical
Gentleness" (written for this book) tell about applying
Focusing to two of the difficult Treasure Maps areas:
action blocks and the Inner Critic.*

The Treasure Maps Story – So Far

Appeared in The Focusing Connection, *November 1997*

Since September 1994, Barbara McGavin and I have been on a remarkable journey that has included profound inner transformation for each of us, mind-bending theoretical insights, and deep connections with hundreds of people and their journeys. We call the work we are doing "Treasure Maps to the Soul."

Although the roots of it go back further, for me it really started in the summer of 1994 when Barbara sent me an article for *The Focusing Connection* called "The 'Victim,' the 'Critic,' and the Inner Relationship: Focusing with the Part that Wants to Die" (reprinted in this volume). It is an amazing article, and although perhaps one could say that I already "knew" what was in it, Barbara was taking the inner relationship to such extremes of depth and beauty that I found my own work beginning to change. I began to embody the belief that anything in us can be heard with compassion – and that the parts which look the ugliest need to be heard the most.

Little did I know that I was soon going to face one of the greatest challenges of my life to my ability to be self-compassionate. On September 15, 1994, I visited Glastonbury, England, and through a series of openings at the sacred sites there, I was guided to recognize that the way I had been using alcohol was an addictive pattern, and I needed to stop.

The effect of this emotionally was like being thrown in a bathtub of ice water, while feeling that I had lost my best friend. Fortunately, or angelically, Barbara and I were about to teach a series of Focusing workshops together, so I had one of my favorite Focusing partners right there when I needed her. I really needed help to listen compassionately to the part of me that still wanted to drink – I tended to feel ashamed of it and want to hide it under the nearest rock instead. We grabbed every free moment to trade Focusing time, and Barbara also worked on tough areas of her life.

Something interesting started to happen – we began to see patterns. After every session we would pull out our notebooks and take notes on the theoretical connections we were making. And, although our work felt too raw and personal to share easily, the people in the workshops somehow asked questions that could only be answered by reaching into the cauldron of new material that was forming.

At that point one key insight was clear: difficult, despised areas of life, like addiction and depression, are not just problems to be resolved. They actually point to treasure. They are signposts, indicators that something valuable and positive is hidden away, waiting to return to one's wholeness. Seeing them that way gave a whole new slant to inner work. That was when we began to use the phrase "treasure maps to the soul."

In the months after that, back home in California and England, we began to write a chapter outline for a book. It was my poet-colleague Barbara, as I recall, who started giving metaphorical names to the difficult areas of life. Most of those names have survived intact in our work today: The Dragon for the Critic, the Fog for Confusion, the Swamp for Action Blocks, and the Pit for Depression.

It was right at this time that New Harbinger Publications asked me to write a book about Focusing, so Barbara and I put the Treasure Maps book on hold while I wrote *The Power of Focusing* (with her help).

In August 1995, Barbara and I spent nine days together with absolutely nothing else on the agenda but Focusing, thinking, talking, and mind-mapping. During this time the area of Addictions was named the Wilderness and Unfulfilled Desire became the Mountain Top. More importantly, we discovered that there were three powerful processes underlying all our Treasure Maps work. They were explications of processes found in Focusing but more specific, more pointed. We called these the Three Parts of Magic – the Inner Relationship, Standing It, and Wanting. (We now know that all three work together and integrate into a powerful change process which we call the Alchemical Marriage.)

Since that time, we have taught Treasure Maps in workshops in various parts of the world, together if possible, separately if necessary. Every time we teach together, the Treasure Maps material grows. We added the River to express the difficult area of Overwhelming Emotion which can sweep you away, then realized that rivers could also dry up, and that Too Little Emotion is also a Treasure Map. We added The Edge of the Cliff because there had to be something about fear and excitement, and found that we were actually talking about situations of Impasse, where it feels impossible to move forward or back – yet there is an urgency, like something *must* happen.

Because we are very different, our collaboration is based on our taking complementary roles. Barbara tends to be the one who can grasp the concepts long before they can be articulated. I'm slower; but once I finally catch on, I can usually articulate them so that others understand as well. For example, when I arrived in England in August 1996, Barbara announced, "The Edge of the Cliff is part of the Magic." "What do you mean?" I asked, mystified. "I can't explain it yet," she said, "I just know it's true." Two weeks later, in the middle of a workshop in a different country, I woke in the middle of the night. "Oh! The Edge of the Cliff is part of the Magic!" I finally got it. Now we teach it that way – and The Edge of the Cliff continues to evolve.

How is Treasure Maps different from straight Focusing? Of course Focusing helps you find the treasure in the difficult areas of your life. But the Treasure Maps work makes it explicit. We've identified typical parts found in each of the areas, and we've developed processes (or "protocols") for working with the parts. We have a model of how natural change and growth happens (The Edge), and a metaphor for what gets in the way (The Amoeba and the Cookie Cutter). We have a step-by-step method for turning the Dragon (Inner Critic) into the Visionary Lover. The work with addictions alone is revolutionary. Imagine asking the part that wants to drink (smoke, watch TV...) what positive feeling it wants to help you experience.

Other people have contributed to the development of Treasure Maps. All of our students and colleagues who have come to workshops have made an impact on our thinking, but perhaps the most influential has been Larry Letich, who identified five levels in the Pit (of Depression) and how they connect to the Wilderness (of Addiction).

Afterword to
The Treasure Maps Story – So Far

As I read this article now, seven years later, here is what stands out for me. This sentence: "I really needed help to listen compassionately to the part of me that still wanted to drink – I tended to feel ashamed of it and want to hide it under the nearest rock instead." Do you see what I see?

That's right: there's an unacknowledged part. The part of me that still wanted to drink is acknowledged, but the part of me that "tended to feel ashamed of it and want to hide it under the nearest rock" is identified with. I'm saying "I want to hide it under a rock" instead of "Something in me wants to hide it under a rock." Even though our Treasure Maps work has disidentification as its central theme, and even though we had been doing it for three years at the time I wrote this article, I did not notice the identification in what I wrote. To me that fact embodies how far Treasure Maps to the Soul has come in the seven years since this article was written in 1997, and how much clarity Barbara and I have gained since then. (As well as illustrating how difficult it can be catch one's own identifications!) We've been teaching retreat-length Treasure Maps workshops three or four times a year since 1996, and every time we teach, the process deepens and we learn enormous amounts. We hope to write a book about it someday – if the process ever holds still!

Perhaps the greatest leap has been in the concept of Presence. (If I had known about Presence when I wrote this article, I doubt if I would have missed acknowledging that hide-it-under-a-rock part.) We took the word "Presence" from the writings of John Welwood, with apologies, because we're not using it in quite the way he would. When Presence came into the Treasure Maps work, around 1998, the whole process opened, becoming easier to do and easier to understand.

In 1999 we changed some important wording. What we'd been calling The Magic, we started calling The Powers. The Magic of the Inner Relationship became The Power of Presence. The Magic of Standing It became The Power of And. The Magic of Wanting became The Power of Not-Wanting/Wanting. To have a "power" is to have an ability, an ability that can be practiced and exercised and can grow. This is more in line with reality than calling it "magic." The results may seem magical, but the abilities are not; they are well within the range of human possibility.

We had a big development in our concept of the Inner Critic, which we called "The Dragon." At first we didn't realize that The Dragon had a counterpart, that every time there is a part that is criticizing, there is also a part that is criticized. We began to see this around the time that the concept of Presence came in, and for the same reasons. Presence would never feel criticized, so the inner critic must be attacking – not me, but something in me. From here our understanding flourished as we began to talk about "controllers" rather than Critics, and to understand the qualities of this interesting key dynamic. (See "Radical Gentleness," in this volume, for more about this.)

The Power of Not-Wanting/Wanting has developed quite a lot, as we learned how to iterate the not-wanting invitation, and later the wanting invitation (2001), to facilitate each side in an inner conflict reaching its essential quality of aliveness. We saw, with anyone we worked with, how every part, no matter how ugly or dangerous it appeared at first, held a positive life-forward energy to contribute to the person's whole life. How exciting: this was not just theory! It was true in practice, over and over again.

Perhaps our greatest breakthrough was in understanding more about the origins of difficult life issues in the roots of trauma. Crossing writers such as Peter Levine with Gene Gendlin, we developed a model of what happens when an organism moving forward encounters a persistently insoluble problem, which is what a trauma is.

In 2004 we discovered the work of Richard Schwartz on Internal Family Systems Therapy. There were amazing similarities to what we had already developed, and we felt we had discovered a kindred soul. Schwartz's writings helped us distinguish more clearly than we had before between a reactive part that doesn't seem to care about the consequences of its actions, and a traumatized part whose unhealed pain provides the source and the reason for the out-of-control behavior of the reactive one. His concept of Self was interestingly different from Presence; we found it helpful in important ways, and have begun to talk about the Self, with appreciation to him.

We didn't adopt Schwartz's methodology, however, and there are still interesting differences between our view and his. The dialogue continues. And so does the development of the work called Treasure Maps to the Soul.

Since this article was written in 1996, some of our terminology has changed. But the ideas and experiences expressed here remain essential to our work, both Treasure Maps to the Soul, and our approach to Focusing itself.

The phrase "Standing It" has changed: we have another name now for this process; we call it "The Power of And." But I still have a fondness for the name "Standing It." That phrase captured the difficulty of holding two parts of us in Presence at the same time, poignantly expressing that it requires a kind of steadfast enduring, like staying by a hot stove because you need to do the cooking. Sometimes it's important to acknowledge that the moves we need to do, for our healing, are not so easy.

You will also find an expression used often in this article that we use less frequently now: "part of me." We have realized that the phrase "part of me" is difficult for many people, because they tend to resist the sense of inner division that it evokes. In any case, it isn't the best phrase for what we mean. Far more serviceable is the lovely Focusing expression, "something in me," and that is what we teach now. "Part of me" is still welcome when it arises naturally, for those occasions when it does fit, but "something in me" ("something in you" from the Companion's point of view) is what we offer routinely.

"Standing It": The Alchemy of Mixed Feelings

Co-authored with Barbara McGavin
Appeared in The Focusing Connection, *July 1996*

When we have opposing feelings, when we are pulled in two different directions, when we are engaged in an inner struggle, the hardest thing to do is just to be with both sides in a Focusing way. Yet this is the one thing that will allow a resolution of a conflict in the right timing and with all parts of the self included and honored.

In our body of work called Treasure Maps to the Soul, "Standing It" is the term we use for the inner process of allowing two seemingly opposing parts to be there, in the body, and being with both. For example, if the Focuser is feeling both fear and excitement about moving forward, Standing It means allowing the fear to be there *and* allowing the excitement to be there, and hearing from each one. If the Focuser is aware of a part of her that wants to leave her job and a part of her that wants to stay, Standing It means giving inner breathing room to both parts, and allowing each one to tell its story.

Standing It is hard. It is much easier to become identified with one of the parts than to stay with both. When one is identified with a part, one says, "I am afraid," or "I am excited," instead of "Part of me is afraid, part of me is excited." Being identified with a part is like taking sides. Instead of being able to listen fully to each one, the Focuser becomes a partisan. We call this process "falling off" into one side or the other. If I actually have both fear and excitement and I have fallen off into fear, then I am only aware of fear. *I* am afraid. There is no room for the excitement, no company. And although the fear has lots of room, in a way, it too has no company. There is no inner "I" who can say hello to the fear and ask it to tell more about itself. The universe of me *is* fear.

Fortunately, if the Focuser falls off the balance point of Standing It, it is usually easy to climb back on again. One simply acknowledges the part that one is identified with *as* a part. "I am afraid... OK, a big *part* of me is afraid!" Typically this allows room for the other part to be acknowledged as well. "And now I'm realizing that another part of me is excited." Now the Focuser chooses to stay with both. "I'm going to let both the fear and the excitement be here."

In the community of Focusing, acknowledging both parts and then listening to each is not new. Standing It includes that and more. Formerly, we might have said, "I'm feeling both fear and excitement. I'm saying hello to each and sensing which one needs my attention first." With Standing It, we would say, "I'm saying hello to each and allowing both to be there. I'm sensing how it feels in my body to have fear *and* to have excitement." Only after a time of staying present with both parts would we begin to explore one or the other. And even that exploration is done within the larger awareness that both parts are there, somewhere.

Before saying more, we need to place Standing It in the context of our theory of Inner Relationship. In Inner Relationship, there are three modes of relationship between "I" and "it," between Focuser and Focuser's experience. The first mode, already alluded to, is *identification.* Identification is expressed as "I am..." The second mode is *dissociation.* Dissociation is expressed as "I am not..." The third mode is the middle position: "Part of me is..." In contrast to the first two modes, the third mode involves *disidentification* and *association.* Neither "I am sad" nor "I am not sad" but "Part of me is sad," "I have sadness," "Something in me is sad," "There is a sad place in me." This third mode is the position from which Focusing can happen. To enable Focusing, we need to help the Focuser's inner experience move from identification to disidentification, and from disassociation to association. Both moves are accomplished when the Focuser can say, for example, "Part of me is excited, and part of me is afraid."

In difficult, persistently stuck life situations, there is *always* a part of us that is out of awareness (dissociated), and another part that feels like all we are (identified). This is why Standing It is so powerful – and so difficult. The familiar place is the identified-dissociated place. "I am excited! Scared? Not me! I have no idea why I am stuck..."

The process of Standing It can be divided into four moves. First, becoming aware that Standing It is called for – that is, becoming aware that there are two parts that both need company. This alone can be very tricky! If the Focuser is identified with a part, then it doesn't feel like a "part," it feels like "me." Sometimes the best way to recognize this situation is when the "me" is struggling with, or pushing away, or trying to fix or rescue a part. Then what feels like "me" to the Focuser can be acknowledged as another part needing company. "I want to argue with this part of me. Oh! I guess I need to say hello to the *part* of me that wants to argue."

Second, the Focuser needs to acknowledge both parts. "So there's a part of me that wants to leave my job, and there's another part of me that wants to argue with it. I'm saying hello to each one. Both are here."

Third, the Focuser allows both parts to be there without taking sides and without pushing to any decision or premature resolution. This is hard. This is where the name "Standing It" is most relevant. People who are new to Focusing are the most likely to find it hard to "stand the heat" of allowing both parts to be there, and doing nothing more. There is a tendency to say, "I have to stay or go. I can't do both. I should just make a decision and get it over with." But when the Focuser can persist in simply being with all of what is there, the hard work of Standing It is rewarded with a transformation which feels magical, because it could not have been predicted by the logical mind.

Fourth, the Focuser senses into each part with compassion and empathy, and allows each part to reveal more about its point of view. This can be done without taking sides. The Focuser is in the position of the listener to each part. In the larger sense it doesn't matter which part comes first, as long as it is clear that each part will get its turn. At times, it may be preferable to begin with the more dissociated part, because that one has probably been waiting longer to feel heard. At other times, it may be important to begin with whatever is most prominent in awareness. In any case, the trick here is to avoid becoming identified, whether with a part or with the opposition to a part. This is why we emphasize, when listening to the point of view of any felt sense, not to argue or agree. Argument or agreement are signs of identification.

The magic of Standing It comes from acknowledging and hearing from all of what is there. All the parts can contribute to the right next step, which can be felt in a bodily way instead of derived logically. Our culture has not recognized the possibility of a carrying forward from opposites which is not a compromise, not middle ground, not a choice, but actually an inner consensus – a way forward which feels truly right to all. This magic can be applied to all sorts of stuck situations, such as the fear/excitement of being at a new edge, the stay/go of a decision, the attraction/repulsion of a relationship, the want-to/don't-want-to of an action block, and the craving/shame of an addiction.

We need to emphasize that Standing It is a part of a larger work, and can be enhanced by other techniques. But Standing It alone brings with it a special kind of grace, as we feel the gratitude of the parts at being heard without being pushed, and we allow for a larger place that honors and includes all the parts without denying any.

What follows are two versions of "The Dog Story," one by me, written for the handouts for Treasure Maps to the Soul, and one by Barbara McGavin, which appeared in *The Focusing Connection*. (I was listed as the co-author because the story is mine, but in that version the words are hers.) The story itself is one that I started telling at workshops around 1993-4. It's what you might call a "teaching tale." I began to tell it after I read the following words of Gene Gendlin in his book *Let Your Body Interpret Your Dreams*:

> Some self-assertive anger is a perfectly good thing and part of a healthy person. If it has been shunted aside for years, it might seem very strong and violent... You may sense your anger as negative, resentful, old, and corroded, when it comes. Take it as it comes, but expect it to turn into healthy anger or a sense of strength... What is split off, not felt, remains the same. When it is felt, it changes (p. 178).

I was struck by the whole idea that when something returns to awareness, returns from exile, it is at first very ugly ("...negative, resentful, old, and corroded..."). I thought, Well, if it has been in exile, of course it would be ugly! That place of exile, wherever it is, probably has terrible showers and no beauty parlors at all.

I wanted to help people have compassion for the part that has been exiled, and to understand that how it appears when it first returns is not the way it is in essence, but is only a result of its rejection and expulsion. No wonder it would be ugly, if that's what it has gone through. So I imagined a dog who had been sent away by its young owner – and also imagined the story's happy ending.

Today, after the detailed work on parts and points of view that Treasure Maps to the Soul has allowed, I would say that a description such as "ugly" is an infallible sign that one is identified with or at least biased toward another part, the part that fears the exiled part and perhaps exiled it in the first place. (Other such descriptions include: *flawed, defective, demonic, monstrous.*) The Dog Story, with its invitation of compassion for what life has been like for the exiled part, can be profoundly helpful for stepping away from identification with the "exiler" and holding all the parts with gentle acceptance.

The Dog Story

Appeared in the workshop handouts to "Treasure Maps to the Soul," 1997-2003

Once upon a time there was a boy who had a dog. The boy and the dog loved each other and played happily as dear friends. But one day the dog did something that the boy's parents didn't like. To appease his parents, the boy had to send the dog away. Years passed, and the boy forgot there had ever been a dog. But inside him there was still a place where something was missing. When he was a man, the missing place called to him so strongly that he had to go in search of what it needed. His search brought him to the edge of a forest.

Not knowing why, he found himself just sitting, waiting. Slowly, gradually, two burning eyes appeared in the darkness of the forest. The young man waited. Slowly, gradually, a long pointed nose emerged. The young man waited. Finally, out of the forest, slinking, there came an animal: thin, scarred, muddy, matted with burrs. You would hardly know it had ever been a dog.

The young man greeted it softly: Hello. The ugly dog stopped, untrusting. The young man felt in his body the memory stirring of the good and happy times with his friend. He said to this animal before him: I want to know how it has been for you, all these years in exile. And in its own way the dog told him, this, and this. Sad, lonely, scared, bitter... The young man told the dog that he had heard it. He heard all that it had gone through.

And with the hearing, the dog visibly softened, became warmer and more trusting. After some time, it came close enough to be touched. When the young man touched the dog, he could feel the missing place inside him begin to fill in. And soon after he took the dog home, and gave it a bath and a warm place by the fire – after it felt loved again – it was no longer ugly. It was beautiful.

The Dog Story

Co-authored with Barbara McGavin
Appeared in The Focusing Connection, *September 2000*

Once upon a time there was a child. This child longed for a companion to play with her, to run and jump and roll in the long grass. To snuggle up with on a cold winter's evening. To tell secrets to. And she was lucky because one day, much to her delight, she was given a beautiful puppy with a shining coat and sparkling eyes and a big doggy grin on its face.

The child and the dog loved each other so much and they were very happy together. Then one day the dog peed on the carpet. The child's parents were very angry and scolded the dog and told the child that she'd better keep that dog under better control or who knows what would happen!

The child did her best to make sure that the dog didn't get into the good rooms but one day she forgot and left a door open into the living room. Imagine her fear when she came into the room and saw that the dog had chewed almost right through the leg of her mother's favorite chair.

The dog was banished to the porch. If it ever came back into the house, it would have to go.

For hours the child would sit in the cold with the dog, snuggled into its soft warm coat until discovered and told to come into the house and leave that bad dog alone.

One day the door to the kitchen was left open and the dog was discovered with yet another precious possession in its mouth. This was the last straw. The child's father took one look at the dog and went to grab it. The child screamed and yelled at the dog. She ran at it and chased it into the woods at the back of the house.

At first it would try to sneak back into the garden, but her parents would yell at it and yell at her too so she began to watch out for it, chasing it away before her parents would spot it. Eventually it stopped coming back.

At first the child missed her friend terribly, but as the weeks and months passed the memories of how wonderful she had felt as they played together began to fade. She even started to believe what her parents said about how bad that dog had been. Spring came again and other friends came to the house and asked her to come out and play. Gradually she began to forget about the dog altogether.

Several years passed and they moved to a different part of the city. One day the child (who was quite grown up by now) was walking beside the edge of a big wood. Suddenly a movement in the dark undergrowth by the edge of the path caught her eye. It was so slight that she wasn't even sure that she had seen anything at all. But she was curious and although she was busy she thought that she could spare a couple of minutes standing there watching that place. So she stayed very still, watching where she thought the movement had been. Yes, there was something but she couldn't make it out. Something just there, hidden behind some tall grasses, under the trees.

Part of her started to become a bit scared. What if it was a bear? Or a wolf? Or a dragon? (Part of her was still quite a small child sometimes.) Then she took a moment just to acknowledge that scared feeling in her and she became still inside again. She brought her attention back to that place where that something was. Now she could just make out two eyes gleaming in the dark, watching her intently. Very quietly she whispered a greeting to the creature: "Hello. I can see you're there. I'm not going to hurt you. I'll just stay over here." And very slowly, so as not to frighten it, she sat on the ground.

The shadows lengthened and still she sat, motionless as a statue, just watching the spot where the two eyes gleamed. And then her patience was rewarded. A furry face emerged slowly. It was so dirty that it was hard to see what kind of an animal it was. The girl could see that it was scared, but also it was wanting to come closer to her. Gently she said, "I can sense that you're scared and you're wanting to come closer," and she waited to see what the animal would do next. Creeping on its belly, the creature inched its way forward until its head was almost touching the girl. It was filthy. Its coat was all matted with mud and burrs. Part of her wanted to pull away from it, worried about getting her clothes and hands all dirty. But as she looked in its eyes she could sense how lonely it was, how much it was wanting her to accept it just the way it was. She tried to sense how it would like her to be with it. It looked as if it wanted her to stroke it. She tentatively put out her hand so that it could sniff her. It gave her hand a little lick and lowered its head into her lap. Gently she stroked its ears. Now that it had come out of the bushes she could see that it was a dog – a skinny, filthy, frightened, lonely dog.

As she sat with it she started to sense that there was something familiar about this dog. Something familiar about the way it looked into her eyes and laid its head in her lap. As she kept it company the feeling of familiarity grew and grew, like something out of an almost forgotten dream. It reminded her of… what was it?… Oh! It reminded her of *her* beautiful dog. The one that had been chased away in disgrace so long ago. But it couldn't possibly be the same dog. That was such a long time ago. Tears came to her eyes as she remembered how close they had been, how much joy she had experienced as she played with her dear friend. She felt a desire to give this dog a hug but as she moved to embrace it, the dog jumped back and growled. It turned and fled into the dark. The girl was startled, but remembered that it was only doing something like that because it was frightened.

It was starting to get late, the sun was beginning to slip below the horizon. So she stood up – but before she turned away she said into the dark: "Thank you for coming. I'll be back – so if you want to come and see me again, I'll be here."

Over the following months the girl returned to the edge of the woods many times. Sometimes the eyes were there waiting for her. Sometimes they came after she'd been there for a while. Sometimes other creatures came to the edge of the woods. She waited patiently, developing a relationship with all that came. The dog came out of the woods more and more confidently until there was a warm, strong bond between them. She brought food for it and a brush for its coat. Gently she untangled the burrs and brushed out the dirt until its coat began to softly shine again. And before her eyes, her own beloved friend emerged. Its doggy grin returned. It began to bounce and run and play. And one day it followed her home.

My interest in action blocks goes back a long way, and comes first from my own struggle with writer's block.

As long as I can remember I've wanted to be a writer. When I was a child and a teenager, stories and poems flowed out of me. But the flow slowed down as I got into my 20s, and by the time I was 30 I was feeling blocked: full of a passionate desire to write, with a lot that I wanted to say, and just not doing it. My friend Margaret Warner found herself in a similar position, and for several years we were "writing buddies." We would meet every morning, or at other times twice a week, to talk about what we wanted to write, and about our feelings about the process, and then go into separate rooms to write. We got a fair amount written. She published papers. What I was writing (a popular book based on my doctoral dissertation) was never finished (although I'm now planning to publish the dissertation itself, on the 30th anniversary of its completion).

We were both on the staff of the Chicago Counseling Center (my presence there was largely Margaret's doing), and Margaret proposed that we offer a group for people with writer's block. My contribution was Focusing; hers was a technique from Gestalt therapy in which one dialogues with the part of one's self that is blocking. This was a new idea to me: personifying the blocking part. Some of our group members experienced breakthroughs. I, however, found writing as slow and painful as ever, especially when I moved to California and lost my writing buddy.

In California my passion for Focusing grew, and I felt the strong desire to write a book about Focusing. I thought, since Gendlin had already written a book about Focusing itself, I needed to find some special angle. I tried a number of approaches; the one I got the farthest with was entitled *Being a Healing Friend* and was about Focusing partnerships. The process of finishing enough of this book to show to publishers took about ten times as long as it needed to because of my dragging feet, and I also procrastinated about contacting publishers and agents. A number of years passed.

Although I had a regular weekly Focusing partner, Focusing had never helped with my writer's block. I could spend my session sensing into my feeling of frustration at not writing, but that didn't change anything in my life.

Finally one day, in depair, I remembered the Gestalt technique I had learned from Margaret Warner, and I realized there must be a part of me that didn't *want* to write.

This revelation was to have far-reaching implications. I would say that it was the earliest source, in my own work, of what ultimately became Treasure Maps to the Soul. It was the radical notion that what may need our attention is something which is *not* in awareness, but which can be invited into awareness once we have an inkling that it exists – through its effects.

There followed a series of Focusing sessions that were extremely powerful and ultimately transformative: after listening non-judgmentally to the part(s) of me that didn't want to write, being willing to keep listening, to stay with them as long as necessary for them to feel fully heard, I no longer had writer's block. Writing was easy. (If you're curious about how that process worked, read the following article!)

In December of 1994 I got a call from New Harbinger Publications, saying they were looking for someone to write a book about Focusing. I delivered the completed manuscript for *The Power of Focusing* six months after signing the contract.

The second source of my interest in action blocks had to do with wanting to change the world. During the 80s I was part of a network founded by futurist Robert Theobald called Action Linkage. Our purpose was to connect people who were envisioning positive futures, and acting locally toward that envisioned world. We were ecologically aware, community-based, consensus-run, etc. My role was to help people communicate about what they were doing and stay connected with the network. What I found, over and over, was that a lot of people were blocked. They had good ideas, but they didn't get around to acting on them. Slowly the notion began to grow in me that I could contribute best to the world I wanted to see by helping good people get past their blocks.

Note: The section on the Critic in the article that follows is slightly out of date. See the article "Radical Gentleness" in this volume for the very latest on that key topic – but the rest of the "Action Blocks" article is current.

Also, what we call "dissociation" in this article we now refer to by the more evocative name of *exiling*. What we call here "the middle position" is what we now refer to as *Presence*.

Releasing Blocks to Action
with Focusing

Co-authored with Barbara McGavin
Appeared in German in Focusing im Prozess, *2000*

Summary

Focusing provides powerful tools for releasing blocks to action. A "block to action" is an experience which can be described as "I want to do it, but I don't do it." Some examples of blocks to action are: procrastination, writer's block, inability to get organized.

In working with the action block with Focusing, we assume the existence of two parts: the part that wants to do the action and the part that doesn't want to do the action. We guide the Focuser to listen compassionately to the part that doesn't want to do the action. Three typical patterns may emerge, although a particular session may not follow any pattern. These are: the pattern of protection, the pattern of rebellion, and the pattern of wanting something else. There may also be an Inner Critic who needs to be heard with compassion.

Characteristics of Action Blocks

An action block is the felt experience of being unable to do an action. This can be phrased as "I want to do it, but I don't do it." The action may be a single action, such as a phone call to a publisher, but more often it is a general type of action or activity, such as "making phone calls," or "getting organized," or "writing." If a person has the experience that all or many types of action are difficult to get started or to accomplish, this is called "procrastination" or "being stuck."

In working with Focusers, it is useful to identify whether situations that they are facing are action blocks. A young man, for example, tells me that he feels frustrated and lonely for the lack of having any fulfilling relationships with women. As we discuss this, it becomes clear that he is aware of certain actions that he could be taking in order to meet more women, and to get better acquainted with the women he meets, but he isn't taking those actions. So we can approach this issue as an action block. By contrast, another man says he has done everything he knows how to do, and nothing works. There is no action he feels blocked about in this regard. So for him we will need a different approach. [In Treasure Maps to the Soul, the second man would be working with the Mountain Top (Unfulfilled Desire) rather than Swamp (Action Blocks). *Note added 2005.]*

Once we characterize an issue as an action block, we can assume the existence of two parts (or "aspects of inner experience"): the part that wants to do the action, and the part that doesn't want to. Typically, the Focuser is *identified* with the part that wants to, and *dissociated* from the part that doesn't want to. Let us discuss these terms further.

Identification, Dissociation, and the Middle Way

We can describe three types of relationship with inner experience. The first, called "identification with a part," is the experience of *being* one's feelings. The person says, "I am sad," "I am angry," "I am afraid." When a person says "I am…" then he is *identified with* the experience of which he is speaking. When a person says "I am sad," then she experiences sadness as *identical* with *herself.*

The truth is, part of her is sad, and part of her is more than that. But she has become identified with the part that is sad. Instead of being aware of her wholeness, she is aware only of a part.

Identification with a part can feel like "taking sides" internally. This person has taken sides: "I need to get rid of this part of me that's so angry." A person is identified with a part if he finds himself unable to be compassionate with someone or something, especially with another part of himself. "I am impatient with my fear" needs to become "Part of me is afraid and part of me is impatient with that."

The second type of relationship with inner experience is called "dissociation from a part." If "identification" is "me," "dissociation" is "not-me." "I am not sad." "I am not angry."

One might, of course, truly not be sad. Then "I am not sad" is simply true. But if one is sad, somewhere – if something in there is sad – and one does not know it, then one has dissociated from one's sadness.

A dissociated part is something which belongs to you, which is yours, yet you do not recognize it. You are not aware of it. You do not feel it. Or, if you feel it a little, you may be feeling much more strongly that you reject, deny, judge, or despise it.

Identification and dissociation often go together. If you feel both fear and excitement, and you become identified with the fear ("I am afraid") then you are almost certainly going to be dissociated from the excitement. Only after you disidentify from the fear ("Part of me is afraid") do you have the inner space to feel the excitement ("And another part of me is excited"). Or you may be identified with the Critic, taking sides to judge and criticize some other part of you which has been dissociated.

The middle position, neither "me" nor "not-me," is technically called *disidentification* and *association,* but we can call it, more simply, "being with."

In the middle position, I am *with* something that I feel. A part of me feels this way, and I can acknowledge that. There is room for other parts of me to feel other ways.

This middle position is extremely powerful. From here, you can stand anything. You are not overwhelmed; you are not denying. You are present to the truth of how you are right now. You are aware of your inner experiences, you are acknowledging them, they are part of you and you are more.

At this level it is easiest to access the larger part of you, that which can be with what is. If you are identified with anything, it is with the largest accessible self, that Self who is able to be compassionate with whatever needs compassion.

The pattern of identification/dissociation in action blocks

In action blocks, the person is typically identified with the part that wants to do the action, and dissociated from the part that doesn't want to. When I had writer's block, I would say, "I want to write! I really want to write! I don't know why I don't write!" Notice the identification: *"I* want…" I was only aware of wanting to write, unaware of any part of me which didn't want to. As is typical with dissociation from a part, I felt the *effects* of the part that didn't want to – this is the part (in Gestalt therapy, the "Underdog") which is so powerful from its position of dissociation. Some people call it "the saboteur" or "the resistance." It has no voice, yet it has complete power to stop the show. This is the action block dynamic: identified with the part that wants to do the action, dissociated from the part that doesn't want to do the action, and stuck. No action.

Beginning with the part that doesn't want to

The first step of using Focusing with action blocks is to invite the Focuser to get a felt sense of the part that *doesn't* want to do the action. We begin with this part because it is the dissociated part. When there is a pattern of identification/dissociation, both parts can be brought into middle awareness by bringing the dissociated part into awareness. The dissociated part "crowds out" the identified part, which can no longer be experienced as the whole universe and so becomes another part. For this reason, the exile gets the first turn.

Working with someone at this beginning stage might sound like this: "You've been telling me that you have a block about looking for a new job. Let's assume that there's a part of you that doesn't *want* to look for a new job. Would that make sense?"

The Focuser will usually say something like, "Yes, but I'm not in touch with that part," or start to give a "head" explanation: "That part is probably just depressed about going on the job search again."

My response is, "OK, so what I'm going to suggest is that I will guide you to get a feel for that part in your body, and then to have a gentle conversation with it in which you get to know it better and listen to what it has to say. Shall we do that?"

The Focuser agrees, and then I begin the "guiding in" instructions which I use at the beginning of every Focusing session (unless the Focuser already has an immediately present felt sense):

"Take your time to begin letting awareness come into your body. ... Maybe first being aware of the outer area of your body – your arms, and your hands. ... Noticing what your hands are touching, and how they feel. ... Being aware also of your legs, and your feet. ... Noticing what your feet are touching, and how they feel. ... Noticing the contact of your body on the chair [couch] and how that feels. ... Then letting your awareness come inward, into the whole inner area of your body, into the whole area that includes your throat, your chest, your stomach and abdomen. ... And just be there. ... Let your awareness rest gently in that whole middle area. ... Any other part of your body is OK to notice, but maybe start in this middle area, throat and chest, stomach and abdomen."

So far these are the instructions I always give. But here is where I begin to do something different for the action block process:

"And give yourself a gentle invitation in there, inviting that part of you that doesn't want to [e.g., look for a new job] to come into your awareness now, into your body. As if you're saying to it, 'I'd like to get to know you better, please come and be known.' And then wait." (longer pause) "And when you're aware of *something*, you might let me know."

In most cases, the Focuser will report something in the body, like a tightness in the chest or the throat, a band across the abdomen, fear in the chest, etc.

If the Focuser reports nothing coming in response to this inner invitation, I will say something like this: "So you might imagine yourself doing that action, going out to look for a job. Imagine yourself beginning that. And notice what comes in your body to say 'no.'" This evocative suggestion will often bring up the felt sense.

Another possibility is that the Focuser will report a body sensation, but say, "I'm not sure whether this has anything to do with the job issue." Then I will say, "So imagine yourself doing that action, and notice whether this feeling responds to that somehow." Usually the body sense tightens, or loosens, and this is an indication that it is connected with the issue. If the Focuser still doesn't know whether this is a felt sense of that issue, but no other sense comes, I will suggest that we go with this and see what happens.

Sometimes this part is hard to feel because it has been so dissociated, so "exiled" from awareness. There is a special type of guiding instruction that I have developed for this. I say: "Maybe it feels like *something* is there, but it's hiding behind a curtain, or behind a door. Almost like a child, hiding. If you were in a room with a child hiding behind a curtain, you would still be able to sense its feeling, its mood. Maybe you can sense if there might be something like that, something behind a curtain in there."

Once there is some meaningful body sense (felt sense) evoked by one of these means, I then guide the Focuser through the rest of a Focusing process with this part. For me, this includes:

(1) Acknowledging. "You might say hello to that place, let it know you know it's there."

(2) Describing. "And notice how you would describe it" or "Offer it that word 'tightness' and see if that really fits it the best, or if another word fits even better."

(3) Being with. "Notice if it's OK to just be with this."

(4) Inner empathy. "Take some time to sense how *it* feels from *its* point of view."

The "being with" and the "inner empathy" are really the key, and the earlier steps of "acknowledging" and "describing" will help the Focuser come into direct and present contact with the sense, and allow it (the part) to feel safe enough to begin to communicate.

After "it" begins to communicate, the guide has the important job of making sure that the Focuser remains in an empathic relationship with the part, neither arguing nor agreeing but listening. This is done by saying, "Let it know you hear that," whenever there is a communication from the sense. For example:

Focuser: "It says it's been protecting me from rejection."

Guide: "You might let it know you hear that, that it's been protecting you from rejection."

The Pattern of Protection

Since working with so many action blocks, in myself and others, I have begun to see some typical patterns emerge. Almost all action blocks eventually follow one of three patterns. The first pattern is the pattern of protection.

Often the blocking part feels that it is protecting the person from some undesirable (scary) outcome. This often connects to past experiences in which these outcomes did happen. For example, in a key Focusing session on my writer's block, I learned that the blocking part was protecting me from attack. It felt that if I wrote and published, I would be attacked. This connected to memories of my childhood and my father's sarcasm, which he used to "deflate" me when I seemed to be getting "too big." My blocking part was protecting me from my father's sarcasm.

In a Focusing session in a workshop, John had a sense of "creativity" bubbling in his stomach area, wanting to come out. But it was stopped by a block in his chest which felt cold and hard, like concrete. John sat with the concrete block in his chest, with interested curiosity. He brought compassion to it, and sensed its point of view, with empathy. Soon he began to sense that it was trying to protect him. It told him it was protecting him from exposing his creativity to the criticism of others.

This type of block typically shifts when it is heard and acknowledged. The guide's job (a very important one) is to guide the Focuser to hear and acknowledge the feelings and point of view of the blocking part. The guide's language includes: "Let it know you hear it," and "Check with it whether it feels really understood now, or whether that's part of it but there's more." When the part feels fully heard, it changes.

There is no need for negotiation. Evidently there are some methods for releasing blocks which ask the person to negotiate with the part, explain to it that things are different now, ask it to find another way to protect, etc. I have noticed that people tend to expect some kind of negotiation with the part to be the next step of the process. I need to explain to them that negotiation is not needed, and, in fact, in my experience negotiation slows down the change process because it interferes with the part feeling fully heard.

In her first Focusing session Mary told me that she had a "frog" in her throat – a persistent, physically felt block which could actually be heard in her voice when she spoke or sang. She said she knew that a part of her was afraid of self-expression, but she had already done a lot of work on this and she was ready for it to change. In the "describing" part of the session, she said it felt like a "lump." Then we had the following dialogue:

Guide: "You might just sit with that lump, to get to know it better."

Focuser: "It feels very determined."

Guide: "Ah, you're sensing that it feels very determined. And you might just ask it gently, what it feels determined about."

Focuser: "It's telling me that it has saved me many times, by not letting me say something that would have gotten me in trouble. And I'm telling it that I really appreciate that, but now it's time for me to take back the power to protect myself, and give it a different job."

Guide: "And you might notice how *it* feels when you say that."

Focuser: "It's still the same."

Guide: "Well, you know, I really appreciate that you were able to tell it your feelings. But I'm thinking that if I were that lump, I wouldn't be feeling very *heard* right now. See if you'd be willing to try something a little different, just as an experiment."

Focuser: "Sure!"

Guide: "See if you'd be willing to *just* tell it that you hear what it's saying, and then stop. No 'but.' Tell it that you hear it, and invite it to say more."

Mary followed this suggestion enthusiastically, and reported over the next ten minutes that the part kept telling her more. She was amazed at how much it had to tell her, including showing her scenes of specific times that it had helped her in the past. She just said, "I hear you," and kept listening. Then:

Focuser: "It's melting! I'm feeling this lump melting down the sides of my throat! There's a clear channel there now. My throat hasn't felt this good in years! This is amazing!"

Guide: "So really take time to feel and let in the good way it feels now."

The Pattern of Rebellion

The second typical pattern with action blocks is the pattern of rebellion. The blocking part is a rebel, a refuser, an inner "no." The Focuser may describe this part as "the resistance," but I like to translate the word "resistance" into "the part that doesn't want to." This inner rebel is a part that may be feeling passed over or pushed around, and it doesn't like that. It has a stubborn quality, a determination not to be forced. The part that says "no" is often paired with another part that says, "You have to."

In my Focusing with my own writer's block, I found a part like this, just before the block released. It felt very stubborn and rebellious. I even described it as an "inner teenager." This part of me was saying, "I don't want to do anything that I *have* to do." Unlike the part that was protecting me from my father's sarcasm, this part didn't have any objection to writing *per se*. Its objection was to being forced to do *anything*. This part changed after it felt heard and respected for its wishes. In fact, after this part felt that I really respected its point of view, it turned around and became part of the positive energy that helps me to write.

Another example: Teresa was taking an action block workshop, and wanted to try working with something "small." She picked the part of herself that hates to write thank-you notes. She does write thank-you notes when she has to, but she is aware that part of her hates to write them, and another part of her is forcing her to do it, riding over that other part.

The group was guided through a Focusing exercise for action blocks, and afterwards Teresa reported: "The part that writes the thank-you notes, and knows that it should write the thank-you notes, it had a lot to say, and it had a lot of reasons, and the other part, I couldn't get it, I couldn't get it to come out. When you said the part about the little child behind the curtain, it felt like it fit. It felt like that part was really young, and very shy. It finally came out but there was sort of a vagueness about it. It wouldn't let me hug it, didn't want to be touched, was kind of rejecting toward me, didn't want to be forced. It really resented being forced into doing anything, kind of dragging its heels. It needed more time. It just needed more time for me to communicate with it."

In this case something that felt so small, "only" about thank-you notes, turned out to be a shy child who resented being forced into doing anything. Surely this was connected with many more parts of Teresa's life. Although I didn't see the later Focusing on this issue, I believe that the good relationship which Teresa began to establish with this part will bear fruit. The more she is able to listen to this part, and to give it the time that it needs, the more it will transform into a willing ally.

Rebellious and stubborn parts need respect and understanding for their points of view. When there is a rebel part, the Focuser has been locked into a pattern of identification/dissociation. This might be identification with the part that says "You have to!" and dissociation from the part that says "I won't do anything I *have* to do!" Teresa's story sounds like this, when she reports that the part that writes the thank-you notes is easy to find and has a lot to say, but the part that doesn't want to is vague, appearing at first only behind a curtain. Or the Focuser might be identified with the rebellious part and dissociated from the part that says "you should." A third possibility is that the Focuser is flipping back and forth between identification with one and dissociation from the other, becoming the Rebel and the Critic alternately. All three of these patterns of identification/dissociation are stuck patterns; there is not forward movement.

Releasing the stuck pattern requires disidentification from either part. It means finding a position from which to listen with compassion to both parts, usually starting with the dissociated one. The guide's role is fundamentally the same as in the pattern of protection: "Let it know you hear that." "Let it know you hear that it really doesn't *want* to!" But there is also a difference. The existence of a rebellious part points to a breach of trust in the inner relationship, a long-time history of dishonoring and discounting that needs to be healed. Whereas the protecting part is stopping a particular action in order to protect me from the perceived consequences of that action, the rebellious part is stopping an action because it doesn't like the *way* it's being asked to do it. Healing this inner relationship can take longer; to re-build trust takes time. Yet the time that it takes is rewarded because this pattern is very likely not just about one action, but is about the relationship of the Focuser to his or her will and action in all parts of his or her life.

So the guide's role may include inviting patience and gentleness toward the rebellious part, and permission for the part to take the time it need to feel safe and trusting.

Focuser: "It doesn't want to be touched."

Guide: "OK. See if you'd like to appreciate it for telling you that, that it doesn't want to be touched. And maybe just find a way that feels right to sit with it, without touching it, but still letting it know that you're there."

Focuser: "It says it feels a little better but it might need me to sit this way for a long time."

Guide: "So you might let it know you hear that…"

Gene Gendlin writes beautifully about this kind of healing inner relationship when he says (*The Small Steps*, 1990): "The client and I, we are going to keep it, in there, company. As you would keep a scared child company. You would not push on it, or argue with it, or pick it up, because it is too sore, too scared or tense. You would just sit there, quietly… If you will go there with your awareness and stay there or return there, that is all it needs; it will do all the rest for you."

The Pattern of Wanting Something Else

The third typical pattern with action blocks is the pattern of wanting something else. In this pattern, the blocking part is carrying a piece of the person's life energy, and it is stopping the action because it feels that the action is taking the person in the wrong direction, away from the positive direction it desires.

Tom wanted to use Focusing to release a block to completing school projects. "I know what I need to do; I just don't do it." But as he spoke about his situation, it emerged that he didn't like his school program and he didn't look forward to the life that he was preparing for. He had been a creative writer, and had set that aside in order to take a degree in technical writing because he believed that technical writing would be a more secure profession. The projects which he had a block to completing were technical writing projects which would carry him closer to a career as a technical writer. Is it any surprise that these were blocked?

During his Focusing, Tom felt and listened to many parts, including the part of him that wanted him to have a financially secure future, and the part of him that felt disgust at the life of a technical writer. When the session (his first time Focusing) was over, he said that what had meant the most to him was getting in touch with his sadness over setting aside the creative writing. He had spent time just feeling and listening to the part of him that was sad about that. The next steps of this process remain to be seen, but my guess is that Tom will find some way to keep both important "wants" alive: the desire to be financially secure *and* the desire to express his creativity.

In working with this pattern, the guide needs to remember not to take sides, so that the Focuser also will not take sides. It can be tempting to side with the part that is carrying so much positive life energy, that has been set aside. But both parts really hold important aspects of the Focuser's wholeness. For example, a full life needs security and creativity, both. As in the other patterns, the guide helps the Focuser stay in a disidentified position in relation to all parts, to make sure all are fully heard.

One special consideration that often arises with this pattern is the importance of not making a decision prematurely. The guide may need to remind the Focuser not to make a decision about action until the listening process is complete.

Focuser: "This part of me is just so sad that it can't be creative any more."

Guide: "You might let that part know you hear it, that it's just so sad."

Focuser: "But I don't feel I can leave the program. My parents would be so disappointed."

Guide: "Some part of you is saying that this means you should leave the program, and another part is saying you don't feel you can. But would it be OK, for now, to just let go of what all this means about what you should do. Just wait on that. For now, just listen to each part. Do you still feel that sadness?"

Having described these three patterns, it is also important to say that the Focusing work is done with an openness to whatever comes, that any particular session or person may not follow any pattern, and even if the guide recognizes what may be a pattern, the guide remains open to what the Focuser is bringing, realizing that it may be different from what is expected, this time.

Working with the Inner Critic

Working with the Inner Critic is a key part of working with action blocks, because most people use self-criticism to deal with perceived action blocks. They call themselves harsh names in a fruitless attempt to get themselves past the block. Psychological sophistication doesn't really improve matters, it just changes the language from "I'm lazy" to "I have a sabotaging inner child."

The lash of the Inner Critic does not release the block; it makes it worse. Every human has a part that resists tyranny and force, whether the tyrant is outside or inside the self. As the Critic gets stronger, so does the Rebel. A stuck system can be in deadlock for years, with an implacable Critic, an immovable Rebel, and the life energy that wants to flow sitting frustrated, unable to get past this impasse.

To release this stuck system, the *last* thing we should do is make the

Critic into the bad guy. The way out is through acceptance, compassion, and listening—starting with the Critic.

The Critic has been described as "the superego," as a voice from "the head," as a force that sits on the good energy that wants to come. All this may be so. But, as my colleague Barbara McGavin and I have found, the Critic is also a part that has feelings, that wants to contribute, and that appreciates being heard. Or, as I sometimes say in workshops: "It's trying to help. It just has very bad communication skills!"

What we have found helpful is a three-part process. First, when the Critic shows up, have the Focuser acknowledge it, say hello to it. I do not use the word "Critic" unless they do. Instead, I prefer to describe the part by its behavior.

Focuser: "Now I'm hearing a voice from somewhere that says this is stupid."

Guide: "Ah. So you might say hello to the voice that says this is stupid."

In some sessions, this simple acknowledgement is enough to make that part subside or disappear. But when the Critic is persistent, we go on.

Focuser: "Yes, it's telling me I'm wasting my time."

Guide: "See if it would be OK to just sit down with that part, the one that's telling you you're wasting your time."

Now we come to the second part of the process, having the Focuser ask that part what it is afraid of. This is an invitation to the Inner Critic to get vulnerable. The theory here is that any attempt to control comes out of fear, fundamentally. The Critic is certainly attempting to control – so it must be afraid! But this is not about winning over it by proving that it is afraid. This is about creating a safe enough inner climate that the Critic begins to be able to feel its fears and tell about them. When this can begin to happen, the transformation has already begun.

If the Focuser has a particularly tough Critic, it may not be willing to tell the Focuser what it's afraid of for quite some time. But at least the Focuser can intuit that it must be afraid of something. I might say, "Let's say there's a particularly difficult person who's always jabbing at people. You may not be able to get that person to admit they're scared. But if you can empathize or intuit that that person must be afraid, in order to be jabbing at people that way, then at least your attitude toward them will change. See if you can just sense that this part of you is afraid of *something*." This kind of empathy will eventually allow the critical part to feel safe enough to admit its fear.

Once the critical part is able to admit its fear, the guide invites the Focuser to ask it what it doesn't want. Fear easily opens into "I don't want..." For example: "I don't want to be criticized, I don't want to be rejected, I don't want to starve..." The guide invites the Focuser to keep listening. "Let it know you hear that it doesn't want to be rejected. (pause) And see if it feels like it's told you all that it doesn't want, or if there's more." Only when this stage feels complete will it be possible to go on to the third stage.

The third stage is for the Focuser to ask the part, "And what do you want for me?" What we're really asking it is: "What positive feeling or state are you wanting to help me experience?" Other ways to say this are: "How are you wanting to contribute to me?", or even: "What is your gift?"

If this part (which we don't even want to call "Critic" any more) has been thoroughly heard in the second stage, it will be able to answer this new, positive question, and the results can be quite moving and surprising. If it is not able to answer the positive question, then this means more time is needed in stage two.

This is a transmutation process. By the time it can answer the question, "What do you want for me?" it has been transformed, and it is not a Critic any more.

Conclusion

The process described here for using Focusing with action blocks is based on a fundamental philosophy that every part or aspect of the self has a "good reason" for being the way it is, and that when it feels heard and acknowledged for its feelings and intentions, it is freed to change.

I owe more than I can possibly say to the inspiration of Eugene Gendlin, who writes: "What is split off, not felt, remains the same. When it is felt, it changes. … If there is in you something bad, sick, or unsound, let it inwardly be and breathe. That's the only way it can evolve and change into the form it needs" (*Let Your Body Interpret Your Dreams,* p. 178).

Introduction to
Radical Gentleness:
The Transformation of the Inner Critic

I was 22 years old, visiting Danny and Jane for dinner in Danny's grad student apartment in Chicago. When the food was served onto the narrow kitchen table, I happily dug in and began to eat. But instead of eating, my friends reached out for each other's hands and mine, in order to say a New Age blessing. Realizing my mistake, I felt a hot wave of shame wash over me, and I burst into tears. How could I be so stupid and insensitive as to start eating before the blessing? Kindly, they took time to listen to my feelings, and to assure me what I had done was OK, before we could eat our dinner. The judgment had not come from them, but from something inside me.

As I look back on that incident from the perspective of 33 more years of inner work, I feel poignant compassion for the suffering of that younger me. How painful and shameful it was, to make a mistake! If that sort of thing happened now, I would simply smile and reach for the outstretched hands. Sometime in the past 33 years, the shame of making that sort of mistake has lifted and released.

In that 33 years, in addition to all the general Focusing I have done, I have also worked specifically with what has been called "the Inner Critic," developing, with the help of colleagues and in co-creation with Barbara McGavin, a radically different approach to the inner criticizing process that ultimately connects to a theory of how inner parts of us arise and how they become exiled from awareness. This journey has had many stages.

As Focusing is traditionally taught (as I was taught by Gene Gendlin), the Inner Critic is the "superego," an intractable voice of shaming and damning that cannot listen and should not be listened to. Gendlin's primary technique was to wave the Critic away dismissively, saying, "Come back when you have something new to say." Meaning, of course, that since it never had anything new to say, it should never come back.

Gendlin does say (1996, p. 255) "When focusing becomes familiar, the client can sense the superego as a subpersonality. Something like fear, hysteria, or insecurity can be expected behind its attacking front.... From that felt sense we can work on the superego as we would on anything else." But rather than exploring that opening, he goes on to offer "bypassing the superego" as his main recommendation.

For a very long time I believed this view of the Inner Critic. There were early voices to the contrary: Jane Lowell wrote "The Critic: A Despairing, Unattended Felt Sense" in March 1985, and Jane Batt's "The Fearsome Critic is a Panicking Child" appeared in May 1986. (See also Phil Levy's "Is the So-Called Critic a Hidden Door to Our Experience?" and Ray Purdy's "Does the Critic Exist?") But I was still treating the Inner Critic as something to be set aside, "locked in a soundproof booth," as late as 1991 when I wrote my *Focusing Student's Manual.* I did become gentler, in that I began asking the Critic politely to step aside rather than waving it away dismissively, perhaps first acknowledging that it had something valuable to say.

I give credit to Ilehlia LeIndra, a wise and accomplished Focusing teacher who taught with me at Shenoa in 1992 and 1993, for radicalizing my view of the Critic. Ilehlia urged compassion for the Critic, and I began to wonder if it might actually be possible to treat this "critical voice" as just another part of us needing to be held with love.

It's true I can be rather slow to adopt new ideas, but it's still striking how long it took me to accept the possibility that the so-called Inner Critic is not the "bad guy" that it seems to be. Perhaps it was only in the context of the Treasure Maps to the Soul work that this attacking, criticizing part began to be understandable as "something in me which is criticizing right now." In other words, what seemed to be an immutably critical voice is actually an aspect of us in the process of change and transformation just like any other.

Once I got it, though, that compassion for the "Critic" was the fastest way to its transformation, I began to develop methods for facilitating that compassion. When someone feels under attack, compassion for the attacker can be hard to find. I remember saying to one woman under "Critic-attack": "You might want to make a guess about what a hard childhood it had, to be treating you that way now." Ultimately I found a reliable method for awakening compassion: the truth that something which is criticizing is always afraid. I *knew* this was so; it just felt intuitively true in my bones. But when "Critics" indignantly denied that they were fearful, I learned to have the Focuser offer the guess that they might be worried or concerned about something. That worked.

There was one final insight, the kind of "flip" in awareness that one wonders afterward how one could ever had missed, and that is that the Critic is not criticizing "me," but rather "something in me." To really do transformative work with this inner criticizing process, we need to disidentify, not only from the Critic, but also from its "victim," that in us that reacts to it.

Again, we were not the first to explore this territory. In November 1994 *The Focusing Connection* published an article by Dieter Müller, "The Critic as

Signpost: Changing the Focus from Criticizer to Criticized." Dieter wrote, "This inner relationship enables the client to take care of the one being criticized in the same way the client-centered therapist cares for the client." This is the first article that I am aware of that treats *the one who is criticized* as a part of us to be turned toward, listened to, spent time with. Dieter points out that the appearance of an Inner Critic is a "signpost" that such a criticized part exists, and needs compassionate company.

Again, since I did read this article, I'm not sure why it took me so long to "get it" – that the Inner Critic isn't criticizing *me*, it is criticizing *something in me* which also needs attention. When we (Barbara McGavin and I) finally did get this point, it was the final breakthrough we'd been waiting for in our understanding of the inner criticizing process.

This article was written especially for this volume, when I realized that, for all the interest there is in this topic, and all the times that Barbara or I had taught workshops on this, there was no one article that pulled together all our latest thinking and practice. Here it is.

Radical Gentleness
The Transformation of the Inner Critic

Newly written for this book

"It's like I don't deserve to feel this happy."
"I hate this weak, sad part of me."
"Why do I always have to be so stupid?"

No matter what kind of inner work they do, at some point people always encounter an experience that can be called the Inner Critic. This is often (but not always) a voice, often (but not always) harsh and attacking, that often seems to come when the person is close to some positive new steps, or touching on an inner vulnerability. This so-called Inner Critic seems to delight in crushing the small, the tender, the new and positive. No wonder that almost every method I have ever heard of treats the Inner Critic as something to be conquered, pushed away, perhaps even belittled or criticized in its turn. (For a notable exception, see *Internal Family Systems Therapy* by Richard Schwartz.)

When the inner world includes harshness, lack of acceptance, judgment (as in being judgmental), it becomes an unsafe place for a positive healing change to happen. Aspects of ourselves that might have bloomed into what they needed to be, instead are crushed and go into hiding. Obviously this is a sad state of affairs. But there are no true villains or victims here. Everyone inside is doing their best to help us... as we will see.

"A Part that is Criticizing Right Now"

This harsh attacker has been called "the Inner Critic," but I would prefer to call it "a part that is criticizing right now." As always, we want to use our language in a way that opens to the possibility of change. Yes, criticizing parts can change – I've seen it happen plenty of times. So let's call it "a part that is criticizing right now." Once we use this kind of language, we may even find ourselves getting curious about what might be getting it so critical. We have made a crucial shift, from seeing this part of us as *essentially critical,* by its very nature, to seeing it as in a temporary state that has come about for a good reason.

This is parallel to the shift we make when we stop labeling another person as essentially bad and start seeing their behavior as understandable from a certain point of view. When I see the mess in my daughter's room, I can think of her as "lazy," or I can remember how hard it was for me to hang up my clothes when I was her age. This shift in perception will profoundly affect my behavior with her. It doesn't mean I'll stop wanting her to clean her room – but it will change what I say to her, how I say it, how she perceives me, and ultimately the quality of our relationship.

A Process View

When people first hear that Ann and Barbara are suggesting that Focusers might be compassionate to their Critics within, they are dubious. It's as if we are suggesting that they love an abuser. Being compassionate to a criticizing part feels equivalent to being glad that it's there, making our lives a misery.

But again, this assumes that aspects of ourselves are fixed, unchanging. "Once a Critic, always a Critic." This is why I suggest the language: "a part of me which is criticizing right now." This shift in language parallels a profound shift in consciousness. There has been an assumption, built into our current language and worldview, that we are made up of units which do not fundamentally change. As Gendlin teaches (see *A Process Model*), we do not have to see ourselves as made up of units which then interact with each other, but rather as *processes*. Process and interaction are *first*.

In the inner world, and from a Focusing point of view, this is clear: when you sit with *anything*, it changes. Sit with something in you that is fearful, and it changes to being excited, or worried, or angry. There is an evolution in the feeling life that is unpredictable in advance, but makes sense in retrospect.

Why then, do experienced Focusers report an Inner Critic that appears to be the same, year after year? Still criticizing, still saying the same nasty phrases? Because there has been something missing, until now, in the quality of attention given to this criticizing part.

Can I Trust Myself?

The experience of an inner critic is deeply based in a lack of trust in a natural unfolding process that has a life-forward direction. If people have, as Freud thought, a fundamentally wild and primitive side that must be kept under wraps, then an inner criticizer/controller becomes crucial to any civilized person. (Freud called these two parts the "Id" and the "Superego.") If emotional states and behaviors do not evolve naturally of themselves into something more positive, then change must be imposed.

The tragedy of the inner criticizing process is that a part of us has come to lose trust in another part of us. As one young woman put it, "I have a part of me that's very angry with me, my behavior, my choices. It says, 'You're totally out of control, I don't trust you to make good choices.'"

And we see, over and over again, when we peer with compassion into the soul of a part of us that is criticizing, that it believes it is helping us. It has to help by criticizing because it fears that the other part of us which it is pushing or holding back *has no other hope of changing.* This is important, and we will return to it.

Identifying a Criticizing Process

You might think it would be obvious when a criticizing process is going on. But most of the time we are involved in this criticizing process without being aware of it as such, because we are identified with one of the inner characters in the drama. We find ourselves saying things like:

"This is stupid."

"I have to stop being so wimpy."

"I feel inadequate."

"I shouldn't be feeling this way."

An inner criticizing process correlates with any of the following activities:

(1) The use of pejorative language, like "stupid," "wimpy," "inadequate," and similar critical labels is always a sign of a criticizing process. See the next section for more on this.

(2) The use of prescriptive language such as "should," "ought," "have to," "need to," and their negatives – "shouldn't," etc. – usually indicates a criticizing process.

(3) The attempt to change yourself, or a part of you, is probably the sign of an inner criticizing process, especially if there's an assumption that the change has to happen for you to be OK. No wonder the world of self-help is so full of inner critics! It takes a big leap of awareness to understand that personal growth must start with self-acceptance, not self-criticism. (For a refreshingly different approach, see the excellent *I Know I'm in There Somewhere* by Helene Brenner, a book based on the idea that self-acceptance is the road to change.)

Definition: An inner criticizing part is any part of you that believes that you or another part of you has to change in order for you to be OK.

Truth in Labeling

As we've seen, the inner criticizing process often shows itself through the pejorative language we are using to label our experience. This process can be hard to recognize, and therefore hard to deal with. We can be so identified with the part of us that is labeling another part of us, that we don't recognize the labels we are using as weapons in a war. They feel like "the truth." But they are not.

Recently I was the Companion to a Focusing session in which the person who was Focusing was spending time with an inner "something" that didn't feel like talking. She was describing this "something," as we do in Focusing, saying, "It's small and hard, like a lump... It wants me to be here, it's glad I'm paying attention... It wants me to be here, but it doesn't want to talk to me... It feels like a selfish, dominating part..." Whoa! Do you see what happened? From simple direct descriptions like "small and hard, like a lump," the Focuser has moved through empathy with its point of view ("It wants me to be here..."), and then the pejorative language begins. "Selfish" and "dominating" are not simple descriptions. They are levers – devices to pry out a resisted change. They are from a point of view – and it's not the point of view of the part being described.

In this case I responded: "You're sensing something in you that's calling the small, hard part 'selfish' and 'dominating.' You might want to acknowledge *that* part as well." The Focuser, used to this kind of shift back into Presence, was able to do this, and reported: "Yes, that part of me can't understand how something could want my awareness and not want to talk. It really wants this thing to talk."

What a big difference! We've gone from "It feels like a selfish, dominating part..." to "[Something in me] really wants this thing to talk."

And consider this: whenever you find something in the inner process, in your own Focusing or someone else's, and that part doesn't want to talk, doesn't want to come out, doesn't want to reveal itself, chances are, 99 times out of 100, it doesn't feel safe, and it doesn't feel safe because there is another part of the Focuser lurking, ready to criticize it.

So when pejorative labels are used in inner descriptions, they're usually signs that another part is present, hiding in identified position, making the process unsafe and also itself unheard.

Presence Is the Opposite of Criticizing

The environment in which an inner criticizing process can begin to transform is Presence. "Presence" is what Barbara McGavin and I call the ability or state of *being with* any inner experience, with interested curiosity and without judgment.

Presence is in many ways the opposite of the inner criticizing process. In Presence, we are able to turn toward whatever we feel, whatever is going on in us, with gentleness, with trust in its underlying life-forward direction. In Presence, we are not trying to change what we find, but only to hear it, so that it can find its own change if it needs to. (See the introduction to "Facilitating Presence" in this volume for more.)

The inner criticizing process isn't Presence, *but it needs Presence.* If we criticize the critic, we are perpetuating the problem. This is a subtle and very important point, so let me say it again: *If we criticize the critic, we are perpetuating the problem.* Making this part of us wrong for being as it is, means becoming *its* critic – and that simply moves the same dynamic to another level. Almost all approaches to dealing with the Inner Critic are of this type: they marginalize the criticizing aspect, in effect scolding it for being so critical, and ultimately exiling it.

There are two problems with this type of approach. The first problem is that it doesn't work. Pushed away, the Inner Critic always comes back. As we later come to understand its origins and purposes, we will see why it has to come back, stronger than ever, if it is pushed away.

The second problem has to do with the dynamics of *exile*. When aspects of our inner experiencing are pushed away from awareness, they do not really disappear. They function implicitly; that is, they are extremely powerful without being in awareness, which makes our lives feel even more unpredictable and out of control to the part of us which does remain in awareness.

An example of this: Quite a few years ago my good friend R. came to me greatly upset. How could I have done that to her? What? I said. I had no idea what she was talking about. She reminded me: at a conference, I had called out to her as she was leading the group in an exercise, telling her to do it differently. It had felt hurtful to her; she had heard criticism and anger in my voice. I only remembered trying to be "helpful." But, respecting her viewpoint, I did some Focusing and invited something in me that might have had feelings about R. to come into awareness. Sure enough, there was something in me that had been carrying critical feelings about her, from long ago in our history. Because I hadn't been aware of them myself, they had come out in public, evident to her and probably to everyone else, but not to me!

I no longer want to be the last one in the room to know what I am feeling. That's why I do Focusing, and it's why I do Focusing with an Inner Relationship emphasis – because I am inviting back the exiles.

You cannot "get rid of" any of your feelings, no matter how much something in you may want to. You can only send them underground. In exile, parts of us become wilder, darker, lonelier, crueler. When they return from exile, or act from exile, they are not a pretty sight. (See "The Dog Story" in this volume for a metaphorical illustration of this.)

So let's not exile the inner criticizing process! Pushing it away just makes it easier for other people to see it and puts it outside the sphere of Presence, which is where its transformation could happen.

Presence Language with an Inner Criticizing Process

Presence language starts with the words "I'm sensing..." and goes on with "something in me that..."

Someone who says "This is stupid" would change this to "I'm sensing something in me that says this is stupid."

Most people experience a big difference between those two sentences. (You might take a moment to notice what difference you feel.) Usually, the second one brings a feeling of more space, more distance without losing connection, a larger perspective. I am reminded that I am more than this, there is more to me than this. It becomes possible to *turn toward* the criticizing part, and toward any other part, with interested curiosity. Focusing on these inner aspects becomes possible.

Presence language is a reminder to take the space that Presence gives, to remember that we are more than the struggle inside us. From that place of "more," there is a possibility of change.

Presence Language and a Criticizing Process – An Example

Sam had an action block. He was ready to move forward with his business plan but somehow he never got around to making the phone calls or finishing the brochure. When he sat down to do a Focusing session with me, he invited the part of him that didn't want to move forward.

"It's like a tenseness in my stomach... Well, actually it feels like clenching, holding real tight.... And there's fear... I'm scared to let go."

To support Sam in finding Presence, I reflected back his words using Presence language.

Ann: *"You're sensing something in you"* that's clenching, holding real tight, scared to let go."

Sam: "Yeah, it's a part of me that's scared to let go. The world is a scary place, it says. It feels like myself as a little child, when I first found out how harsh the world could be."

Notice that Sam took the invitation into Presence language; after I reflected back, "You're sensing something in you... scared to let go," he said, "Yeah, it's a part of me that's scared to let go." This perspective allowed him to feel into that part of him more deeply, to sense that it felt like him as a little child.

Ann: "You're sensing that it feels like you as a little child, getting hurt for the first time."

Sam: "I get so hard on myself sometimes."

I wasn't sure how this connected with what Sam had been saying. But Focusing is like that sometimes; what comes next is connected but not necessarily in a logical sequence.

What I did know was that his sentence "I get so hard on myself sometimes" needed to be unpacked – he was identified with both sides of an inner struggle, and I wanted to invite him into Presence with those sides.

Ann: "You're sensing something in you that gets hard on something else in you."

Sam: "It's like I have this voice that says, 'You have to. You don't have a choice.' But letting go feels like standing over a huge abyss."

Again, Sam took my invitation, in that now he's describing these two inner combatants in two different sentences, and each one is felt as more separate from him. In the next thing I say, I want to support that separation (and connection).

Ann: "You're sensing something in you that feels letting go as standing over a huge abyss. And you're sensing something in you that says, 'You have to.' And both are there." (See "Standing It" in this volume for more about this kind of invitation and its reasons.)

In the rest of his session, Sam was able to listen with compassion to each of these sides of his process. What behaved at first like a criticizing process ("I get so hard on myself") evolved into a part of him eager for him to succeed. And the part of him that felt so scared needed to be kept company as we would be with a frightened child. When that part felt heard from Presence, rather than pressured and criticized, it began to relax. And when the impatient part felt that its concerns were heard, it also began to relax.

None of this could have happened without Presence.

Sensing How It Feels in the Body

We know that Focusing is a body-oriented process. But what that means in practice is open to interpretation. (See "Body? What Body?" in this volume.) In the session we just reported, Sam had a tenseness in his stomach, clenching, holding tight... Clearly a body sensation. But this wasn't the criticizing part. For him, the criticizing part showed up as a voice. ("It's like I have this voice that says, 'You have to. You don't have a choice.'")

Perhaps this is one of the reasons that a part which criticizes has not been understood to be something that could be focused on, felt into... because it often does not appear as clearly located in the body as the other parts of us, the ones that it is trying to control or change. ("I have this cold rock of dread in my stomach... And I'm trying to get it to loosen up... I shouldn't be feeling that way...")

Sometimes the criticizing part *is* experienced in the body. When it is, it is often felt as a constriction or narrowing or binding of some kind.

"I've got a lot of anger, I can feel it like heat and energy pouring through my shoulders and arms. And I'm also feeling this band across my chest. It feels cold, dense. It's saying to the anger, go away. You can't be here. It isn't safe."

In being with criticizing parts in a Focusing way, we need to be open to any modality they may use to communicate their presence. Voices (auditory) and images (visual) are just as likely, if not more likely, as body sensations (kinesthetic). As always, if we do experience these parts of us as voices or images, we need to keep on being aware in the inner middle body, so that these experiences stay grounded in present awareness.

A Part that Criticizes Is Really Afraid

When I first began experimenting with inviting my Focusing clients to bring compassion to their inner criticizing parts, I encountered an interesting kind of resistance. People didn't want to be compassionate, because it seemed to them that this part of them was "mean," "cruel," or "angry." "It wants to hurt me," they would report. "How can I be compassionate to that?" From my experience with Marshall Rosenberg's Non-Violent Communication, I knew that a human being behaving as those inner parts were behaving could be seen as trying to meet legitimate needs. (In ways, Marshall would say, that were "tragically unlikely to succeed.") I wondered how to understand the behavior of this inner criticizing part in a way that would invite the Focuser's compassionate understanding. How could we understand what was going on, if we looked at it from *its* point of view? And it always came down to this: the fearsome critic was afraid. It was attacking so fiercely because *that* was how afraid it was, that something would go wrong, that something wouldn't get fixed, that other people would be critical, etc.

I began to wonder: What if all inner criticizing parts are really afraid?

They don't feel or look or sound afraid, usually. They sound angry, or authoritarian, very sure of themselves, sure that you are wrong and they are right. But what if the more sure and authoritarian they sound, the more scared they are, really, deep down?

I remembered a time when I was in my 20s, living in Chicago, and my roommate and I were painting our apartment. A rickety ladder was standing in the hall, and Leone's goofy cat Frostbite decided to leap onto the paint shelf. Ladder, cat, and all went crashing down to the floor, and an unearthly yowl arose. We went running over. Poor Frostbite was caught by the tail, entangled in the ladder. I went close to help him get loose, and instead of welcoming me, he attacked me. Ouch! Some gratitude! But it didn't take long for me to forgive him. *Of course* he attacked me; he was terrified, panicky, trapped, and desperate. All I had to do was see the desperation instead of the attack, and my compassion opened up easily, despite the claw marks on my hand.

The same was true of the inner criticizing process. If I wanted to help a Focuser have compassion for a part of them that was critical, what I needed to do was invite the Focuser to consider that the criticizing part might be afraid. This always worked. In fact, it worked so reliably that over time I wondered if there might be some kind of universal law at work. Eventually, Barbara McGavin was able to show me that a part of us that is criticizing is a part needing to *control*, and that fear and the need to control are two sides of the same coin.

The part that is criticizing often doesn't like to admit that it is afraid. To do so would be to show its vulnerability, and of course it doesn't want to do that. But there is a whole raft of synonyms for fear: from panic and terror at one end of the scale to worry and concern at the other. A part that is controlling/criticizing is often willing to admit that it is worried or concerned. And for it to say that it is worried is already a big difference from being on the attack.

The Fearful Criticizing Process – An Example

Here's an excerpt from a session in which a woman with a chronic illness was deeply honest with herself about what her illness was saying – and this brought up a criticizing process. After spending time connecting with the bodily feel of her symptoms, and using Presence language ("I'm sensing... something in me...") to remind herself to *be with* rather than *be in* the feelings, she reported this:

"I'm sensing this part of me that isn't sure it wants me to get well. It's afraid if I get well, I'm going to forget everything I learned in this time. *Another part says I shouldn't feel that way, that's bad.* My symptoms are saying to me, 'If we go away, you're going to go back to being unconscious.' Something in here thinks that I have to be sick or ill to have a sane life. *And something in me is scared when it hears that."*

Notice that in those six sentences, she is hearing from two parts of herself. I've put in italics the sentences that report what the "criticizing part" is saying and feeling. It starts by saying the other part of her "shouldn't" be feeling the way it is feeling. This is the familiar critical voice: judgmental, using "should" and "ought." But a few sentences later, she realizes that this part of her is scared.

We can empathize with this scared part. Of course! It can be scary to realize there's a part that *wants* the painful symptoms that one is experiencing. No wonder this scared part gets anxious and tries to stop those experiences the only way it knows how: through judgment and blame.

Even though we (from Presence) are aware that hearing exactly what is here is the fastest way to allow it to transform – and there's nothing to be afraid of in hearing what is so, because it already *is* so – there is often a part, as in this case, that is scared to hear it, doesn't want that to be true. A part of us that is trying to suppress another part often *behaves* critically. But its *feeling* is worry, fear. And this is important: to make the distinction between the actions which a part of us is taking or urging another part of us to take, and the feelings that are behind its behavior. If we get caught up in the behavior, the actions, we are caught up in a warlike struggle. But if we can sense beneath the actions to the feelings driving those actions, we are much closer to the potential for transformation.

Empathy with the Fear

Once we are compassionately aware of the fear (worry, concern...) in this part of us, we can give it empathy for what it's afraid of. Empathy can often be expressed with the help of phrases like "no wonder" and "of course." This manner of speaking helps to carry and convey the attitude of understanding how *it* feels from *its* point of view.

A man who was starting out to be a meditation teacher was Focusing on a difficult area of his life. Suddenly he reported: "This part of me says, You have no qualifications to be a meditation teacher, because you're so screwed up!" We'd often done inner work on the criticizing process, so I just said: "Wow, it must be really scared about something!" He sensed into it with the possibility that it might be scared, and reported: "Oh... It has a belief that if I'm teaching I have to present myself as having no problems myself."

I suggested he say to it, with empathy, "No wonder you'd be feeling scared or worried, if you believe if I'm teaching I have to have no problems myself."

I saw his body relax even before he reported: "I'm feeling a big relief all through my stomach and abdomen. A strong tightness there just let go."

Notice how the sentence starting with "no wonder" is warm and empathic, without agreeing in any way with the limiting belief held by that part. It acknowledges the feelings ("scared or worried") and their connection with the belief ("if you believe...") without validating the belief itself. This tends to result in a loosening, a freeing up, around the belief, which is often experienced as a physical release.

The Not-Wanting

There is something that this part of us which is criticizing right now is not wanting. And, paradoxically, it often doesn't want exactly what it is predicting. It says "You'll be a failure" or "You are a failure" and failure, as it turns out, is exactly what it doesn't want for you.

This may seem frustratingly illogical, but actually it's a very natural human process. Imagine a parent calling to a child who is going out the door in the wintertime. "You'll catch your death of cold!" Why would a parent predict that a child would die? Obviously, the parent wants the child to do something: to put on some warmer clothes, perhaps. So that statement isn't really a prediction of death. It's really a request with an expression of strong feeling attached: "Please put on warmer clothes, I'm so worried about you!" From this perspective, we understand that "You'll catch your death of cold" is actually an expression of what's *not* wanted.

Is it possible that every time our inwardly criticizing parts predict our doom, or our failure, they are actually speaking of what they *don't* want! What an idea!

It can be a powerfully transformative process to invite a criticizing part to reveal what it is not wanting. In particular, as Barbara McGavin and I have discovered, it helps to invite it to let us know what it is not wanting to happen *to us*. That sounds like this: "I'm inviting it to let me know what it is not wanting to happen to me." Phrased this way, the invitation validates the protective nature of this part of us, and therefore is likely to be a welcome invitation to it.

If you connect first with the fear-type emotion of the criticizing part (fear, worry, concern...), it is rarely difficult for it to begin letting you know what it's not wanting to have happen to you. Without that emotional connection, this step can be more difficult, sometimes impossible. Sensing *its* (fear-type) emotion is a key step; then comes sensing its not-wanting.

The Not-Wanting: An Example

Thea was Focusing with an aspect of herself that she called "resistant." It had a harsh tone, and when she connected with it, she heard, "You're never getting anywhere. Give up." It didn't feel fearful, and at first she found it hard to imagine that it might be afraid, but she decided to try taking it on faith that a criticizing part must be afraid, and see what happened.

She sensed in her body, and saw a dark lurking figure, glowering in a corner. "I'm wondering if you might be worried or concerned," she offered it. There was a slight sense of agreement, not much, but a little. Empathizing with what it might be going through, she invited, "I'm wondering what you might be not wanting to happen to me." Images and words began to flow: *abused, punished, dishonored...* "Punished" felt like the crux of it. She let it know she heard it. "I really hear that you're not wanting me to be punished."

There was a slight sense of release... and she decided to offer it empathy. "No wonder you're feeling worried," she said to it, "if what you're wanting is for me not to be punished." There was a lightening in the sense of this place inside, a relaxing. Thea was able to stay with it and sense more.

The Wanting

Just under Not-Wanting is Wanting, what this part is wanting for you to experience or feel. The good news about criticizing parts is that their Wanting is usually quite accessible, once the Not-Wanting has been heard. (We'll talk about the exception to this below, in the section on "Severe Inner Criticism.") And by the time a part is willing to tell a Focuser what it's wanting, it rarely feels critical anymore. It often feels like a concerned protector. This is another reason to let go of the term "Critic" and name this part by the way it is behaving, changing its description as its behavior changes.

Let's follow the example of Thea, just given, into Wanting. Staying in contact with a part of her that was criticizing, sensing that it's not wanting her to be punished, Thea feels a lightening when she acknowledges that. She takes time and senses a readiness in that part to allow its Wanting to be sensed into. The image of being punished is still with her, what is not wanted, and now over that image comes another one, of being... "embraced with pride" are the words. "It wants me to be embraced with pride," Thea reports.

Thea's Focusing partner invites her to sense what that part is wanting her to be able to *feel* from being embraced with pride. Getting in contact with the Wanted Feeling is/brings a deep level of awareness that can be quite transformative. Thea invites the body sense of what that part wants her to be able to feel from being embraced with pride. There is a bodily sense of warm... protected... connected... This is deeply satisfying to feel, and Thea stays with it for quite some time.

Yes, this is the same part that Thea first encountered saying, "You're never getting anywhere. Give up"! Like the parent who says, "You'll catch your death of cold" while really meaning "I'm worried about you, I want you to be safe," the very part of us that seems to be attacking is actually a supportive protector. But it needs to be taken through a process that allows its protective side to emerge.

Review of the Process So Far
(1) Becoming aware that an inner criticizing process is happening
(2) Coming into Presence with all aspects of experiencing, including the inner criticizing process
(3) Noticing how the inner criticizing process feels in the body, or how it presents itself, as sensation, voice, image
(4) Sensing if it might be afraid or have some form of fear such as worry or concern
(5) Inviting it to let me know what it's *not wanting* to have happen to me
(6) Inviting it to let me know what it's *wanting* for me to experience or feel

The Criticizer and the Criticized
In the following examples, I invite your curiosity about who is this "I" that the speaker is identified with. Is it Presence? Is it the criticizing part? And

if neither of those, then who?

"I feel bad about messing up my life."

"My inner critic is huge, and I'm so small."

"A critical voice is calling me 'stupid,' and that feels true."

"A critical voice is calling me 'stupid,' and I'm telling it to shut up and get out of here."

"I feel ashamed."

In all our talk about a part that criticizes, we have been ignoring another key character in the drama – the part of us that is being criticized. If I identify myself with Presence, the state of being able to be with anything that arises, then it is clear that I am not the one being criticized. Robert De Niro's character in the movie *Taxi Driver* says, "Are you talking to me? *Are you talking to ME?*" Who is the criticizing part talking to? Who is it criticizing? Me?

When I am in Presence, I don't feel criticized.

So, if there is an experience of being criticized by a criticizing part of me, then that must be another part of me that also needs to be acknowledged, the one that feels criticized, and has feelings about that: anger, rebellion, guilt, embarrassment, shame.

We can be *identified* with the criticizing part, as in "This is stupid," or we can be identified with the criticized part, as in "I feel inadequate." We may be identified with the criticized part yet have some awareness of what is happening, as in "A critical part has showed up and is telling me I'm never going to get anywhere with this." Rarely are we in Presence with this criticizing process. If we were, we might say something like this:

"I'm sensing something in me that's being critical of this other part of me, and I'm also sensing the part of me that's feeling criticized."

Coming into Presence is the first and most essential step for shifting out of the deadlock between criticizer and criticized. To find Presence when "you" are under attack, remember that you are not the target, you are not the one being criticized. *Something in you* is being criticized by *something in you.*

The part that's feeling criticized can be called the reacting part. Barbara McGavin and I have identified three styles or modes that this reacting part assumes from time to time.

(1) **Collapsing.** This is an attitude that says, "You're right, I am that bad, and I feel so bad about it." This may be a difficult part to detect, if we are identified with it. It can feel like the truth, simply the truth. The queasy hollow feeling in the stomach (or some other unpleasant body feeling) may feel like no more than I deserve. Barbara McGavin and I used to call this part the "Critic's Victim," before we decided that the word "victim" was too much of a pejorative label itself. But sometimes "victim" is exactly what this part

feels like, even to itself.

The felt experience of shame is the territory of this collapsing reacting part. If something in me is ashamed, then there surely is another part of me shaming it. The same is true of guilt and embarrassment. "I feel guilty" can become, in Presence language, "Something in me is feeling guilty, and something in me is saying I should feel guilty." We will then be able to sense into and hear the not-wanting and wanting in each one.

(2) **Rebelling.** This reacting part says, "I am NOT!" or "I *won't*, and you can't make me!" It often has a stubborn teenager quality to it. In fact, the relationship of the reacting part to the criticizing part is often like the relationship of a teenager to a parent, with all the comedy and drama that entails.

The criticizing part is controlling, pushing, managing (of course, as we have seen, for its own good reasons). The reacting part is something in us that doesn't like being controlled, pushed, or managed. (And who would?) When the two come head to head, sparks fly... and the body is the battleground.

(3) **Escaping.** When it feels itself under attack, something in us may respond by running away, escaping. Experientially this could be going blank, forgetting, getting confused, going to sleep, etc. Behaviorally, this escaping reacting part could be the part of us that indulges in what are called "escapes": watching TV, playing computer games, eating too many snacks, etc.

One indication that you may be *identified with* the Reacting Part is if you find it difficult to sense the fear, worry, or concern in the Criticizing Part. If you find it hard to imagine or feel that this criticizing part of you is anything but angry, harsh, mean; if it seems really big in relation to you; if it's hard to empathize with it at all – this is a very reliable sign that you are actually identified with the recipient of that criticism. You feel it is criticizing *you*. Which means you are not in Presence – which is good news, because once you get into Presence again, things are going to feel a lot better!

Being in Presence will enable the Focuser to *be with* both the part that is criticizing and the part that is reacting to the criticism. Each side will have an emotional quality, a not wanting, and a wanting, that need to be felt in the body in their own timing, and acknowledged and heard. This way lies healing.

Severe Inner Criticism

Some experiences of inner criticism are especially hard to understand with the benevolent analogy of worried parents predicting what they don't want to have happen to a beloved child. "It hates me." "It wants me to die." "It's so vicious, it wants to tear me apart." Of course we need to facilitate disidentification from the "me" in these statements. Still, how can we understand the force of this seeming inner hatred?

In our body of work called Treasure Maps to the Soul, Barbara McGavin and I have come to see that the nature of trauma can lead naturally to this kind of harsh criticizing process. Put simply, when overwhelmingly frightening or painful events occur at a time when there are not resources to handle them, either from within or without, the emotional process becomes frozen – unprocessed – and encapsulated in a part that is then exiled from awareness. Various other parts take on the job of keeping this so-called dangerous emotional "stuff" out of awareness.

So there are two main types of inner criticizing process, or two ends of a continuum, depending on how severe is the trauma, or how much fear there is in the system of what may be contacted or felt. At the lighter, less severe end of the scale, we have an inner criticizing process that is more easily felt as protective, that reveals what it is wanting *for us* without too much fuss. At the more severe end of the scale, we have a harsher criticizing part that is driven by a profound fear of what may be allowed to be felt if it doesn't do its job. In this case, the not-wanting is more complex: we have the not-wanting of the criticizing part, which is for something not to be felt, and we have the not-wanted feeling that it doesn't want felt. Ultimately, both need to be contacted in a felt bodily way, but it is counterproductive to rush this process; retraumatizing can occur. Go slowly, and respect any inner signals from parts that need to stop and come back to the process later.

A Harsh Inner Critic – An Example

George said he had been experiencing a harsh inner voice all week, saying to him, "You dumb shit! You can't make a difference! Don't you know any better than that? You're powerless!"

He had been determined to turn around a situation in which a sales promotion wasn't doing well, by writing a well-crafted email to a carefully selected mailing list of key people. He was proud of himself for taking action. But then there were *no* responses to the email. As soon as he realized this, the inner attack started.

When George acknowledged and brought awareness to this inner attacker, he sensed it as a "dragon-creature" with big wings, and its emotion was anger. "It's furious with me!" I invited him to sense what might be getting it so furious. "It's furious that I dared to think I could be powerful. It doesn't want me to be powerful." However, it wasn't George's powerful actions that enraged the dragon, but the fact that they hadn't worked. "It wasn't a problem while I was writing the email and sending it out. It was only after it didn't work that I started hearing what a dumb-ass I was."

It was unbearable to some part of George that he took powerful actions that were rejected. "It's like I can hear those people whispering, who does he think he is, thinking that important people like us would respond to his silly little email." As he sat with the feel of all this in his body, a memory came from junior high school days: He had written in the yearbook of a very popular girl that he liked her. Later she had come up to him and insulted him cruelly in front of her friends. "They must have teased her about what I wrote," he says now. At the time, it was devastating.

George sits with the body feel now of the memory of that devastating rejection. That memory is joined by others, other times, other rejections. He is staying with the body feel as these memories come, getting a sort of inner permission to feel it as much as he is feeling it. "It's like a punch in the stomach," he says. "No... it's like after a punch. Like nausea and not enough air." He stays with that feeling, acknowledging it.

"This is what that dragon was not wanting me to feel," George says. He acknowledges both: the feeling itself, just as it is right now, and something in him not wanting him to have to feel it. Slowly a peacefulness grows in him. "It's not so bad," he says. "I was afraid it would be worse."

"Yes," I reflect, "something in you was afraid it would be worse."

Richard Schwartz's Manager and the Treasure Maps Controller

Our conception of the criticizing process is very close to the conception of the "manager" in Richard Schwartz's finely worked out Internal Family Systems Therapy. A manager is a type of part that "tends to be highly protective... and interested in controlling the environment to keep things safe" (*Internal Family Systems Therapy*, p. 46). Managerial parts may be perfectionistic, striving achievers, bitingly critical taskmasters, worriers, sentries... "The point to remember is that the primary purpose of all managers is to keep ... the feared feelings and thoughts from spilling over the inner walls, so that the system remains safe and the person is able to function in life" (p. 49).

In Treasure Maps to the Soul, Barbara McGavin and I call the critical type of part described in this article a "Controller," because it may or may not criticize, but it always feels desperate for an inner control. There is much more in both Internal Family Systems Therapy and Treasure Maps to the Soul than can be described in this brief paper, but the main differences are in the way of working with the parts: Treasure Maps to the Soul, as a Focusing-based method, uses contact with the bodily felt sense as a central part of the change process; for IFS the body sense is used as an anchor, and change comes in other ways.

A Glimpse of Possibilities

I used to cringe when someone, in a workshop, let's say, raised a complaint or a dissatisfaction. As a peace-loving Nine (on the Enneagram), I wanted to avoid conflict at all costs. Anger was the scariest emotion I could encounter. Now I turn toward angry complaints with delight. I'm excited about encountering the real person who is feeling the anger, and finding out what that person's needs are. It's because of Focusing with my own inner criticizing parts that this has changed.

It's possible to imagine a state where we cannot be criticized, either from within or from without. I'm not talking about being closed to information or feedback. We would be open to receiving information, and to taking in feedback and making changes. But none of it would make us feel bad about ourselves, our essence, who we really are.

If you can't imagine such a state, you're not alone. Many people who are tormented by inner criticism have a hard time picturing a time when they'd be truly free of it. Don't fret; this brave new world is not something we can think our way into; it's the result of process. Doing Focusing as described in this article, turning toward inner criticizing parts with compassion each time they arise, and when they feel ready inviting a sense of what they're not-wanting and wanting, will bring lasting and deep change.

Focusing
Partnership

We see each other weekly, and perhaps we tell each other our deepest secrets, yet no money exchanges hands. We experience profound therapeutic change, yet neither of us may have professional degrees. We are part of a revolutionary movement in human relations, yet all we are doing is sitting across from each other and exchanging turns at being the Listener and the Focuser.

Being a Focusing partner is a privilege and a gift. In this section are two of the articles I've written about this special relationship, addressing the questions of what agreements and guidelines need to be in place to make a Focusing partnership a safe place for inner work.

In the Focusing community we emphasize Focusing partnership. People learn not only Focusing for themselves, but also the process of being a companion to another person who is Focusing. The Companion mainly uses the method of Listening (see "The Power of Listening" in this volume) to reflect back the essence of what the Focuser says. The Companion offers no advice or guidance of any kind; does not even ask questions. Yet – or perhaps "therefore" – the Companion's presence is enormously facilitative.

In the Focusing email discussion list recently, someone asked, "Why do you discourage people from Focusing alone?" It had never occurred to me that our emphasis on partnership could look like a discouragement to Focusing alone. It's not. Believe me, if I knew a way to teach people to Focus easily by themselves, I would be doing it! I've simply observed over the years, as have many others, that people have a hard time Focusing by themselves, especially when starting out with Focusing.

There are exceptions. Some people take to Focusing alone, do it easily. By my informal estimates we are talking about 5-10% of people here. I myself am in the 90-95% category. I would *never* have learned or stayed with Focusing if it hadn't been for Focusing partnership. My first experience of Focusing alone successfully – as far as I can remember – came eighteen years after I learned Focusing! And that was in a crisis situation in which I *had* to Focus immediately and had no partner nearby. To my astonishment, it worked. And I still prefer Focusing with a partner.

Think of it: partners provide or enable so many processes that otherwise we would have to do for ourselves. They provide a quality of containment; they provide a structure for staying with the process; they provide a nonjudgmental quality of interested attention. That's powerful. Sure, we can give those things to ourselves. We can also massage our own shoulders! Which is more fun?

Safe Focusing with (Almost) Any Partner

Appeared in The Focusing Connection, *July 1992*

It always seems like a minor miracle: that I can sit in a class of beginners, with a new person listening to me for the first time, and have a fantastic Focusing session. And often in only ten minutes! Isn't this remarkable? If I tried to convince someone from another tradition that I do some of my best Focusing in front of a group of relative strangers, accompanied by a brand-new Listener, in such a short time, they might check me in somewhere for a long rest. But it's true!

So if I try to explain the process that lets me feel safe enough to have a great session with a new Listener, then this might help us understand how to feel safe as a Focuser with almost any partner.

First, we have an agreement that only Listening responses will be given; no guiding. This means that I am in charge of guiding my own process. I know that I have a nice open space in front of me, without interference from the other person. I can take the time I need to find something, and not have to worry about being interrupted; as long as I am silent, the Listener will be silent, too.

I know that the Listener is just going to follow where I am, not try to interpret, analyze, anticipate, tie together, or even worry very much about understanding. The simplicity of our task together brings me a great inner peace. I am just going to be with myself, and the Listener is just going to be with me.

Second, we have an agreement that my turn is mine and "The Focuser is the boss." This reminds me that it is not up to me as the Focuser to take care of the Listener. I don't have to be interesting or productive for their sake. I can be silent the whole time and that would be OK. Or I can talk a mile a minute (I probably wouldn't, but I *could)*, and it would be up to the Listener to figure out a way to keep up. That is our deal.

Third, I know it is my job to check what the Listener says with my inside place, and to either speak up or ignore it if it's not right. That way, it's really the inside place that is guiding the session, and *it* won't let anything happen that isn't safe for me. Sometimes (very rarely) I have to say, "Please stay closer to what I'm saying," or "I feel like you're making a suggestion and I'd just like you to say what I said." So even if the Listener forgets our first agreements, this agreement keeps me safe.

Fourth, we have arranged a hand signal so I can stop the Listener without even having to speak, if they begin to talk while something important is coming in me. It is part of our agreement that this is not something they need to feel defensive about, but a natural possibility in any session, that something may come in the Focuser that needs silence from the Listener *now*, and that's OK.

The result of all these agreements is that I start the session by carefully taking time to be with myself inwardly and inviting "something" to come that wants to be known. When I first feel it, it's usually very faint and hard to describe, so I describe it in a very approximate way. When the Listener says back those words, I use them to pay closer attention to the sense. Better words come, and once again I hear them back and check them inside. Each response from the Listener takes me deeper and deeper into my process.

By the end of the session, when we give feedback to each other, I often have to say that in a positive sense I hardly noticed the Listener. By following the agreements and really being a mirror for me, they became transparent: still present as a person, but not at all clouding the vision.

But there is a dimension of feeling safe with a Listener that doesn't usually arise with a new person in a class. What happens if I know this person well enough to have some feelings about *them*, positive or negative, that might interfere with my experiencing them as a good clear mirror? Then the session must start with some clearing of that. I would ask my inside place how much of what I am feeling is safe and right to say right now. Then I would say it, and the other person would reflect as a Listener, and notice in turn if there's something they need or want to say to me.

(There is more that could be said about this whole territory of interpersonal space between the Focuser and Listener, and I hope that someone will address it, especially Barbara McGavin and Rob Foxcroft, whose illuminating conversation inspired me to write this much.)

In most cases, this interpersonal clearing at the beginning of a session will take only a few minutes, and then I ask my inside place if it feels safe to continue. When I let *it* guide me, and my Listener is being guided by *it* as well, the session almost always feels both safe and productive to us all.

Focusing partnership doesn't always go as easily as the last article makes it sound. We aren't magically freed of our interpersonal issues just because we are Focusers! And sometimes the very instincts that serve us well in another context (such as friendship), are exactly what we don't want to do in the partnership relationship.

Since my mission is to make Focusing as an ongoing connected practice available to everyone who wants it, I feel sad whenever I hear that someone stopped doing Focusing because their Focusing partnership went sour. "I stopped feeling safe" is something I have heard, not often, but more times than I would like. And when I delve a little deeper, it turns out that often that loss of safety doesn't come from anything major, but from a simple stepping past the boundaries into expressions that would be perfectly ordinary in a friendly conversation – but which feel "too much" in the delicate context of Focusing.

So I decided to write another article, and in the spirit of the times, this one emphasized the "perils" rather than the ease of Focusing with a partner. I used such strong language because I wanted to alert people to the importance of the ground rules. You might think, I wanted to say, that a little thing like chatting about the content of your partner's Focusing process couldn't possibly hurt anyone. Think again.

Why is this? Why can't we say whatever we want? Why do we have to be so careful?

The context of Focusing is special because we are giving each other something we don't get anywhere else: space with connectedness. I am going to sit here and give you my absolute undivided attention for the whole time we have set aside, and I am not going to mix in my stuff – my opinions, my interpretations, my needs. The space is all yours, and I'm here to help guard it for you.

Ordinarily, we have to entertain or please or cater to another person in order to keep their attention. We have to pay for connectedness by being interesting... or something like that. But in this special turn-taking agreement, I have agreed to stay connected with you without you having to do *anything* to keep my attention, and in return, half an hour from now, you are going to do that same thing for me.

This quality of attention from another person creates the maximally facilitive environment for us to give the same kind of attention and space within ourselves. As you help guard my space and attend to me, I can offer that same space and attending within myself. This is precious. This is worth working for. This is worth the effort of changing our usual habits of friendly chatting, just for this one hour a week.

(And yes, when I wrote: "You are a real person, not impervious to being moved or touched or shaken or stirred by what the Focuser is working on," the humorous reference to James Bond's famous martini request *was* intentional!)

The Perils of Focusing Partnership – and Some Rules for Safety

Appeared in The Focusing Connection, *January 2000*

They make it sound so easy, Focusing partnership. "Just start exchanging Focusing and listening turns with a friend, or with someone you met in a Focusing workshop." They talk about how rewarding and satisfying Focusing partnership can be, and how much easier it is to Focus with someone else than by yourself. Well, that much is true. Focusing partnership can be very rewarding and satisfying, and much much easier than Focusing alone. But it also has its perils. What felt easy and safe when you practiced it in a workshop, or when you read about it in a book, starts to feel like a danger zone. And that's when the safety guidelines that your Focusing teacher taught you become so crucially important. They aren't just good ideas – they can actually save your Focusing partnership, and even your Focusing practice.

1. Never never *never* mention the content of the Focusing session, even after the session is over, unless the Focuser brings it up. This is really important. Many a Focusing partnership has broken up on the rocks of this one. A seemingly innocent, well-intentioned comment can compromise the safety of the partnership for both people. And it's so tempting to do it! You have to be really clear, and really conscious, on this one, because the easiest thing out of your mouth is probably something that will violate this rule. We have thousands of times more practice being social in a non-Focusing setting than in a Focusing one. What could it hurt? Answer: a lot.

Let's say your partner is Focusing on feelings around an argument with their spouse. During the session you scrupulously follow the guidelines, and just reflect their feelings and their point of view, without putting in any opinions of your own. But after the session is over, when the two of you are still sitting there, or standing up to go, or in the kitchen sharing a cup of tea, you find yourself saying, "X [the spouse] is really a difficult person." What happens? The next time your partner wants to focus on that issue or a similar one, there is a tilt, a slant. A part of them thinks it can win you to its side. Another part feels unsafe, like you have taken sides against it. You have shown your *bias*, and bias creates an unsafe space.

It's even worse if your casual comment implies some judgment or criticism of the Focuser, like: "I would never put up with the kinds of thing you put up with from X." Now the bias includes a judgment of the Focuser, and the space is even less safe for Focusing.

Worst of all: advice of any kind. Giving advice unasked-for implies both judgment and lack of trust. Think about it! When you say, "Why don't you try..." or "Have you thought about..." or "What I would do if I were you is...," you're actually saying that you don't believe they can handle this situation wisely without your input. Is that what you actually believe? You may want to Focus on that – with another partner!

It's another matter if advice is *asked for.* "What do you think?" or "What would you do?" are clear invitations to give your opinion. The problem I think for many people (and I'm not just talking about Focusing partnerships now) is that they hear the statement of a problem *as if* it were a request for advice. Y was talking about her painful wrist during a Focusing session and her listener, Z, after the session was over, started asking, "Have you tried orthobionomy? I can give you the name of a really good practitioner." There is no doubt that Z had the very best of intentions. But the loss of safety from the intrusion was a greater cost than the possible gain from the good advice. Y has plenty of people to give her advice, but only a few Focusing partners.

No matter how you met your partner – whether they were a friend to start with, or someone you met in a workshop – this close relationship will start to feel like a friendship. And then there can be a clash between the rules and mores of friendship, and the stricter ones of Focusing partnership. It might be good to recognize the potential for conflict within yourself, the part of you that wants the ease and flow of a regular friendship, the part of you that wants the safety of a Focusing partnership. Friends express opinions, friends give advice (although probably a lot more than they need to!), friends share stories of similar experiences. You have to ask yourself, is the feeling of relaxed unstructured friendship with this person really worth the risk to the Focusing partnership? I'd say no, don't risk it. A good Focusing partner is not that easy to find!

"What do I do if my partner mentions the content of my session and I'm uncomfortable with that?" If you catch it at the moment it happens, you might say something like, "It feels like you're talking about the content of my session, and I know you mean well, but I'd like to leave some space around that." Or, "....but I'd like to leave that whole topic alone now."

If, as often happens, you only realize later that you were uncomfortable with your partner commenting on your content, that's a trickier situation. You might ask yourself, in a Focusing way, if your sense of safety with your partner needs for you to bring up the subject of what has already happened. If not, you could just resolve to catch it if it happens again. But if you do need to bring it up, you might say, "Do you remember last time when we were chatting after the session, and you said, 'I would never put up with the kinds of thing you put up with from X'? I realized later that it felt like you were commenting on the content of my session, and I'd like to make a request that we not comment on the content of one another's session unless the Focuser brings it up. Would that be OK?" There are two key points here (with appreciation to Marshall Rosenberg's Non-Violent Communication, even though I'm not following his system exactly). One is to quote, to the best of your ability, exactly what your partner said, as opposed to something like: "Do you remember last time when we were chatting after the session, and you criticized my relationship?" Two is to remember that your partner was well-intentioned and this is not to judge their behavior as wrong, but just to let them know that you would like something different in the future.

"What if the Listener gets triggered by the Focuser's material?"

First answer: Good! What a great opportunity!

Second answer: As the Listener, you are responsible for your own feelings and reactions, of course. You are a real person, not impervious to being moved or touched or shaken or stirred by what the Focuser is working on. But your feelings are *yours*. I'd recommend saying "Hello, I know you're there," silently, to any feelings of your own that come up while you're listening to the Focuser. That may be enough. There is no need to share them. In fact, better not, not even after the session is over. They're too likely to infringe on your partner's content.

If your turn is next, there may be a way to sensitively Focus on your issues that were triggered by your partner's work. If you can really own the issues as yours, and not in any way "about" your partner, it should be OK. If you're in doubt, you can check with your partner by briefly describing what you want to work on and asking if that would or wouldn't violate their space. This sort of mutually inspired work can actually be rewarding for both people.

The most dangerous type of "being triggered" is when you don't realize it, so that instead of you taking responsibility for your reactions, they emerge as criticisms, judgments (of the Focuser or others in the Focuser's life), advice, or rescuing behavior. Earlier, I said that giving advice is probably out of social habit or because you mistakenly believe you've been asked for help. Actually, the urge to give advice, rescue, help, or judge may well be coming from a place in you that is having a hard time just being with the Focuser's process. *Be alert for the urge to help, fix, or rescue.* These urges can be golden signposts that there is something in you that needs some company.

2. Remember that it is the Focuser's session, and it is not your responsibility as Listener/Guide/Companion/Ally to make something good happen in their Focusing, or even to make sure they're Focusing at all.

This used to happen quite frequently: We would finish the Level One

Focusing class, and the people would go forth to practice with each other as partners. Then I would start getting the phone calls: "I'm not sure that my partner is really Focusing. What can I do about it?"

My answer: "Nothing. There is nothing you can or should do about it. The Focusing is your partner's responsibility. You're there to listen, hold the space, be present. That's all."

I got tired of the phone calls, so I got smart, and now I teach this in the course. The locus of responsibility between Focusing partners is this: when someone is Focusing, it's their session. It's their time. Period. If they want to use it to talk about instead of sense into, that's their business. If they want to use it to brainstorm or set goals or meditate, that's their business. Just ask how they would like you to be with them. Then you don't have to worry about your role.

"I get bored when my partner tells long stories about other people. I keep waiting for them to get a felt sense." Here we have a paradox. On the one hand, we teach you that what really brings change is to do Focusing: to bring interested awareness to a felt sense. On the other hand, we say, it's the Focuser's session, whatever they want to do, just be with that. How to resolve this? How about this: what if you really knew, what if you really *trusted*, that your partner's stories are part of a holistic process? Would you still be bored? Or would you, perhaps, sit back and watch curiously, interested to see where and how that process would unfold?

There is one legitimate way to influence your partner's Focusing, and that is, when it's your turn, do great Focusing yourself. If they really aren't getting satisfaction from whatever they're doing, and they see how much you're getting from Focusing, they'll change. In their own time, in their own way.

3. Divide your time together into equal turns.

I had a lovely and precious Focusing partnership that lasted, weekly, for fourteen years. For approximately the first eleven years of that time, I would drive up to my partner's house, switch off my car's ignition, and think, "Too bad nothing's going to come up for me tonight." Week after week, without fail, that same thought would come, even though week after week, without fail, I had Focusing sessions in which something *did* come and unfolded and brought insight and relief. (Even though you can trust the Focusing process, you cannot necessarily trust your thoughts about it before it starts!)

If my partner and I had not had the rule, "Divide your time together into equal turns," I might have been tempted to say to her, "I don't need to Focus tonight, why don't you take all the time." And that would have been, as I hope you can feel, profoundly undermining to the partnership relationship. It also would have been a shame, because I would have missed all those great sessions.

People are different. Some have a lot going on, a lot of the time. We call that (as I learned from my first Focusing teachers, Elfie Hinterkopf and Les Brunswick), "Close Process." Some people, like me, usually think that nothing will come. That's called "Distant Process." Both kinds of people can and do get a lot out of Focusing. They can even get a lot out of being partners for each other. But the Distant Person should not, repeat not, be tempted to give away their time to the Close Person because the Close Person seems to need it more. They don't. Everyone needs Focusing. (Besides, a person who is upset or going through a tough time can get a lot out of being the Listener – a feeling of centeredness, the self-esteem of being able to be there for someone else...)

"Equal turns" can be equal in time, or simply equal in opportunity. For example, if two people make an agreement that they will each Focus as long as they want to, that's equal, even if one session is forty minutes and the other ten. Also, the turns don't have to be at the same time: some partnerships have a deal where one week is one person's turn, and the next week is the other person's turn. That's OK. It's even OK if one of you always wants to go first and the other one always wants to go second. The only thing that's not OK is not taking your turn, because that alters the power relationship of the partnership, and marks one person as "needier" and the other as "the giver." Giving away your turn is not a trusting thing to do, neither trusting in the other, nor in your own process. Trust, and take your turn.

On the other side of the coin, if you happen to be the partner with the Close Process, be scrupulous about finding a comfortable stopping place for your session when the agreed ending time has come. If you're full of feelings, of course there will be a temptation to go over, especially if you're enjoying the space your partner gives you. Don't. It's a dangerous indulgence, because – maybe not the first time, and maybe not the second time – but if this happens too often, then you will have become the "needy one" and I guarantee you won't like how that feels. Unless you are really sure that the other person feels relaxed about time, as you do, better to respect time boundaries as agreed. It's part of the "care and feeding" of a Focusing partner.

Of course we are not machines and it should always be possible to renegotiate time agreements if needed. If I give a two-minute warning and my partner says, "It feels like this needs five more minutes, is that OK?" I feel much better about being asked, like that, than if my partner goes over time without asking. I also feel better if such a thing is asked for only rarely, as a special request, rather than regularly. Others may feel differently. The key is to respect your partner's needs – and your own.

The Art of Facilitative Language

I've always been fascinated by language. That love carried me through a Ph.D. in Linguistics, and stayed with me even when I switched careers to become a teacher and guide of the Focusing process. Where these two loves meet is in the intriguing field of "facilitative language" – choosing and using language to facilitate inner process.

Whether we use that language with ourselves, or with a Focusing partner, therapy client, etc., we are still drawing on the awesome power of language to open and invite experiencing.

Although every article in this book is about facilitative language to some extent, the articles in this section center on it.

In the Focusing community, we use the word "Listening" with a special meaning. It stands for "active listening," or "empathic responding" – saying back (the essence of) what the other person is saying. This is not silent listening. The Listener speaks.

I learned Listening at the same time and place I learned Focusing: in the Changes community that met at the University Church on Sunday nights, in the Hyde Park neighborhood of Chicago, in 1972. (I was 22.) My first Listening teacher was Les Brunswick, who had us sit in a circle and each in turn say a sentence to the person to our right. The person to the right was to "take it in and say it back." We were not to be parrots, this wasn't simple repetition. We were to imagine a clear pool in front of us, into which the other person's "meanings" could fall and be reflected back. I found this simple process tremendously exciting. I was good at it. I loved it.

At Changes, you could go up to another person and say, "Would you Listen to me?" It meant that you wanted them to sit with you while you did Focusing, or explored some issue both verbally and emotionally, and they would keep you company by saying back your words, or the essence of your words, or the sentence you said just before you stopped talking. No advice! No help! No interference! No judgment!

For a person like me, coming from a family background that seemed to leave me tangled in a morass of unspoken obligation and expectation every time I interacted with anyone, this way of being was astonishing – and as welcome as fresh air. I quickly acquired three or four Focusing partners, people willing to Listen to me every week, and all I had to do was Listen to them in return. Both roles, giving and receiving, felt wonderful.

Being a good little girl who liked to be helpful, I had some habits to unlearn. I remember one early practice session when I was Listening to Elfie Hinterkopf, another early teacher of mine. Rather than saying back what she was saying, I was taking each thing she said a little further, adding something to it, in a kind of "I understand you so well I can even take the next step for you." She nipped that tendency in the bud, and I got it: in Focusing, people take their own steps. The Listener takes the step that the Focuser just took, and no more.

I loved Listening so much I used it everywhere I could, which meant I sometimes used it inappropriately. I found out that in ordinary conversation people often didn't want just to be repeated back. Too bad: my wonderful new skill didn't apply to every moment of life! Conversations with friends were the place for that "adding a little" that hadn't been right to do with Elfie. I learned that a new tool doesn't replace the old tools, but joins them in the toolkit.

The Changes community that met in the University Church was a remarkable social experiment. Sometimes as many as a hundred people would crowd into the cafeteria (known on weekdays as "The Blue Gargoyle," a popular low-cost lunch spot) to hear from Gene Gendlin or some other speaker, followed by announcements, socializing, and small groups. The special time called "Announcements" wasn't just a dull reading of notes from a list. Often the highlight of the evening, it was a time when anyone could stand up and ask for anything. I heard people ask for rides, places to stay, help with moving, homes for kittens, jobs, hugs, and Listeners. This was also the time when small groups were formed, sometimes impromptu ("I'm so upset about what Nixon is doing in Cambodia and I need a small group to discuss possible actions"), sometimes ongoing.

The small groups changed their nature and composition every week, but one constant was the "New People's Group," a kind of orientation group for first-timers – of whom there were always some. After I'd been attending Changes for a month or two, someone stood up in the Announcement time and announced that the New People's Group needed a facilitator that night. There was a silence. No one jumped in. I heard myself saying, "I'll do it."

What happened in the New People's Group was very simple. We taught Listening. In addition to the few principles which were obvious to anyone – that this was an open group, with little or no centralized planning, in which people were considered equally able to give and receive help – Listening was what they needed to know in order to participate in the life of the community. Interesting: we didn't teach Focusing. We taught Listening.

That was my first teaching gig. Every week there would be anywhere from two to ten new people, of all ages and backgrounds, interested in learning enough Listening to participate in this unusual community. I never tired of giving the spiel about Listening. It went something like this:

"This Listening-Focusing thing has two sides, and both are important. The person who's Focusing is in charge of what the session is about, how much to say or how little. You can Focus without saying what it's about, if you want to. The Listener waits until the Focuser speaks. Then you let in what they said. You don't just say it back quickly, like a parrot. You let it in, so you can say it back from really getting it. And you can change their words, especially the unimportant ones, as long as you keep their meaning. You say back what they said, or the essence of it, and not as a question. Let your voice fall. Then wait. The Focuser has the next job, the job to compare the Listener's words with what you feel inside. Not just with what you said; with what you actually have in there right now. You need to be willing to say, 'No, that's not quite right,' and then sense what is right instead." (This is almost how I teach Listening today, on Sunday mornings of my weekend Level One Focusing workshops.)

Then we would go around the room and each pair of people would take a brief Listening-Focusing turn, there in front of everyone. We learned so much! I learned the most, of course, since I was there week after week. I learned something profound that has stayed with me always – to respect the power of Listening. Over and over again, I saw people have insights, releases, amazing shifts, just from another person, often a stranger, saying back to them exactly what they had said. I lost any awe I might have had for the "expert" who helps another person have insights or make shifts, because I saw those insights and shifts happening before my eyes, with no experts in sight. In fact, when a Listener slipped past my careful instructions and gave advice, I saw the "shut down" happening for the Focuser, as fast as a slamming door. And I was experiencing these same truths in my hour-long partnership exchanges three or four times a week. Listening without advice, adding nothing, brought the most powerful movement. Having an agenda for the other person brought a dead end. There were no exceptions.

Thirty-two years later I remain convinced of what I learned there. Now, I would say it this way: if someone is Focusing – in Presence, contacting an unclear felt sense with interested curiosity – the most facilitative thing that a Companion can do is be in Presence too, and do Listening. If the person is not Focusing at all, and would like to be shown how to do it, they need gentle suggestions, "guiding," in addition to Listening. And if the person is close to Focusing, almost doing it, then the Companion can use advanced Listening techniques (still Listening, not adding anything, yet making choices about what to say back), that can gently invite Focusing for the other person. That's what this article is about.

I presented this paper at the 13th International Focusing Conference held in Shannon, Ireland, in May 2001. That presentation was videotaped, and the video made from it is available as *The Power of Listening*, from Nada Lou Productions, www.nadalou.com.

The Power of Listening

Presented to the 13th International Focusing Conference
Shannon, Ireland, May 2001

Abstract

We discuss the purposes of Listening, and compare Carl Rogers' stated purpose for "reflection of feelings" with Eugene Gendlin's purpose for reflection within a session that includes Focusing. Three purposes for Listening are given, corresponding to three ways that Listening facilitates Focusing process. Listening is then defined as making a statement that says back what the other person (Focuser, client, partner) just said, exactly or in paraphrase, with no intention of changing or adding anything essential or of making any change in the other person's experience. Listening, as defined here, is not asking questions or making suggestions. We note that the linguistic form of Listening responses changes as the purpose changes. We explore some linguistic forms that help Listening do its work and accomplish its three purposes. We conclude that when Listening is used with sensitivity and skill, little or no guiding is needed, especially between Focusing partners.

The Purpose of Listening

Why would we say back what someone else is saying? In ordinary life, repeating another person's words is just as likely to get you an angry look as a grateful one. Yet in the special world of Focusing therapy and counseling, and the even more circumscribed world of Focusing partnership, repeating back is the key, the essence, the *sine qua non*. Why?

Carl Rogers was not the first to repeat back a client's words, but he is the one who made it a well-known technique, taught in counseling courses and practiced worldwide. During his lifetime, the technique called "reflection of feelings" became so widely used, and in many cases so misunderstood, that a backlash was created, detractors mocking the therapist who merely repeats a client's words. Responding to this backlash, Rogers (who wrote in 1980 that the word "reflect" had come to make him cringe) clarified the purposes for repeating someone's words:

> I have come to a double insight. From my point of view as therapist, I am not trying to "reflect feelings." I am trying to determine whether my understanding of the client's inner world is correct – whether I am seeing it as he or she is experiencing it at this moment. Each response

of mine contains the unspoken question, "Is this the way it is in you? Am I catching just the color and texture and flavor of the personal meaning you are experiencing right now? If not, I wish to bring my perception in line with yours."

On the other hand, I know that from the client's point of view we are holding up a mirror of his or her current experiencing. The feelings and personal meanings seem sharper when seen through the eyes of another, when they are reflected. (1986b)

So Rogers saw the therapist's purpose for Listening as checking with the client to make sure the therapist's understanding fit or matched the client's "inner world." At the same time, he saw that the client was receiving something more from having their "feelings and personal meanings" reflected, something more than could be predicted from the simple activity of checking understanding.

Eugene Gendlin, once Rogers' student, became interested in what he called "the client's side of the therapeutic process." (1984) He became interested in why some clients were vastly more helped by therapy than others. An important part of this question was why some clients were more able to get positive benefit from the therapist's reflection of their "feelings and personal meanings."

What do we assume the client will do with a Listening response?

We hope and assume that clients will *check* the response, not against what they said or thought, but against some inner being, place, datum… "the felt sense"; we have no ordinary word for *that*.

An effect might then be felt, an inward loosening, a resonance. What seemed to be there was expressed and heard. It need not be said again. For some moments there is an easing inside. (In theoretical terms the interpersonal response has carried that forward.) Soon something further comes. What *was* there turns out to have more to it.

We hope that clients will check not only what we say, but also what they say, against *that inward one*. (1984, p. 82)

Gendlin called *that which the client needs to check with* the "felt sense." He was the first to identify and name this essential move: that the client checks what comes with something inside, directly felt. His research showed that this checking made the difference between success and failure in therapy. (That Rogers was impacted by Gendlin is shown by the fact that, writing about empathy in 1980, he cites Gendlin's work as a key reason empathy is effective.)

Gendlin shifted the therapist's purpose for Listening. For Rogers, the purpose was for the therapist to check his or her understanding. For Gendlin, the purpose of Listening is to support the client in checking within, checking with that inner "something." The words Rogers used, to express the therapist's attitude toward the client, now fit the client's attitude in offering words and images back to the "felt sense."

> *"Is this the way it is in you? Am I catching just the color and texture and flavor of the personal meaning you are experiencing right now? If not, I wish to bring my perception in line with yours."*

Presence

There is no disagreement over this key insight: Attitude is far more important than technique. Rogers was appalled when his non-directive approach was reduced to a technique of reflection of feelings, and fought back by putting forth empathy as an attitude or "way of being" rather than as anything one "does." Edwin McMahon and Peter Campbell, beloved and influential Focusing teachers who emphasize the caring and gentle aspect of Focusing, have this to say:

> Remember, the greatest gift we give to someone whom we accompany in Focusing is a caring presence that is non-manipulative. Technique can be very helpful, but in the long run is of little consequence if this presence is missing (1991, p. 21-22).

There is no question that Listening (reflection) should not be done as a technique, but as an expression of an attitude of presence with and for the client. Having said that, however, we can acknowledge that Listening is an unequalled way to express the attitude of nonjudgmental presence.

> A safe and steady human presence willing to be with whatever comes up is a most powerful factor. If we do not try to improve or change anything, if we add nothing, if however bad something is we only say what we understand exactly, such a response adds our presence and helps clients to stay with and go further into whatever they sense and feel just then. This is perhaps the most important thing that any person helping others needs to know. (Gendlin, 1996, p. 11)

Expressing one's nonjudgmental presence is the second purpose of Listening.

The Inner Relationship

My own work, building on Gendlin's, has added one more purpose for Listening. In addition to supporting the client in checking inside, and expressing one's own nonjudgmental presence, the third purpose for Listening is to support the client in facilitating and maintaining a positive inner relationship with "something" that is there for them.

Although Gendlin doesn't mention how reflecting can support this inner relationship, he has eloquently described the relationship itself:

> The client and I, we are going to keep it, in there, company. As you would keep a scared child company. You would not push on it, or argue with it, or pick it up, because it is too sore, too scared or tense. You would just sit there, quietly. ... What that edge needs to produce the steps is only some kind of unintrusive contact or company. If you will go there with your awareness and stay there or return there, that is all it needs; it will do all the rest for you. (1990, p. 216)

This "unintrusive contact" that Gendlin describes is not even a checking; it is simpler than that. It is much more a "being" than a "doing." Even something inside that is "too sore, too scared or tense" to be checked with can still be kept company. And this is not only, and not primarily, the therapist's company. It is the client's "I" keeping company with the client's "it." (Gendlin, 1990, p. 222: "Focusing is this very deliberate thing where an 'I' is attending to an 'it.'")

We have spoken of the therapist's presence. The ability of the client to *be with* what is there, not merged with their experience but Present for it, can be called the client's Presence. (To distinguish the two, I will capitalize the word "Presence" when referring to the client's inner Presence with what is there for them. Barbara McGavin taught me to use the word Presence in this way, and showed me much about this beautiful concept. Much of my work with the Inner Relationship is our shared work.)

Supporting this keeping company from Presence is the third purpose of Listening.

The Purposes of Listening: Recapitulation

We can say that there are three ways Listening facilitates the Focusing process for the client. These correspond to three purposes for giving Listening reflections.

(1) We listen to support the client in checking what comes with something inside, directly felt.

(2) We listen to offer our nonjudgmental presence for the client's process.

(3) We listen to support the client in "keeping company" from Presence with something inside.

Definition: What is Listening?

The word "Listening" has many meanings and many uses. In this paper, it is being used in its technical and specific meaning of making a statement that says back what the other person (Focuser, client, partner) just said, exactly or in paraphrase, with no intention of changing or adding anything essential or of making any change in the other person's experience.

The Listener says something back to the Focuser (client) that has the purpose of "saying what they just said." It is in the form of a statement. It is usually not solely the exact words they said, yet even when the words are different, they are not different in essence. Nothing from the Listener is being added, no opinions are being given, no change is being intended.

I would like to make the case that the process of Listening does not include asking questions, not even by tone of voice. I am aware that not all Focusing teachers would agree with me on this, and I respect their opinion and their work. However, this has been my experience: that when the Listening response includes a questioning tone, the Focuser tends to be drawn out of direct contact with their process, towards contact with the Listener. The classic instance is where the Focuser has closed eyes until the Listener's question, and upon hearing the question, the Focuser opens their eyes and looks at the Listener. Of course if the Focuser *wants* to open their eyes and look at the Listener, there's nothing wrong with that! But it's unfortunate if the Focuser is drawn out of an inner contact which is otherwise going well, because the Listener framed their reflection as a question. This goes against one of our main purposes for Listening: that it facilitates the Focuser in staying in relationship with something inside.

Furthermore, the nature of questions is such that, unless they are carefully framed, they can sound as if what is being questioned is not whether the word fits, but whether the Focuser is right to feel or think the way they do. A striking example is this one from Kevin Flanagan's *Everyday Genius:*

> Paula: No, I can't take it … I just seem to fold inside … I don't have the stomach for it anymore. Maybe I'm a coward.
> Listener: A coward? (p. 153)

The Linguistics of Listening

When the purpose for Listening evolved, so did the form. When the primary purpose of Listening is to check the therapist's understanding of the client, as it was for Rogers, then sensitive paraphrases are better than word-for-word reflections.

> Jan: And yet people say to me, "Jan, you're in your prime. You've got everything going for you!" And little do they know inside what I feel.
> Carl: That's right. So that outside and to an observer, you are in your prime and you have everything going for you. But that's not Jan inside. Jan inside is quite different from that. (1986a, p. 145)

But once we are aware of Focusing, then at those moments when we sense that Focusing is happening in the client, repeating back the client's key words so that they can check them within becomes more important. In fact, the more the client is in contact with something inside, and the deeper and closer the client's contact, the more the exact words are needed and will even be insisted on by the empowered client.

> C: I can hardly touch it. There is something and it is right here on the edge. I can hardly touch it; it is – I cannot want my mother, I can hardly say it.
>
> T: You cannot want her. (Silence)
>
> C: That is where I feel the noise like darts. (More silence.) It is real, real early.
>
> T: It feels like a very early experience. (Silence)
>
> C: I cannot want anything. (Silence…) This needs to rest and it cannot rest. If it lets down and rests, it will die. It needs to keep its guard up.
>
> T: There is such a big need and longing to rest and let down and ease; but somehow also this part of you cannot rest. It feels that it will die if it stops being on guard. (Silence…)
>
> C: Maybe it could, if I could trust something.
>
> T: It could rest if you could trust something.
>
> C: No, no. MAYBE it could rest if I could trust something.
>
> T: It is important to say 'maybe.' "Maybe it could rest if I could trust something." (Gendlin, 1990, p. 219)

But of course the client is not always in deep, close contact with something inside. What then? In the rest of this paper, we will explore linguistic forms that help Listening do its work and accomplish its three purposes. It should go without saying that any talk about linguistic form assumes that the Listener's attitude is one of unconditional presence, or at least of acknowledging any parts of him- or herself that are not able to be unconditionally present. Tone of voice and pace/timing are also important, and not in the scope of this paper.

There are those who would say that, once the Listener's unconditional attitude is in place, it doesn't matter what words are used. I don't agree. Just because attitude and presence are more important than words doesn't mean that words are unimportant. There are those who feel that conscious attention to word choice changes the relationship between Listener and Focuser, makes the Listener somehow inauthentic or a manipulator. I respectfully disagree. I can understand the problem, and in some instances I share it: I have a long-standing dislike of techniques of rapport-building (as in Neuro-Linguistic Programming) where, for example, the therapist consciously breathes along with the client. I believe that, in most cases, helpful tone of voice, pace, and timing of Listening responses can be trusted to arise naturally out of the Listener's presence. But when it comes to words, I feel we can be conscious of making facilitative word choices *and* be in an attitude of presence with the client. The suggestions that follow are offered in this light. They are by no means a complete list of all types of facilitative Listening forms, but are simply those which I find most interesting from a linguistic point of view.

The Power of "Something": Pointing to Felt Experience

The Focuser needs to sense into a place inside. When the Listener's response includes the word "something" used appropriately, this helps to make a place inside the Focuser that can be sensed into. The word "something" is an invitation to be aware of a place which is already implicit; therefore the phrase "make a place" in the previous sentence isn't quite right. At the same time, until the word "something" points to the place, there's a way in which it isn't there yet. So both are true.

> How may we help a person to find and attend to that unclear edge in the border zone between conscious and unconscious? One way to do so is to respond in a pointing way toward an unclear "something." (Gendlin 1996, p. 47)

C: I had a dream… I was alone with this guy, ah (silence)… and the dream was real nice, it was a real nice relationship. When I thought about it next day I thought, why don't I have a real one! I don't think he could really see anything wrong with me. I was also thinking why I was absent in school so much. When it comes to the end of the line I don't have a paper, I hold back. I get jittery and then I pull away from it.
T: You're saying there is *something* similar about those two things.
C: Yeah, I have all these excuses about why I never do my best, uh –
T: You come right up to the line and then *something holds back*. (pp. 41-42, my italics)

Gendlin points out that the therapist could have reflected without pointing at a "something." Instead of saying "You're saying there is *something* similar about those two things," T could have said, "not handing papers in is like not getting with a man" – which surely qualifies as understanding what the client is saying. So this "pointing at a something" is a special Focusing move, informed by our awareness of how powerful it is to be at an unclear edge, a fuzzy not-yet-fully-described experience that is like a door into unfolding.

F: I keep going back to that incident with Jan.
L: There's *something* about that incident with Jan…

F: It's puzzling… it was when she wouldn't agree to the meeting, that was it, but I don't know why…
L: There was *something* about when she wouldn't agree to the meeting….

Saying Back What Is There; Not Saying Back What's Not There

It is obvious that the Focuser can only feel into what is there for them; they can't feel into what is not there. Yet people talk all the time about experiences that they are not having, or not able to have:

"There's also something vague. I can't get what it is."

"I don't know where this is coming from, but I'm getting the sense that this part of me needs support."

"I'm not sure how to describe this feeling in my throat."

I would suggest that the way to support the Focusing process is to say back what is there, but leave out what is not there.

F: There's also something vague. I can't get what it is.

L: You're sensing something there that's vague.

F: I don't know where this is coming from, but I'm getting the sense that this part of me needs support.

L: You're getting the sense that this part of you needs support.

When the Focuser doesn't use a word to refer to what is there, and yet something clearly is there, the Listener can supply the word "something" to point to what is there.

F: I'm not sure how to describe this feeling in my throat.

L: You're sensing something there in your throat.

Reflecting Fresh Air

Whatever is fresh, new, something stirring, always needs support. The Listener gives that support simply by saying that part back.

The following sequence occurred in a partnership session between two experienced Focusers:

F: [Something here] needing to rest. And needing privacy. That's strong – doesn't want to be seen, or to relate.

C: It doesn't want to relate, or be related to.

F: It could be gently touched, but doesn't want talking. Doesn't want to have to respond.

C: You're aware of something there that could be touched, just that much is possible. Gently touched.

The Listener, Chris McLean, had this to say afterward: "I chose this part to mirror – the touching – even though the last thing that the Focuser had said was 'Doesn't want talking. Doesn't want to have to respond.' I think I sensed a movement in the whole thing, a movement forward. We had already been with the part that didn't want to respond, and here was this new thing, so I reflected just that."

Often, the "fresh air" can be found not so much in the literal words the Focuser says, but rather in the *positive implications* of a negative statement. This would be a sentence which means the same as what the Focuser said, a paraphrase, but with no "not" in it. (By the terms "positive" and "negative," I am pointing only to a linguistic fact, whether or not there is a "not" in the sentence. I am not otherwise evaluating the statement.)

F: It doesn't know how to settle down.

L: It wants to find a way to settle down.

Here's another example, from the Focusing/Listening session given as the Appendix to this paper:

> A: … my awareness bounced over to the woman in the battlefield to invite her to sense what she would want as well. And she said "Don't rush me. I'm not finished yet."
>
> B: Yeah, she has something she needs to do first. She's not finished with something.

Here the Listener re-phrased "Don't rush me. I'm not finished yet." as "She has something she needs to do first." This illuminated the positive (i.e., containing no "no" or "not") inside the negative. The Listener then reflected the Focuser's words more closely ("She's not finished with something") to make sure they were heard.

Disidentification

I cannot overemphasize the importance of disidentification. We've spoken already of the power of the Inner Relationship and the Focuser being in Presence with what is there. Disidentification is the first key that opens this big realm of inner Presence.

Gendlin says, "Focusing is this very deliberate thing where an 'I' is attending to an 'it.'" Yet people often speak, and experience themselves, as all "I."

"I want to run."

"I'm afraid I'm never going to get over him."

"I want to go and I don't want to go."

"I don't seem to like myself very much."

There is no "it" in any of these sentences, and we don't know whether there is an unspoken "it" in the person's awareness – perhaps not. Without an "it" in awareness, Focusing is often harder, so a Listener can facilitate Focusing by offering a candidate for "it," for the Focuser's consideration.

Here is one way to do this:

F: I want to run.

L: There's a wanting to run.

"I want" has become "there's a wanting," and thus more of an "it" to feel into.

Our favorite word, "something," offers another way:

F: I'm afraid I'm never going to get over him.

L: Something in you is afraid you're never going to get over him.

When the Focuser is clearly experiencing parts, they will probably appreciate receiving a reflection using "a part of you."

F: I want to go and I don't want to go.

L: Part of you wants to go and part of you doesn't want to go.

This clear separation of parts can be especially valuable when the Focuser is locked in an inner struggle.

F: I don't seem to like myself very much.

L: There's something in you that doesn't like something in you very much.

Fritz Perls and the Empty It

People who've studied with Perls (father of Gestalt Therapy) or his students are sometimes taken aback at our Focusing love for this little word "it." Perls is famous for insisting that his students own their feelings, using the word "I" in places where they'd previously said "it." "It's sad" would become "I'm sad," "It's depressing" would become "I'm depressed," and so on.

I've had people say to me, "I'm working hard to own my feelings, and now you seem to want me to go back to saying 'it' again!" My response is that I'm happy they've learned to own their feelings – and now I want them to go, not back, but even further. The disowning "it" which Perls and others so rightly dislike is not the "It" of Focusing.

In the structure of the English language, every sentence requires a subject. Sentences which describe processes where there is no actor are given "empty" subjects: "It's raining," "It's dark out." The "it" here means nothing, refers to nothing. These sentences would be just as meaningful without it – "Raining." "Dark out." They just wouldn't be grammatical.

We speakers of English have made use of this empty "it" to distance ourselves from feelings and opinions, making them seem as impersonal as the weather.

"It's interesting."

"It's scary."

"It's impressive."

"It's overwhelming."

"It's depressing."

Each of these sentences gives the illusion that it is not about the speaker, but about some condition outside of the speaker. I can say that the book was interesting, the movie was scary, the bridge was impressive, the task was overwhelming, and the loss was depressing. When, actually, in every case I am speaking of my own feelings: it's I who is interested, scared, impressed, overwhelmed, depressed.

But this empty "it" is not the Focusing "It," because the Focusing "It" refers to something felt in inner experience. It is not empty. It refers. So if I start by saying "It's scary," then own the feeling by saying, "I'm scared," I would then move in a Focusing way to sense the *scared* in my body, and say, perhaps, "In my stomach I'm sensing something that's tight. It's scared." "It's scary" – empty it – has become "I'm scared" – owned feeling – has become "It's scared" – something to be with in a Focusing way.

We certainly never want to go backward, and turn a Focuser's "it" back into an identified "you."

F: "This place in my stomach is angry."

Not recommended:

L: "You're angry."

Preferable:

L: "That place in your stomach is angry."

"Something" Is Alive

Earlier we quoted from a client session cited by Gendlin (1990), as an example of how the therapist follows the client's words very closely if the client is in deep contact with something inside. But there was one place in this example where the therapist varied the client's words slightly and significantly.

> C: I cannot want anything. (Silence…) This needs to rest and it cannot rest. If it lets down and rests, it will die. It needs to keep its guard up.
>
> T: There is such a big need and longing to rest and let down and ease; but somehow also this part of you cannot rest. *It feels that it will die* if it stops being on guard. (Silence…)

What the Listener has done has somehow *enlivened* the part. Where the client said "it will die…", the Listener responded, "It *feels* that it will die." "It will die" could have been an outer description, an objective assessment. The Listener responds from inside a "living It," from the Its own point of view.

As a Focusing session continues, the "something" in awareness often takes on more and more of the qualities of being alive. Ideally the Listener recognizes that this is happening and responds in a way that supports the aliveness.

F: It's tired. It doesn't want to speak.

L: *It's letting you know* that it's tired and doesn't want to speak.

Who's Saying It?

Linguistic theory tells us that every sentence uttered is situated in time and place and oriented as to its speaker and hearers. This is why we can use relational words like "I," "you," "now," "then," "here," etc., and have them understood, even though "I" refers to me when I use it and to you when you use it. If we don't know who said the sentence (or where or when), then we don't know what or whom these relational words refer to.

The most obvious way this applies to the linguistics of Listening is that we change these relational words when we say back the Focuser's sentences.

F: Something in me is angry.

L: Something in you is angry.

F: I'm sensing a heaviness right here.

L: You're sensing a heaviness right there.

Although since we're speaking at the same time as the Focuser, we don't need to change their time-reference words.

F: Now it's starting to change.

L: Now you're sensing it starting to change.

There are some practitioners of Listening who do not change the other person's words at all. To me, this sounds quite strange, but I can understand it if I imagine the Listener is saying back the Focuser's words in quotes.

F: Something in me is angry.

L: "Something in me is angry."

It's quite true that sometimes the Focuser says words that sound so powerful and meaningful that we hesitate to change them, even an iota. When that happens, I prefer to make the quote explicit, by saying something like, "What comes there is…" or "The words that come are…"

F: I never have to put up with that again!

L: The words that come are: "I never have to put up with that again!"

Whenever the Listener feels it would sound odd to repeat the Focuser's words, it's usually because, without any preamble, it would sound as if the Listener agrees with what the Focuser is saying. Rather than reports of body sensations or emotions, these are usually value statements. There's rarely an "edge" for sensing into in a statement like this. Often it issues from a part that would like to close a door rather than open one. So it is helpful if the Listener can point to that part, the one who is speaking, using our favorite word for pointing to edges: "something."

F: There's nothing that can be done about people like that.

L: Something in you is saying: "There's nothing that can be done about people like that."

Whenever it is clear that the words are coming from a part, from something inside, not from the Focuser's "I," it's especially helpful to put the Focuser's words in quotes and state who is saying them. "Something in you is saying" is generally useful if the part is unidentified. But sometimes you can make a pretty good guess who is speaking.

F: I'm feeling this part of me that's so . . . angry, I guess. Like a little kid who hates everyone.

L: That part of you feels like a little kid who hates everyone.

F: Just get away from me!

L: It's like that kid is saying, "Just get away from me!"

Presence Listening

We've said that the third purpose for Listening is to support the Focuser in "keeping company" from Presence with something inside. We've talked about the importance of disidentification, and how Listening responses can support the Focuser in remembering that they are not their anger, not their fear, not their tightness, not their judgment, not any of their temporary states.

But what *is* the Focuser, if they are not their temporary states? Barbara McGavin and I call this Presence: the state of being able to *be with* anything, without taking sides, without judgment or agenda. Qualities of Presence include: compassion, allowing, spaciousness, openness, acceptance, patience, gentleness...

Gendlin calls this "being friendly toward a felt sense, and the friendly reception of whatever comes from it (1996, p. 55). McMahon and Campbell call it the "caring-feeling-presence" (p. 11). Clearly it's something that helps Focusing happen. How can a Listener help engender Presence?

What the Listener can do is to *reflect* the Focuser's presence with what they are saying, making it explicit. Each time the Focuser describes something they are experiencing, it is understood that they are experiencing it, sensing it. By making that sensing explicit, the Listener confirms, supports, and deepens the Focuser's experience of Presence. We recommend doing this with the words "You're sensing...", though "You're aware of...," "You're noticing...," and, in appropriate cases, "You're realizing..." will work also.

F: This place in my stomach is clenched with anger.

L: You're sensing that place in your stomach is clenched with anger.

F: I've got a tight band across my chest.

L: You're sensing something in your chest like a tight band.

F: Oh, I see! This part believes that no one can ever help.

L: You're realizing that that part believes that no one can ever help.

When the Focuser doesn't feel compassionate or patient or accepting toward some part of themselves, they are not in Presence. Yet Presence is always there, available, behind the temporary identifications. So if the Listener reflects what the Focuser says *as if* they were in Presence, it functions as a kind of subtle invitation – which, like all invitations, can be refused – to find Presence again.

F: I don't like this heavy part of me.

L: You're sensing a part that feels heavy, and you're sensing another part that doesn't like it.

F: I'm angry!

L: You're sensing something in you that's angry.

F: No, I'M angry!

L: Oh, YOU'RE angry!

Combining this "you're sensing" with "something in you" is what Barbara McGavin and I call "Presence Listening." The effect is often to illuminate that two parts are there, and to offer to the Focuser the opportunity to acknowledge and be with either or both.

F: This part needs to change quicker.

L: You're sensing something in you that's needing this part to change quicker.

F: It's scary.

L: You're sensing something in you that's feeling scared, and something that it finds scary.

The Power of Listening

My personal belief is that Listening is underused and underappreciated. I feel that when Listening is used with sensitivity and skill, little or no guiding is needed, especially between Focusing partners (people who already know Focusing). When the Companion uses all or mostly Listening, and little or no guiding, this respects the Focuser's process by staying out of its way, and it increases the Focuser's sense of empowerment. It also decreases the Companion's sense of taking responsibility for the session. For all that we've said about the gifts of skillful Listening, it is still the Focuser's session.

We could even speculate on the possibility that a need for guiding indicates a failure of Listening. Or, to put it more positively, when Listening is done well, there is less need for guiding.

An example of this occurred recently in a training session in my Center in Berkeley. The session seemed to go well, except for one moment when the

Focuser felt stuck and needed help from the teacher. In the discussion afterward we went back to that moment and wondered if there was anything the Listener could have done, with Listening alone, to help at that moment. What we discovered was that there was little that could have been done at that moment, once the Focuser felt stuck. But when we went back earlier in the session, to what came right before the stuck place, we saw that the Listener had missed saying back a presently felt body feeling, and we could trace the "stuckness" directly back to that missing.

F: I sense *a kind of heaviness on my shoulders and upper arms*. Might be related to carrying something, kind of a burden.

L: Something in you seems to be carrying some kind of burden.

F: Yeah, something in my shoulders and arms. That's where I sense it. I'm saying hello to that sense of carrying a burden and asking it to tell me more about that, what feels like a burden. (long pause) I'm sensing another part of me that wants to rush this process... (At this point the teacher offered help, inviting the Focuser to sit with what was there with interested curiosity and sense from its point of view before asking it any questions.)

Later the Focuser agreed that if the italicized phrase had been said back – something like: "You're sensing something like a heaviness in your shoulders and upper arms..." – it would have helped her stay more directly in contact with the felt sense, rather than moving into her thoughts about it.

In an earlier draft of Eugene Gendlin's book, *Focusing-Oriented Psychotherapy*, there is a beautiful metaphor about Listening. I haven't been able to find it in the published book, so I'm quoting it here from the draft:

> [Listening] is something like adding to the motion of a fly-wheel. The wheel is already moving and you want to add movement to it. Therefore you don't stop it first, so that you can push it. You give it short spurts that can go with the movement it has already. (p. 372)

Listening is like touching an already turning wheel, in the same direction that it's moving. Nothing dramatic appears to be happening. Yet a space is created for the greatest of all human miracles: how much more happens when we allow what is to find its own unfolding, than when we try to make something happen.

Appendix: A Listening Session

Note: This session is on the phone, between two experienced Focusers and longtime Focusing partners. In fact, A is me, and B is Barbara McGavin! When the partner makes a short sound, like "m-hm," that is indicated in parentheses (m-hm) within the other person's paragraph. Pauses are indicated with ellipses. Nothing has been omitted.

A: OK. So I'm bringing my awareness into my body. And I'm sensing, like there's a person inside me, a part of me. I feel her as a "she," who feels – the word is shellshocked, and also – there is a sense of her coming back, almost like maybe even from a coma or emerging from a long period of illness (mmm) still weak and then coming out into a place where, uh, she's looking around and there's a sense of something she doesn't even understand. Other things are kind of coming at her dragon-like, like: why didn't you do this yet? Why didn't you do this yet? And, uh, a little bit of a sense of being overwhelmed and behind and weak and confused – and I'm just sensing what really feels central in all of that. ...... Her – it's interesting, her emotion isn't fear or guilt or any of those things. She's really – bemused maybe more than confused. Like an innocent. She has an innocence about her (uh huh)

B: You can sense that there's an innocence about this girl, female, woman, person.

A: Yeah, she's a woman, she's not a child. She's walking through a battlefield where the battle is over. She's touching pieces of cannon and bodies and things. Touching them with an innocence as if she were touching flowers. Like, just curiosity.

B: You're seeing her walking through this battlefield, touching the dead, cannons, whatever with a kind of innocence like they are flowers, curiosity.

A: Makes me remember a poem I wrote when I was sixteen or something. I don't remember it but the first line was: And if we pick our way through a battlefield...

B: Yeah, that comes there.

A: And tears are here.

B: You can sense tears.

A: ...... So many of my clients have been working lately with a part that's stunned with pain and another part that's anxious with moving forward with life. And so I'm looking, or beginning to get a sense of a counterpart that's anxious.

B: Uh huh, so you're starting to sense a counterpart right there that's anxious.

A: That says "Come on, we can't take any more time with this, we have to get moving!"

B: Yeah, you're hearing it say, "Come on. We don't have any time for this. Got to get moving!"

A: And that woman in the battlefield, she can't be hurried. There's no way. She doesn't even hear, or she vaguely hears those urgings to move but they hardly penetrate. She's much more involved in what she's doing.

B: Mm hm, you can sense how she can't be hurried. She's involved in what she's doing. The other voice is just… she hears it but just barely.

A. Mm hm. So I'm saying to the other voice, "Yes, I know you're scared. You're scared something will be damaged or fall apart if attention isn't paid."

B: You're really letting it know you hear how it's scared.

A: … That part, yeah, it's beginning to show me its wanting as well, at least one level of it. It's like there's a yearning, it feels like that part is carrying that right now. A yearning to express our messages into the world and have them be heard there. Like even, I have, even as I do this session there's something in me that says, "You know this could be animated!" (laughter) Technology isn't that hard anymore, and we could animate lots of these typical parts and counterparts, and people could really relate to that. And that would really help. And it's like (uh huh) [big sigh] a sense of a big, at least that part feels, a big gap, a distance between what I feel capable of …

B: Yeah, you can sense how this part is carrying the longing for all the potential…

A: Yeah, the gap between the reality and the potential feels really big (yeah) right now. And this part feels like one of the problems is this woman in white who's looking…

B: It's like from its point of view this woman is the problem, or a problem…

A: – one of the problems, right –

B: …in between the potential and where you are right now.

A: Right. And I want to just acknowledge the feeling of the gap and acknowledge to that part that it's so much wanting that to change that it's so much trying to figure out what the problem is.

B: Mm hm. Yeah, you're really letting it know you can sense how much it's wanting to reduce that gap.

A: Yeah. Huh. The way you said that made me want to ask what having a reduced gap would feel like.

B: Mmmm.

A: And I felt that for just a moment, and my awareness bounced over to the woman in the battlefield to invite her to sense what she would want as well. And she said "Don't rush me. I'm not finished yet."

B: Yeah, she has something she needs to do first. She's not finished with something.

A: Yeah. And saying that way, and hearing you say it back that way, she shifts a little. She was looking really dazed and again, what was the word at the very beginning? Shellshocked. And now she looks more purposeful. (mmm) She has something she needs to do. That's right. (uh huh) And she's wanting to do it and not be rushed, because it wouldn't be right to rush. (uh huh) It can't be done in a rush.

B: Uh huh, whatever this is that she needs to do, it can't be done in a rush, and you can sense there's a purposeful quality to her now. (yeah) Sounds like there's a kind of strength there.

A: Yeah, I feel – well I'm feeling really touched. And not only by that but I also went over to the other one (uh huh) and it shifted too (ah) 'cause in the presence of her purposefulness, it's sensing that its purpose right now is to just hold the intention and hold the awareness of the potential, and it's feeling good and proud that it has that purpose.

B: Yeah...

A: All of that is touching me. [tears]

B: You can sense how that other part is holding the potential. It is like a container for it - or something like that.

A: Yeah, yeah.

B: And it's feeling proud (yeah) that it has this purpose.

A: Yeah, it's feeling much more able to be patient.

B: Uh huh. As it senses her purposefulness, her needing to do something.

A: Yeah, and again as I feel its willingness to be patient, I feel touched. Tears come. (yeah) I feel touched by the willingness to carry the purposes of both these parts. (yeah) Oh, fabulous.

B: Yeah, you're sensing touched by the willingness to carry the purpose of both these parts.

A: Yeah... we're coming to a good stopping place.

B: And there's about two minutes.

A: [big sigh] Yeah, I think it's the whole thing about being heard that this anxious part shifted from being anxious (yeah) to being honored. Its job is to remember the potential. That's still true, it was true before. But when it's heard, then it shifts from being anxious about remembering the potential (uh huh) to being honored to remember the potential. Cool.

B: And it doesn't have to be pushy.

A: Yeah, yeah. And it doesn't have to – there's some kind of being part of a larger team and it doesn't have to feel alone (yeah) and the "anxious" comes from feeling like nobody is going to hear it.

Introduction to
Focusing with a Family Member with Lung Cancer

The story of my sister Mona's experience with lung cancer is naturally an emotional one for me. She died of her cancer, and I miss her. Her children and her friends and her community miss her. I can sense tears in me right now, as I write about this, nearly six years after her death. I can also sense a peacefulness. Both are here.

I've included this article in this volume for three reasons.

(1) Many people wonder how to be helpful to friends and loved ones who have serious illnesses. If people are open to it, Focusing can be an ideal way to be present with someone, and help them be present with themselves, in a compassionate and healing way, yet without interfering. My sister Mona taught me that people facing serious illness can be justly sensitive to the barrages of well-meaning advice and intrusive sympathy that so often come at them. Focusing may be welcome precisely because it is not that. But it needs to be offered without being pushed, of course.

There's a great article on this subject by Judy Hart, another Focusing friend we lost to cancer. ("'It Stinks, Doesn't It?': Ways to Connect without Fixing." See also Ellen Kirschner's article "When a Friend is Diagnosed with Cancer.")

(2) For those who are interested in how I use the language of Listening and guiding to help people be present to their own experience, these sessions are great examples. Even separated from their theme, assuming nothing about who this Focuser is and what she is facing, these sessions show a person coming into deeper and deeper contact with her own implicit process, and experiencing change, relief and release because of it.

I've put this article here in the book, just after "The Power of Listening," because it provides a demonstration of many of the points I made there. When I typed out these sessions, I did not include everything that was said, but I did type out my responses as fully as I could. I wanted to show what I do, hoping that these examples are illuminating and inspiring.

And finally, (3) Mona asked that we not forget her. A painting that she made hangs on the wall of my study; I see it every day. I feel her smile inside of me. It's a pleasure to include her in this book. Let us remember her.

Focusing with a Family Member with Lung Cancer

Appeared in The Folio: A Journal for Focusing and Experiential Therapy, *Vol. 18, 1999*

In March 1997 my sister Mona was diagnosed with lung cancer. At the time of diagnosis it had spread through her lungs and had already metastasized to her liver and a bone. She has approached her treatment with humor (disliking the word "cancer," she renamed her condition "Clarence"), courage, and a profound faith in God. At this time of writing she has been through a number of courses of chemotherapy and is doing very well, but is not yet cancer-free or in remission.

In October 1998 I offered to do Focusing with her on the phone (we live on opposite coasts). Why did I not offer sessions before? Why did she not ask me, knowing this is what I do? Nobody knows!

The following notes were made after our first three Focusing sessions. Each one was about an hour.

Session One

Mona had chemo today, so she was tired. When I invited her to bring awareness into her body, she became aware of a place near her right breast which has been very troublesome—often hardens up, often is painful, and also has been the site of some procedures. "Tight" was its description.

I invited her to say to it, "Yes, I know you're there," and then sit with it gently, to get the feeling of just keeping it company, just sitting with it like a friend. Then to slowly sense its mood, from its point of view.

"It's very sad. So much has been done to it, it's been invaded. And it's sad because it feels like it will never be the same again."

I gently invited her to let it know she heard it, that it felt sad from being invaded, and from a sense of loss.

Then I invited her to sense if there might be more that it was feeling.

"It's a little angry," she said. "But it's more that it's hurt. It's angry because it's been hurt."

—And maybe you could let it know you hear that as well.

"It's eased up some. It liked hearing me acknowledge its hurt. I guess I've been—not denying it exactly, but just trying to be in the place where everything's OK."

—You're realizing that you've been maybe passing over it some, trying to be in the place where everything's OK.

"It wants me to know that it didn't bring on the disease. It wants me to know that *it's* there, *under* the disease. Like it was there, before the disease came. And that's why it got so hurt."

—Ah, so you might let it know you hear that, that it's still there, *under* the disease.

"It wants to be soothed. It wants to be held, and stroked gently."

—Now you're sensing it wants to be soothed, and held, and stroked.

"It wants to be thanked, for hanging in there."

—And you're sensing it wants to be thanked, for hanging in there.

Soon afterward we respectfully ended the session. Later that day Mona reported that she was feeling pretty good, more "together," more relaxed, since that session.

Session Two

Mona told me that she is scheduled to have a CAT scan next week, which will let her know how the latest chemo has been working. Then we started the session.

"Well, I have some pain spots, and I have a pressure in my solar plexus, like a weight."

—So we'll have you say hello to those pain spots, and then hello to that pressure like a weight in your solar plexus.

"I think it's fear."

—Yeah, so maybe we could say that's a place in you that's feeling scared right now. And gently check with it, and see if that's right, that it feels fear.

"It's like I'm seeing a person with their knees drawn up, waiting. They're wanting to know an outcome, being hopeful but tentative."

—Maybe you could just stay with that person, keep sensing what more that person is feeling.

"It's like the person is not knowing what to do, maybe feeling powerless."

—Not knowing what to do, powerless, maybe check if it fits, if that is how that person feels in there.

"No, not that it is powerless, but only unable to do anything for right now. I think it's because of that CAT scan next week, and I'm powerless over the outcome. The last time I saw my doctor I asked him, How much cancer do I have? I hadn't wanted to know, before. He said I have five spots in my liver, and in my lungs there are cancerous cells all through. I didn't get upset, it's like I already knew it." (pause) "That person in there is waiting because it thinks it has to keep working. It's so tired."

—Ah, you're sensing it's so tired. You might let it know you hear that.

"It's tired because it's had to work so hard. I've been wanting so much to take a rest, but I feel like I can't. Somewhere in me I feel I have to keep working, pushing."

—Yes. You've been feeling like you have to keep working, keep pushing, And you might just stay with that place gently, open to sensing more about that, whatever it wants you to know...

"It's afraid I'll die if it doesn't keep working."

This touched a place of tears for Mona, and she sobbed for a few minutes. I was really happy to sit with her, it felt like a healing kind of crying, as a deep fear was being acknowledged. While she was crying I didn't say anything but I did make murmurs to let her know I was there. As the tears subsided I invited her to let the place know she could hear how scared it was, and to say to it, "No wonder you would be tired, if you feel like you have to keep working or we'll die."

Soon afterward she said she'd like to stop and take a nap. I urged her to do so, and didn't try to chat or talk about our next phone time; I wanted her to be able to go right into sleep.

Session Three

Mona started by telling me the results of her CAT scan. She had called her doctor because her breathing was getting labored, and she wondered what it was about. He told her it was probably both anxiety and symptoms starting. Then he told her the CAT scan results.

The little cancers (in her lung) are growing. The big tumor in the lung and the tumors in the liver are not growing. He is switching her to a different chemo regimen (Taxol). It will be harder, take longer prep time, and her hair will probably start thinning again. She told me she was concerned about how hard this might be to go through.

When we invited her awareness into her body...

"I'm feeling full, from lunch...also that labored breathing..."

—You might just acknowledge that labored breathing, and stay with it, sensing how it is.

"It's like a reaching..."

—Yeah, just acknowledge that it's like a reaching. Sensing into it, sensing how it is.... And maybe there's a sense of something more right there, that's hard to put into words...

"There's a sense that I've been having, that the treatment I've been getting is not enough. This reaching is like that. Like it's that feeling, this hasn't been enough."

—Oh, yes, you've been having a sense that the treatment was not enough, and the reaching is like that.

"Kind of a relief, too, because I knew it was coming and now it's here."

[the CAT scan results]

—You're also noticing it's kind of a relief.

"Remember that last session I felt the part of me that thought it had to work so hard? Well, now it's relaxing. It had to work hard because it knew the treatment was not enough."

—You can feel that part of you relaxing now.

"I thought I was feeling bad about the new treatment, but I'm actually feeling good. It's like my life force won't be as strained."

—Oh, that's how it is, like your life force won't be as strained. Maybe you're feeling that life force in there right now?

"Yes. It's mixed. There's a part of me that's not happy and a part of me that is happy."

—So maybe we can acknowledge both, and let both be here.

"The part of me that's not happy is not just about the effects I'll have from the new chemo, but because I've lost another treatment. Because you can't go back on one after you've done it. Very mixed feelings."

—Yeah. That part feels unhappy because of an option closing, you've lost another treatment.

"I still wonder about the labored breathing. The doctor said he thought it was both anxiety and the symptoms starting. I wonder which it is."

—That might be something you'd like to ask it, inside.

[taking time] "It feels like it's the symptoms starting, and it feels like they're starting so I'll really know that this new treatment is the right thing to do."

—So you might take some time to check that with your body, see if that's right, that the symptoms are starting so you'll really know this is the right thing to do.

"Yes. It's like my body is saying, yes, you do need this. And I don't feel any anxiety. I feel sadness, and hopefulness, but no anxiety."

—No anxiety. What's there now is sadness, and hopefulness.

"You know, I have a lot of cancer. And people tell me they can't believe it because I look so good. And I think that's my life force."

—Ah, your life force!

"Yes. I've come to peace with a lot of things. I don't want to die, and I don't think I'm going to die, but I'm not afraid of it." (pause) "Also my labored breathing gives me a reason to really take the week off. It *is* a relief."

—You can feel the relief there.

"That's surprising to me. I thought I would feel upset. But when I really feel in there, right now, there's relief."

—Feeling in there, right now, you feel the relief. Yes.

"And there's a knowing that this will work, that I'll be closer to being well. It's a very comfortable and peaceful feeling."

—Ah, so that's great to take time to feel, this knowing that this will work.

"My body loves me!"

—How great to feel that!

"I'm breathing much easier, Anny. At least for right now!"

As an ending step she thanked her body, and then she thanked me, and I told her that I was feeling overwhelmed with gratitude and privilege to be able to share with her at this level.

Reflections from Ann

I myself haven't had to face life-threatening illness, but I know from friends who have gone through it how hard it can be, making choices among treatments and often getting conflicting advice. How wonderful if people in those situations could sense into a level of body-knowing about what would be right! I could tell, from the peaceful quality that my sister was radiating at the end of the third session, that she was in touch with a knowing about what is right for her. That doesn't mean that chemo is the right way for everyone. What's wonderful about Focusing is that it lets a person get in touch with "right for me, right now" and find a sense of balance and peace amid all the conflicting outer messages.

Also, it feels deeply exciting and encouraging that Mona could get in touch with her "life force" as it feels in her body, in the Focusing session. This could only be good!

We have continued to have weekly sessions, and all kinds of issues have surfaced, including the spiritual purpose of the cancer, and Mona's anger at the cancer ("How dare you!"). For me, these sessions are doubly joyous—not only whatever healing they may bring, emotionally and (dare I hope!) physically, but also the closeness between us as sisters which has deepened so much from being able to share at this level.

Reflections from Mona

It feels like I'm so much more in touch with my feelings, more than just feeling them. Not an analysis really, just a deeper understanding. Sometimes I really don't feel like Focusing, but when I do I always feel better, quieter, more calm, secure and serene. I love the relaxation. I dearly love the closeness with Anny, and I love that she calls me every week. Her guiding is very helpful, and always seems to go in the right direction. There's no struggle or guessing about it. I just seem to know, and it feels right. Thank you Anny for that, and for loving me.

Keep me in your prayers. Don't forget me.

Appendix: Starting the session

Some people may be interested in the words I use to help start the session, referred to briefly in the accounts above as "when we invited her awareness into her body." (Mona calls it "the relaxation.") This actually refers to about three minutes of talking, and it goes something like this (with pauses indicated by …):

—So let your awareness begin coming to your body… And maybe first the outer area of your body, like your arms, and your hands… Noticing what your hands are touching, and how they feel… Being aware also of your legs, and your feet… Noticing what your feet and touching, and how they feel… Being aware also of the contact of your body on what you're sitting on… And then letting your awareness come inward, into that whole inner area of your body, that includes your throat… your chest… your belly… Taking your time to rest your awareness in there… And any part of your body may be calling for your awareness, and that's OK, and we'll just start in this middle area… And maybe give yourself an inner invitation in there, like you're saying, "What wants my awareness now?"… "What would like some attention, some company?"… and then wait… … And when you're aware of something, you might let me know."

Afterword

These sessions took place in October and November, 1998. On Christmas Day, Mona was taken to the emergency room with a piercing headache. It was discovered that the original metastasis of the lung cancer had included tumors in the brain. She began receiving radiation and chemotherapy for brain tumors, and although we felt hopeful at first, Mona never really recovered after those treatments. It became more and more difficult for her to lift herself and to speak. On March 20, her husband and her doctor made the decision to stop treatments and ask for the help of Hospice. When I called from Japan and heard this news, I flew immediately to New Jersey, and spent six heartful days at Mona's bedside, talking to her, singing to her, and often just touching her face. Mona died at home, peacefully, on April 7, 1999, holding the hand of her son.

My friend Frans Depestele, the Belgian experiential therapist and Focusing theorist, often urges me to write more about the use of language to facilitate process. I can see his point. There aren't many people in my position: trained academically in linguistics, and with 24-plus years of experience facilitating Focusing. When I gave up my career as a college teacher of linguistics after two years, at age 27, I thought I was turning away from linguistics forever, and that was sad. I had gone into linguistics because I loved studying the patterns of language, and I left it because the academic world, with its rigid hierarchies and relentless politicking, did not nourish me. I remember the joy and astonishment I felt, years later when teaching a Level Three class, to find myself reaching for linguistics concepts: I still needed my linguistics!

For teaching Focusing itself, linguistics is not so obviously important. But for teaching Focusing teachers and therapists – for teaching how to facilitate a Focusing process – I have found my linguistics to be invaluable.

What we are really talking about here is *the therapeutic use of language* – when language is used to facilitate a process in another person, as in almost all psychotherapy, hypnotherapy, guided meditation, guided imagery, and many other emotional healing techniques. While the area that I know best is Focusing guiding, I'm convinced that the insights in this paper apply across the board, to all facilitative use of language.

There are many many therapeutic and spiritual practices involving questions. There are methods of various sorts called "Inquiry." There is something called an "enlightenment intensive" in which one is asked "Who are you?" over and over again. I have been told that the purpose of repeated questions is to put one off-balance, or to put "the Superego" off-balance. That may be so. For me, it goes deeply against the grain to do a process that tricks or silences any part of the being.

I challenge any practitioner using questions to try the gentler, slower process of proposing suggestions. I assume that if you are such a practitioner, your first reaction to this paper will be to hold to what you already know how to do. Questions have been working fine for you! I hope that you stay long enough to have a second reaction, and I hope that your second reaction is one of curiosity. I hope you'll go into your sessions with a fresh eye and ear, to notice what is happening with your questions.

Recently I did a Focusing workshop with a group of people, many of whom had had previous experience with other Focusing teachers. One young woman came up to me at a break and thanked me for helping her with a problem she'd had with Focusing. "I keep going up in my head. In my session with X [a well-known Focusing teacher], she asked me what was the quality of what I was feeling, and I just went right into my head." I smiled and told her I was glad she was learning how to stay in her body. But inwardly I was thinking: I wonder if X has any idea what she did when she asked, "What's the quality of that?" I wonder if she connected this young woman's going away from the body with her own use of a question, and if she considered saying, the next time, "You might take some time to sense the quality of that."

All I ask is this: When you are facilitating someone in an inner process, and things don't go the way you hoped, listen to what *you* just said. And if what you just said was a question, consider the alternative!

Questioning Questions

Appeared in The Focusing Connection, *March 2001*

Recently my 81-year-old mother was telling me about the exploits of a friend of hers. I wasn't listening attentively (sorry, Mom!), and I missed the name of the friend – though I knew she'd said it. "Excuse me, Mom," I said. "Who are you talking about?" She went blank. "I know I said her name a minute ago," she told me, "but I couldn't tell it to you now to save my life."

People who are 81 tend to assume that any memory lapse is a problem of aging. But because I've been thinking about the effect of questions, I noticed something else about that incident: her memory had been working fine until I asked her a direct question. Could it have been the question that stopped her process?

I had occasion to test this hypothesis a few weeks later when I was talking to a friend about a musical event I had missed. "What songs were played?" I asked. "You know," he said, "when you ask me, I can't think of any." "OK," I said, "let's try it another way. I bet they played a lot of good songs." "Yes," he said – and immediately started naming them.

The question is this: Are questions the best way of facilitating inner experience in another person (and in one's self)? My answer: in most cases, no.

Of course, many excellent Focusing guides do use questions, and people have wonderful and profound sessions with them. In questioning questions, I do not mean to question the wisdom or skill of guides who use them. On the contrary, my admiration for such people (Gene Gendlin is one) is even greater because I am aware of what remarkable Presence they must have, to counteract the difficulties of questions.

Let me also say that I am profoundly convinced that Presence is more important than any technique, including the linguistic distinctions which I will make in this article. As Gendlin says in his paper "The Small Steps..." (1989): "All that is needed... is to be a human being, with another human being." Even using the most facilitative linguistic forms will be fruitless if one is not first able to be present to the other, as a person who is there, willing to trust the process and follow where it goes, willing to take back "brilliant" moves which did not happen to be helpful to this real person in front of us.

Having said this, I want to discuss the three main reasons why I prefer to use suggestions rather than questions when facilitating inner experiencing

(Focusing) in another person (and in myself).

To summarize:

(1) Questions are conversationally *strong*, that is, demanding. (I will say what this means in a sociolinguistic context.) Because of this, questions (a) give fewer choices, (b) are difficult to refuse, and (c) can be experienced as intrusive.

(2) Questions tend to draw attention to the questioner and to highlight the interpersonal relationship between the questioner and the questionee.

(3) Asking a question as a way to facilitate a process is cognitively complex, that is, it requires more steps to be performed internally, and therefore the process which is being facilitated is less supported and more liable to break down. The commonest types of breakdown are (a) questions being answered from the head, and (b) questions being answered with "I don't know," "Nothing," etc.

I will discuss each of these more fully.

Questions are conversationally "strong"

In 1991 I was watching a session between a student guide and a new Focuser. At a number of places, the guide asked questions, and it seemed that the questions were more difficult and less facilitative for the beginner than the corresponding suggestions would have been.

For example, the guide asked: "What are you feeling there, in the middle of your body?" and "What's the quality of that tightness?" rather than saying: "Notice what you're feeling there, in the middle of your body," and "Maybe you could sense the quality of that tightness."

After the session, I invited the guide to sense into her reason for asking questions in preference to making suggestions. She responded that she had a feeling that questions were more tentative, and therefore offered the Focuser more choices. Somehow I knew that was wrong; that in fact, questions close down choices. But I didn't know how I knew.

Then I remembered a whole body of research from my days as a student and teacher of linguistics. Two researchers from the University of California at Irvine, Harvey Sacks and Emmanual Schegloff, had studied turn-taking in all sorts of conversation, from job interviews to friends chatting on the phone. They described a conversational move as "strong" if it constrains (limits) the conversational choices of the next speaker. They discovered that the quintessential strong conversational move is a question.

So, contrary to popular belief, questions are not more tentative and they do not offer the other person more choices. In fact, a question at any point in a conversation strikingly narrows the conversational options of the other person. Even not answering the question is not really a choice, because any kind of non-answer will be interpreted (in a process Sacks and Schegloff call "strong inference") as a refusal or inability to answer the question, and the other parties to the conversation have a right to draw conclusions about why.

Why is it rude to ask a person about their sexual habits or their age or how much money they make? Not only because it's none of our business, but also because asking a question puts them "on the spot," makes whatever they say next somehow "about" the question.

A: "How old are you?"

B: "It's a lovely day."

A: "Your age is nothing to be ashamed of!"

You may feel that we have strayed far from the gentle mood of a Focusing session, where questions are framed with a quiet voice and a tone of permission to answer or not. Indeed. But tone and permission can only mitigate the effect of questions, not remove it entirely. It is the question *form* which carries the effect, not (only) the intention of the speaker. Because questions are conversationally strong, they have a demanding effect. They place the questioner in a subtly one-up position. They narrow the options of the one questioned to those defined by the questioner.

If this were the only problem with questions, surely we could get around it. But there is more.

Questions tend to draw attention to the questioner and to highlight the interpersonal interaction

I first noticed this effect when I was teaching Listening in Level One Focusing classes. I always encourage beginning Focusers to stay in touch with their inner process and resonate the Listener's words in there. The Focuser speaks, the Listener takes in and then says back what the Focuser said, sometimes the exact words, sometimes summarizing or saying the essence or just the "feeling" words. But unlike in a regular conversation, the two are not looking at each other. The Focuser typically closes his or her eyes, to pay better attention inwardly. It's especially important for beginning Focusers to learn that they can concentrate on their inner process rather than trying to "take care of" the Listener.

I noticed that when the Listener reflected the Focuser's words as a statement, with falling voice at the end, the Focuser's attention tended to stay inside, with their own process. But uncertain Listeners tended to raise their voices at the end of sentences, as if asking the Focuser, "Is that right?" When the Focuser heard the questioning voice (even if the words were in the form of a statement), their awareness tended to move away from their inner process and out toward the Listener. At these moments, the Focuser would often open their eyes and look up as if answering the Listener.

Focuser: "I'm sensing this heavy place is sad."
Listener: "You're sensing that heavy place is sad."
Listener: "You're sensing that heavy place is sad?"

Further observations showed me that the same is true of questions vs. suggestions in guiding. When asked a question (e.g., "How would you describe it?"), Focusers tend to answer *the guide,* as if the guide is asking for his or her own information. On the other hand, a guiding suggestion to sense inwardly ("You might sense how you would describe it") facilitates the Focuser's attention to stay inward.

Asking a question as a way to facilitate a process is cognitively complex

When I was about 13 years old, I went to dinner at the home of a friend whose parents had a different cultural background from mine. At one point the father, sitting at the other end of the table, asked me, "Ann, would you like some more spaghetti?" The spaghetti bowl was sitting near me on the table. I was full, so I answered politely (I thought), "No, thank you." My friend nudged me with her elbow. "What is it?" I whispered, mystified. "He wants you to pass him the spaghetti," she whispered fiercely.

This social *faux pas* illustrates what I mean when I say that asking a question as a way to facilitate a process is cognitively complex. Because I wasn't asked directly, "Please pass the spaghetti," I needed to go through a series of steps: (1) he is asking if I want more spaghetti, (2) the bowl is near me, and (3) perhaps *he* wants more. I didn't make the connections, and the process broke down.

The more steps there are, the more possibilities for breakdown. When a question is used in a Focusing session, and what is hoped is that the Focuser will access inner experience, this is cognitively complex and liable to break down in a very similar way to the "spaghetti" incident.

A question is a request for information. As such, it assumes that the information is there to be given. When the information is not there, the "questionee" must go searching for it.

Q: "What time is it?"
A: "Wait, I need to find my watch."

But, because questions are demanding (see #1 above), the search must be as brief as possible. Also, if there are several places to search in, or several ways to search, the question gives no help as to which one to choose. Which makes a question ideal for testing whether a student has achieved a competence.

Q: "What's the square root of thirty-seven?"
A: "I missed the class where we learned how to do that."

So a question, such as, "What does that heaviness seem to want you to know?", implies a process, but it does not actually facilitate one. The person must already know how to connect in a gentle way with the "heaviness" and sense into it. They must already know that this is a process that takes time, and they must be willing to take the time despite the demanding nature of the question form. This is a lot to expect, especially from an inexperienced Focuser.

There are two corollaries to this point. The first is that questions tend to be answered in the head, as many people have pointed out. Because questions are demanding and imply that the answer should be accessible, the person questioned will tend to look in the place where answers are stored when already known: the head.

Questions tend to be answered in the head *because* the question merely asks for information – it does not facilitate a process of accessing the information. The person who is asked the question has to figure out for themselves how to access the requested information. Because the head-process is faster than the body-process, the person will first attempt to access the information in the fastest place, the head. Some Focusing teachers have solved this problem by teaching Focusers to answer questions from the body and not from the head, and this is commendable. However, it is still a lot of extra work – like teaching people to clean up a mess rather than showing them how not to make the mess in the first place.

The second corollary is that questions (compared with suggestions) will tend to result in a higher percentage of answers like "I don't know" or "Nothing." Again, this is because, although the guide is intending to facilitate a process, the question actually does not support a process which may take time. Instead, the implication of the question form is that the answer should be already there, available to be given back. When it is not there, the person, especially someone not trained in Focusing, will tend to report, "Not there." They have looked, and found nothing, and reported that. They are not being resistant – they have done *exactly* what was requested!

Guide: "And what do you feel in your body as you think of that issue?"

Focuser: "Nothing."

Guide: "Take a little more time, if that's OK – let the issue be here... notice what comes in your body..."

Focuser: "I start to feel a tightness..."

About suggestions

If questions are not the most elegant way to facilitate a process, what is? I propose suggestions.

Compare the following:

Question: "What does that heaviness want you to know?"

Suggestion: "You might take your time to be with that heaviness and sense what it wants you to know."

In contrast to the question, the suggestion "You might take your time to be with that heaviness and sense what it wants you to know" is relaxing and supportive because it supports the Focuser through each step of the whole complex process: to take time, to be with, and to sense for something.

Suggestions are both more direct and more facilitative, because they reduce the amount of extra work that the Focuser needs to do. This is particularly important for people who are new to Focusing. As a full-time Focusing teacher, I give many first sessions, so the problems with questions loom large for me. People who are being guided as a way to show them Focusing can be significantly supported in this process by receiving suggestions rather than questions.

The primary objection I have heard to suggestions is that they seem like "giving orders." I prefer to think of them as "invitations" or "offers." I encourage the use of "cushions," which are phrases expressing the invitational nature of the suggestion.

"You might..."

"See if it would be OK to..."

"See if it would feel right to..."

"Take some time to..."

"Maybe..."

I would recommend avoiding, however, cushioning phrases which turn the suggestion into a question, such as:

"Would it be OK to...?"

"Can you...?"

"Could you...?"

Although they cushion, they are still questions, and share the problems of questions that we have seen.

When to use questions

Do I avoid all questions? Not at all! I use questions when (1) I want to connect interpersonally (usually before or after a Focusing process), and (2) when I believe the information requested is there, ready to be reported.

Focuser: "That part feels done, I'm not sure what to do."

Guide: "Are you still wanting to explore the connection with your room-mate?"

Focuser: "Yes, let's do that."

So you still want to ask questions...

When I shared the thesis of this article with the Focusing Discussion List last year, I was surprised by the number of Focusing guides who defended their practice of asking questions. This led me to some further thoughts.

I do believe that questions have more of a place in therapy than they do in non-therapy Focusing. Because questions highlight the interpersonal relationship, they are more appropriate for the therapist/client relationship than they are for a guiding relationship (including between peers in partnerships). So perhaps it is the fact that I am not a therapist, and my Focusing teaching is primarily aimed at getting people into peer Focusing partnerships, that has led me to such a clear stance on questions.

I also find that questions are much more problematic for a person who has never focused before than for a person who knows how to do Focusing. If a person knows how to do Focusing, then their reactions to questions will probably be more a matter of personal preference than actual interference with their process. But even experienced Focusers can be interrupted by questions. A friend of mine, well trained in Focusing, had these reactions to a recent session with a guide who questioned: "I felt put on the spot, pressured to come up with the answer. Like he knows something I don't, and I'm supposed to guess what it is."

I had a therapist who asked me questions when she intended to facilitate process. Every time she said something like, "How does that feel now in your body?" I forgave her, translated what she said, and sensed into my body. But there was always a little pang, a little bump. Yes, I could do it myself. But how nice it would have been to just sink deep, undistracted, invited by the words of the guide into gentle and intimate relationship with my own being.

For Focusing Teachers

These are articles that I feel would especially benefit those teaching Focusing one-to-one, as well as therapists, coaches, bodyworkers, and others who are using the Focusing process as part of a helping profession.

First I address "The Difference Between Focusing and Therapy" — it's good to get clear on that! Then, in an article written especially for this book, I talk about my way of working one-to-one, how that developed in the process of working with people. Next I compare Inner Relationship techniques with Finding Distance techniques.

In "Body? What Body?" I wrestle with the question of the different conception of the body in Focusing, and what that means for Focusing teaching. A four-fold view of process types emerges. "The Full Felt Sense" offers an earlier view of those four types. And "Focusing on Childhood" offers one view of how childhood functions in — and illuminates — our present pain.

People tell me that they appreciate the way I can make clear distinctions. I believe this article is an example of that.

I had so often heard people express confusion about the difference between non-therapists doing Focusing sessions, and therapists doing therapy with a Focusing orientation, that I felt this was a much needed clarification. I eventually found eight differences between these two situations. Taken all together, these eight differences point to a very clear distinction: guiding someone through a Focusing process, even if done for money and week after week, is not the same as therapy.

When this article appeared in *The Focusing Connection* newsletter, it generated a bit of controversy. Most of the reactions came from Focusing-oriented therapists who disagreed with one or the other of the distinctions that I made between doing Focusing as a non-therapist and bringing Focusing into therapy. They told me that they too did not bring up topics and/or they too did not diagnose or analyze. I could empathize with the fact that their way of working was not fully recognized by my distinctions. However, I stand by my article. I think when you take all eight points together, as a whole picture, you find a clear distinction between therapist and non-therapist as Focusing guide. The fact that a particular therapist may not match one or two of the points exactly doesn't negate the whole picture.

What is the Difference Between Focusing and Therapy?

Appeared in The Focusing Connection, *March 1997*

I am often asked the question, "What is the difference between Focusing and therapy?", and it always startles me a little, as if someone were asking the difference between breathing and making apple strudel. Because of course Focusing is something that we hope is happening in therapy, especially in the client but ideally in the therapist too.

So I ask, and it usually turns out that what the questioner is really wanting to know is: "What is the difference between guiding a person through Focusing as a non-therapist, and doing therapy as a therapist using Focusing?" This is a question which interests me greatly, and to which I have given a great deal of thought over the years, since it is clear to me that I am not a therapist even though I do one-to-one Focusing sessions with people, and charge for them.

If you exchange Focusing sessions with someone, and don't charge, then that is a Focusing partnership, and it's fairly easy to see that the *exchange* of roles makes this a relationship that is different from therapy. So if Focusing guiding sessions (paid, one-way) are different from therapy sessions, it must also be that something about the relationship is different. I would say, yes, very much so.

In general, what distinguishes Focusing Guide from Focusing Therapist is the *quality* and the *character* of the relationship. The Focusing Therapist is concerned with the "interpersonal space," as Gendlin calls it, and attends to the quality of that space as a key part of the therapeutic process.

(As an aside, I need to mention that there is some controversy over what to call a therapist who uses Focusing as a primary modality. "Focusing Therapist," "Focusing-Oriented Therapist," and "Experiential Therapist" are three possibilities. I apologize for using the shortest for convenience in this paper.)

In his paper "Focusing Therapy: Some Basic Statements," Johannes Wiltschko writes: "I now have to mention the importance of the *specific relationship between client and therapist.* This is, besides working on the felt sense, the main aspect of Focusing Therapy.... The relational space between client and therapist is the living space in which the client's developmental process can occur."

Of course there are many different ways of doing Focusing Therapy, so any one of my generalizations about Focusing Therapists may not apply to a particular Focusing Therapist. But I hope that these distinctions make a cluster which, as a whole, distinguishes Focusing Therapist from Focusing Guide.

A. The Focusing Guide Primarily Facilitates the Inner Relationship

The Focusing Guide has the job of helping the client to focus. This is primary. Focusing is an *inner relationship*, so in the office of the Focusing Guide, the inner relationship, the relationship of the client to the felt sense, is primary.

The Focusing Therapist has a larger job: being present for this whole person's (emotional, spiritual) growth at this time in their life.

For a Focusing Guide, process is not only more important than content – as I'm sure it is for many therapists – process is *supreme*. It would be rare for a therapist to say to a client, as Focusing Guides often do, "You don't need to tell me what just came. Just be sure you really receive it for yourself." The therapist would usually consider it therapeutic, and a valuable part of the relationship, for the client to share what came. The Focusing Guide considers the communication between client and guide to be relatively unimportant next to the communication between client and client.

B. Therapists Need to Pay Attention to Relationship Issues

Therapists need to be alert for transference and countertransference, and use the awareness of these issues therapeutically in the work with the client. As a Focusing Guide, if I encounter transference and countertransference, it's no more strongly than in any teacher-student relationship. If I did encounter them – if a client got very upset or very closed down at the prospect of my taking a planned vacation, for example – it would suggest to me that we needed to discuss a referral to a therapist.

The therapy relationship makes a place where relational issues can come up, as part of the process of healing. A few years ago I entered psychotherapy as a client for the first time, after twenty-two years of Focusing in partnership relationships. I noticed that I had reactions to my therapist that I *never* had to my Focusing partners. For the first few months, I didn't want her to have any other clients but me. I knew she did, but I didn't want to know about them. I felt terribly jealous if I saw any other clients in her waiting room. I didn't want to tell anyone her name for fear that they would go see her. The strength and irrationality of these feelings was embarrassing to me, and yet at the same time it was comforting to know that this relationship was a place where it was OK to feel like a child jealous of my brothers and sisters, and to explore those feelings of "there's never enough for me."

C. The Focusing Guide Does Not Bring Up Topics

A Focusing Guide does not choose the topic that the client will work on. A Focusing Guide does not look for gaps in what the Focuser is bringing up, and ask about them. The Focuser is totally in charge of the content of what she works on.

When I was a therapist and did couple therapy with a co-therapist, at some times with some couples we might bring up the question of their sex life. "How is it going?" we'd ask. "Can you talk about it to each other?" For a couple in couple therapy to not be talking about the sexual side of their relationship was a significant omission, and it was a legitimate part of a therapist's role to bring it up. But with my Focusing clients I would not do that. I help them pursue whatever they bring up.

I worked with one woman for a year in what was paradigmatically a Focusing guiding relationship. She chose the issues that she worked on. Primarily, she worked on the question of what she wanted to do with her life. After about a year, she told me she was in great pain because she was breaking up with her lover. At that time, and not before, I discovered the gender of the lover.

I believe, and I've checked this with several people, that a therapist would have been justified in feeling that something was missing, in working with someone for so long and never hearing about their love/sex/relationship life. A therapist might have been right to ask, "Is that part of your life really perfectly OK, or is there some other reason why you're not telling me about it?"

But as a Focusing Guide, I considered that to be outside my scope. It was understood that my client was completely in charge of the topic of the session. I was willing to go with her along whatever path she (and her felt senses) indicated.

D. A Therapy Client Would Usually Have Only One Therapist at a Time

Because of the special qualities of the therapy relationship already described, it would usually be considered confusing and unhelpful if a client were to have more than one therapist at a time.

On the other hand, a person could have many Focusing relationships. When I first learned Focusing, it was part of a peer community (Changes) in Chicago. I was so enthusiastic about the process that I did it at every opportunity. During my first year, I rarely had fewer than two sessions a week with different people – and sometimes as many as five. When I sat down to work with someone, I didn't need to explain what had come in the four other sessions that week. Nor did they feel the need to know. I just began at my own edge. I was the guardian of my own process.

As a Focusing Guide, I don't need to know what other growthful work the Focuser has done in the past week. I remember one man who did tell me that he had worked with another guide a few days before, and we were fascinated to discover that the sessions were totally different, in both theme and tone. In my opinion, the choice to do this is totally up to the Focuser. In this sense, I feel that Focusing guiding is more like bodywork than like therapy. I feel free to schedule sessions with different bodyworkers, and even several in a week, without needing to inform them about each other.

E. A Focusing Guide Can Work with a Friend

There is no difficulty in being a Focusing Guide to a person who is also a friend. On the other hand, it would be difficult and inappropriate to form or maintain a friendship with a client currently in therapy, or to become a therapist for a friend. I would feel, as either the client or the therapist, that the two relationships competed with each other. If I felt that this was a person who *could* become my friend, I wouldn't pursue the friendship, since I can have many friends, and I would want to set the friendship aside in preference for the therapy relationship for as long as the therapy continued.

F. A Therapist Makes a Long-Term Commitment

Although this too can vary in special cases, most therapists make a commitment to the client that goes something like this, "I will be here for your growth, for as long as you need me."

When I was a therapist, and I decided to move from Illinois to California, I informed my clients as soon as I began considering the move, about six months in advance. Their reactions to my potential move became one of the issues which they explored in therapy. I felt I owed them the chance to "get used to" the idea of my going, and to report and explore the feelings that this raised in them. The same was true of going on vacation. I informed my clients of my vacations well in advance, and welcomed their exploration of feelings and reactions they might have to my absence.

As a Focusing Guide, I plan my travels at times when I don't have classes scheduled, but other than that, I don't need to take my Focusing students into consideration. If someone calls for an appointment at a time when I am away, they can either wait until I get back, or call another Guide or Focusing partner. There is little likelihood they they will have feelings of upset or betrayal about my absence.

G. A Therapist Uses Everything that Works

Having made a commitment to this person for their whole growth, it would of course be nonsensical for the therapist not to use any method that they know about that might help the client. My therapist uses techniques from Focusing, Gestalt, EMDR, and a dash of Buddhist/Hindu spiritual guidance. Mostly she uses her own personal presence – she is *there*.

As a Focusing Guide, I assume that the person has chosen to come to me because they want to be guided through Focusing. If they want something else, they'll go somewhere else. Of course I too try to give the Focuser my full presence. That part is not different.

H. A Focusing Guide Does Not Diagnose or Analyze

Of course, neither do many therapists! But even therapists who hate to diagnose may have to, at least to fulfill requirements for third-party (insurance) payments. And some therapists do find themselves living up to their training in "Advanced Labeling" (as my friend and teacher Marshall Rosenberg calls his psychology degree) by naming some clients "borderline," "dissociative," "alexithymic," etc. Focusing Guides don't.

What Both Have in Common

It might be good to mention some of the factors that Focusing Therapy and Focusing Guiding have in common. I have already mentioned *presence* – being there as a whole person. There are also ethical considerations in common.

Confidentiality of all information learned from the client or student is an important ethical consideration. I believe that neither a Focusing Guide nor a Focusing Therapist should reveal information about a client or student to any other party without the client/student's permission. A Focusing Guide is unlikely to have to face the special exceptions to this, involving danger to another person or to the client's own life, that some therapists have to face.

Romantic or sexual activity with clients or students would be another area requiring great care. Romantic and/or sexual feelings have such great power and force, and can be so interwoven with personal needs and unhealed wounds, that they can "drown out" (like loud music) any other relationship which is present. Some ethicists forbid such relationships entirely. I would at least recommend great care and much Focusing before such feelings might be acted upon.

There is a distinction to be made between clients/students with whom one was in another kind of relationship before the Focusing relationship started, and clients/students who were met first through Focusing. One can be a Focusing Guide for one's spouse, for example, or a dear friend. However, a Focusing partnership or trade would probably be more appropriate to the reciprocity of the relationship.

What Does Not Distinguish Focusing Guide from Focusing Therapist

A. Length of Time

It has been suggested that if a Focusing Guide works with a client beyond a limited number of sessions, say four or five, then the work is no longer Focusing teaching and is, to call it by its right name, therapy.

I don't agree that the number of sessions defines whether a relationship is or is not therapy. A relationship can be definitely therapy-like in the very first session. I can remember having a first session with someone, and feeling the red flag go up – This person is experiencing transference with me!

I can understand that defining a relationship as limited in time might be a way that some people maintain the boundaries between Focusing Therapy and Focusing Guiding. But a certain number of sessions doesn't make a relationship into a therapy relationship, any more than keeping below a certain number makes it not one.

B. Focusing "Teaching" Doesn't Have to Happen

It has also been suggested that after a certain number of sessions you are no longer teaching Focusing, because the person has learned Focusing, so you must be doing therapy. I agree with the first half of this statement but not the second. My experience has been that there is a kind of relationship which is not teaching Focusing in an explicit way, and is also not therapy. In this relationship I am a companion to the person's process, using my expertise as listener and guide. No new teaching may be happening; in fact, this may be a person who already "knows" Focusing, having taken a number of workshops. Perhaps they called me up for a session because an issue felt especially difficult, or they had a feeling that a session with me would help. I'm happy to get a call from someone after months have passed, and then not know, at the end of a session, when or if they will ever call me again. Not a very therapy-like attitude!

One more positive aspect: as a Focusing guide, I am not burdened by society's expectations of the therapy relationship. People don't come to me expecting to be told whether they're good or sane. I'm not given the power to wave a magic wand and analyze someone's problems. I don't face the educational process that client- and person-centered therapists face, of explaining that that magic wand won't be forthcoming!

I feel that Focusing Therapist and Focusing Guide are two honorable professions which can support each other in harmony and mutual respect. I'm happy that Focusing Therapists exist, and I'm happy to refer to them anyone who is looking for therapy that includes Focusing. For myself, my own profession suits me perfectly!

Introduction to
The Origins and Development
of Inner Relationship Focusing

There are "strands" of Focusing teaching. Everything which is alive evolves, and certainly Focusing teaching is alive. I hope *my* students too will change what I teach them as they meet new circumstances and those circumstances interact with the unique people they are.

When I moved to California in 1983 for personal reasons, my strand of Focusing teaching began to separate from Gene Gendlin's strand. I didn't know at the time that this was happening; I just knew that I had to teach Focusing in the way that was called forth by the people coming to me to learn.

The development of that strand continued, in evolutionary steps, and I was joined in it by Barbara McGavin in 1991. Today it is clearly distinct enough to have a name: "Inner Relationship Focusing."

Since I'm telling so many stories in this book, I definitely want to tell this one: How and why Inner Relationship Focusing was born.

The Origins and Development of Inner Relationship Focusing

Newly written for this book

When I moved to California in 1983, after assisting Gene Gendlin with Focusing workshops in Chicago for three years, I wanted to become a Focusing practitioner. I wanted to be, not a therapist, but a person who teaches Focusing in one-to-one sessions and in workshops. At the time, this was barely a profession that anyone had conceived of, but I had an inner sense of wanting to do it. It takes a while to gather enough people for workshops, so teaching Focusing through one-to-one sessions was where I started, and where I concentrated for a number of years. (I still do more "first" Focusing sessions than anyone else I know, often two or three in a week.)

Of course I wanted to give people successful Focusing experiences, partly because I wanted that for them and partly because this is how I wanted to earn my living, and who would pay me if the sessions weren't helpful? This need – to be effective rather quickly – led to a number of new learnings for me. I can say with confidence that these generous people who came for sessions taught me much more than I taught them!

My way of approaching and teaching the Focusing process grew out of these "first" sessions. Taking someone from "no Focusing" to "Focusing" is an absorbing challenge, quite different from giving sessions to people who already know Focusing. There can't be just one method, since people start in different places. At the same time I learned that some suggestions I could make tended to work even for people who were different from each other (for example, people who get images easily vs. people who get body sensations easily), and I began to make a collection of these generally helpful suggestions.

Guiding someone through a first Focusing session has always been a fascinating dance, a balance between meeting this unique person, creating/inventing what this person needs at this moment, and drawing on what I'd learned in the past from others who'd been helped by certain ways of saying things. I think all Focusing teachers go through this process, enriching what they can do with each person they work with. But for me, landing in California with the dream of making my living helping people learn Focusing, the first thing I had to do was "un-learn" some of what I myself had been taught. How that happened, and what I learned instead, is what this article is about.

In the research that led to the development of Focusing (Gendlin, et al., 1968), some therapy clients were naturally doing something that connected them directly with their presently-felt experiencing, and others were not. Focusing as a process was developed as a way of teaching the people who weren't natural Focusers how to do this direct connecting. I have seen this myself over the years, as a Focusing teacher, that some people will find Focusing no matter what you say to them! They are the easy ones.

Since I myself was not one of the easy ones, my passion has always been to explore ways of teaching Focusing that work for "the rest of us." I'm convinced that Focusing is a natural birthright, that everyone has the potential to be able to do it (barring brain damage and similar barriers to natural function). The challenge is to find the way to Focusing for each person. This is in essence what my life's work has been about.

One of my goals has been to find a way of taking people through the Focusing process without explaining very much to them ahead of time. I didn't want to tell them before the session what the "steps of Focusing" were, or teach them what specialized words like "handle" or "felt sense" meant. To do that would be to engage their intellect, which I felt would be counterproductive at the beginning. It would also, in my experience, tend to raise up parts of them that doubted whether they could do this, and wondered if they were doing it right. I wanted to take them through the process without previous explanation, to let them have the experience first before they did any thinking about it. (Teaching offered in short segments during the process, as needed, didn't seem to share the drawbacks of explanations in advance.)

Perhaps the most important reason not to offer explanations in advance has been my realization that people come to Focusing from such different places, comfortable in different modalities, experienced in different previous methods, that the same explanation will not work for everyone. And we won't know until the process starts what they do need to know.

So come with me back to my session room in the years from 1983 on in California. People are sitting across from me to learn Focusing, yet they are doing all kinds of non-Focusing things, and the facilitative words I had learned to use did not help them to find Focusing. I had to come up with something more helpful. Gradually, with their feedback, I did – though this process hasn't ended, and I make no claim that I've found the most helpful suggestions for everyone.

What is interesting, though, and most relevant for this article, is that this process of learning from my students/clients what would help them find Focusing led me in a coherent direction, toward a conception of the Focusing process as an inner relationship. And that in turn led to a supportive structure that people can follow on their own, in their own Focusing and in facilitating the Focusing of others.

I'm going to discuss what I learned not in the order I learned it, but in the approximate order of a typical Focusing session, beginning, middle, "deeper middle," and end.

Leading In

I found that most people could be helped by getting into better contact with their bodies at the start of the session. (See "Body? What Body?" in this volume for some thoughts on the people who aren't helped by this.) I developed a way of starting that eventually came to be called "Leading In." I had once received a session from Joan Lavender in which she started by having me sense the periphery of my body, and I liked it so much I incorporated it in my own way of starting. (Although I didn't use the word "periphery," because on principle I try never to use words that a 12-year-old wouldn't know.)

This was quite a development, because what we had been doing before this was saying something like "Take some time to get settled and go inside." As a "Thinker" type, I wasn't helped by this at all. There was a lot of "inside" in my head! I needed, and was greatly helped by, someone actually mentioning parts of my body one by one. After the periphery of my body (which I needed because sometimes I was so far away from sensing my body that all I could feel were my hands), I really appreciated hearing someone say "throat... chest... stomach..." Then I could feel in there. (See p. 242 in this volume for the text of a typical Leading In script as I might do it today.)

Not Clearing a Space

For the next stage, what we had been doing before was saying something like: "Ask yourself in there what's in the way of feeling fine about your life." This was a preliminary to Clearing a Space, and was a way to find life issues to set out or move.

I had to drop this fairly soon. People were coming to me willing to pay for one session, to find out if Focusing would help them, and if three quarters of the session was taken up with setting things out, people tended to wonder when we were ever going to get to the good stuff – and usually didn't come back. A lot of people, myself included, simply didn't need to do Clearing a Space. (Later I discovered other problems with it. See "Relationship = Distance + Connection" in this volume.)

I needed another way of starting, so I studied what experienced Focusers did at this stage if they didn't Clear a Space. They seemed to sort of wait expectantly in the inner body space, open to sensing what wanted awareness. I put that into words: "So you might give yourself an inner invitation in there, like you're saying, 'What wants my awareness now?' And wait."

Something Comes

Gene Gendlin called his next step "Finding a Felt Sense." My expectant waiting was my version of that. There was a variation if people wanted to use the session to work on a particular issue known in advance. I would say at this point: "So you might invite that whole thing (about _____) to sit down with you here, and invite your body to give you its whole sense about that."

Describing

Traditionally, the next step is to Find a Handle. That was good. But I realized, for almost everyone, this "Handle" finding process was greatly helped if it started with a physical description. The benefit of finding a handle was greatest when it enabled the Focuser's awareness to stay and deepen at the bodily level. Let me give some examples to show what I mean:

"I'm sensing something... I'm finding a handle... the handle is 'rejection'... I don't know why he rejected me like that!"

"I'm sensing something... I'm finding a handle... the handle is 'tightness'... I'm staying with that sense of tightness... The tightness is like a pulling in... This is about the way he treated me... Something in me feels like protecting, not to be rejected again...."

The first example is what I would call leaving the Focusing type of contact, going into thoughts and interpretations. The second example shows a person staying in a Focusing type of contact. As I watched people doing the first kind of thing over and over again, I felt the need to offer a supportive type of guidance that would help them find and stay in Focusing contact. As I've said, this almost always involved finding first a body sensation description. (See "Body? What Body?" in this volume for the cases in which it didn't.) The words "find a handle" didn't enable this process to happen reliably. I stopped using the word "handle" because, as a new specialized term, it required too much thinking and remembering on the part of the Focuser.

Instead I said, "Maybe you could take some time to describe what you're sensing there... what it feels like, even just at the physical level..."

Checking the Description

Gendlin spoke of Resonating the Handle, and I believe that this powerful and important move is central to the Focusing process: to let the symbolizing of what is felt continue to interact with the directly felt experience. I just needed to change the language so that people could do it easily, without too much explanation.

"So take that word 'tightness' back to your body and check if that's right, if 'tightness' is the best word for what that feels like, or if another word fits even better."

Staying in Contact

As I compared what experienced Focusers did with what I saw these new people doing, one thing that stood out for me was what I've been calling "staying with the process" vs. "leaving the process." Experienced Focusers knew how to stay with what they were experiencing, with a quality of gentle interested curiosity. New people "popped out" into all kinds of other activities: speculation, analysis, rumination, argument, distraction...

I realized that one of the functions of finding a description for what was felt, and then checking the description, was to stay with the inner experience. If a person was finding a description and checking it, they weren't doing all those other things I've just listed.

Once they had a description, though, what then? "Just being with what was there" wasn't a step for Gendlin. He probably assumed it would go without saying. My new people needed it said. Since they weren't used to the notion that simply staying with something in awareness was a powerfully helpful thing to do, they "popped out" into other activities unless they had the support of a gentle invitation to stay.

I realized that I had to suggest, invite, or "guide" them to do what experienced Focusers did naturally, to stay with the process. Once they had "popped out," it was harder to take them back in, so I tried to anticipate (gently) the moments when they might pop out... and to give a guiding suggestion right then, before it happened.

I said to them, "See if it would be OK to just be with that." Or, "... just stay with that." Or, "...just keep that company." And I added: "...with interested curiosity."

The Inner Relationship

What I have said up till now has been the background, the foundation, for what happens next, the heart of Inner Relationship Focusing. This point in the session, when they had come into body contact, invited something, described it, checked the description, and were staying with it, with interested curiosity... this was the point where some people had breakthroughs, and others became completely stuck.

Gendlin's step that I had learned to offer at this point, Asking, wasn't as helpful as I would have liked. As always, people who found Focusing easily also found Asking helpful. But those who didn't, those whose inner contact was tenuous and who easily popped out of the process, let asking inner questions take them on all kinds of wild rides.

"I'm asking it what it needs... It needs me to be strong and tell him what I think of him... It needs me to call up his wife and warn her that her husband is a jerk... It needs me to just forget about all these emotions and try to relax..."

It was clear to me, listening to these diatribes, that "What does it need?" didn't help. Without more assistance, people took questions like that right into their heads and said what they were thinking. Even the careful cushions I had been taught ("If your head answers, let the answer go, and ask again in your body") weren't as helpful as I wanted them to be – they told people what to do, but didn't really help them do it. How was an inexperienced person to know whether it was their "head" answering or not? And if asking didn't work the first time, why would asking again work better?

So again I watched experienced Focusers and asked myself to put into fresh words the essence of what they were doing at this stage. And what I frequently saw was people entering into a kind of empathy with the "it" that they were in contact with. They sounded like this:

"I'm sensing it here... It's a tightness... It's a pulling back... It's like it doesn't want any more hurt... I'm checking... that's right.... it's like it's letting me know that it's been hurt enough... there's more... ah, yes, it's been hurt enough and it also feels like it's been betrayed... 'betrayed' is the word that fits... yes... [big sigh] ... that's right."

It was as if they had become empathic listeners to an inner "it" that had begun to have feelings and needs of its own. How to facilitate this for people who didn't find it themselves?

I found the answer one day when I was sitting across from a man who had gotten to that stuck spot. He felt something in his body, he had described it and was sitting with it, and now what? Nothing more was happening. As I remembered experienced Focusers, and I reached for words to help him do what they did, I found myself saying, "Maybe you could sense how IT feels from ITS point of view." That was it, that worked... for him, and for many others in the weeks that followed. I learned that although some people easily and naturally found the place of listening empathically to the inner "it," others needed to be guided there. And this invitation to "sense how IT feels from ITS point of view" was extremely helpful. It facilitated inner empathy in a way that "How does it feel?" did not. Asked "How does it feel?" people told me how *they* felt. "It's uncomfortable," said a woman on one memorable occasion when I asked her how a tightness in her throat was feeling. "Oops," I said to myself inside, and re-phrased my invitation to her: "Maybe you could sense how IT feels from ITS point of view." She closed her eyes for a moment, opened them in astonishment, and reported, "Oh, IT feels scared!"

I realized that what I had been developing was a rather close type of guiding that didn't allow people to stray too far from the Focusing path. Experienced Focusers didn't need this kind of guiding, nor did some new people – reflective Listening took them right inside, and they did all the rest. But for the people who did need it, it seemed enormously helpful, as far as I could tell. And when people wanted to learn how to do what I was doing – "guiding" – I began to find ways to teach that as well.

Although I based my guiding on the process of experienced Focusers, this close inner empathy wasn't the only type of process that experienced Focusers had. Others took leaps, for example from a wholistic awareness to a realization that the whole problem was really different from what they had thought. But this type of process was harder to facilitate for a new person. There were too many other things they might do.

An analogy: Imagine there is a little valley, and where you want to go is on the other side of the valley. People who know how to get there use two different ways. Some walk step by step down one side of the hill and up the other side. Others take a leap and find themselves on the other side. Your job is to take a new person to the other side of the valley. You could just take them to the top of the near bank and say, "Leap!" But there is fog; the other bank isn't visible. If they leap, they're far likelier to end up in the wrong place, and have to be brought back to try again. Maybe they'll be discouraged or ashamed at their wrong attempt, and after enough wrong leaps may even give up. Or you can choose to show them the step-by-step method. It isn't the only way to go, true, but it works more reliably – and once they know the other bank, leaping will be available to them too.

I was developing a way to take people into Focusing "on the ground," so to speak. I could guide them in baby steps, and let each increment of deeper contact prepare them for the next one. If something I suggested didn't work, it was such a tiny addition from the previous step that it was fairly easy to see what hadn't worked, and backing up to try another angle was hardly a hiccup.

I realized that what distinguished what I was doing from the facilitation ("guiding") that I was taught was a kind of "inner relationship" that was the touchstone all through the session. The Focuser's "I" was being with an "it," and it was the "it" which spoke, opened up, had feelings, and revealed its depths, held in the gentle containing presence of a "I" which was curious, interested, accepting, spacious, and non-judging.

"Inner relationship" was a perfect metaphor for this whole process, because we could talk about the qualities of that relationship – gentle, accepting, interested, etc. – and we could show how that relationship was enhanced and deepened at every stage, by describing, by "being with," by sensing how it feels from its point of view, etc.

The Focuser, in the role of the "I," was the ideal listener, just saying back to the "it" what it was saying. I could support this role with guiding suggestions like, "Let it know you hear it," which also prevented the Focuser from sliding into other activities like arguing, interpreting, apologizing...

The Living "It"

What I saw as I observed closely was that, in many Focusing sessions that were satisfying for the Focuser and clearly in close contact with a deep process, the "it" that the Focuser was in contact with seemed to be alive, or to come alive in the course of the session. The Focuser said things like, "It wants..." or "It needs..." or "It says..." or "It doesn't want...." In fact there was often a *developmental process* for the "it" (the felt sense) in the course of the session, in which at first it was rather simple and rather simply described, from an external point of view, and then, as it was empathically connected with and sensed as inwardly complex, it seemed to come alive. I called this phenomenon "The Living 'It,'" and of course I was interested in how to facilitate this coming alive which so often seemed to correlate with the Focuser being able to deeply hear what the felt sense needed to express.

In *A Process Model*, Gendlin writes of an "interaffecting process" in which "[The Focuser] *interacts* with some 'feel' even before *it* is quite *there*. She seeks it, looks for it, waits for it, lets it come, pursues and points to what has come... Interaction is usually (and as discussed so far) in relation to a person or a thing.... Now something like such interactions [is] occurring in a new space made by these activities..." (p. 219, italics in original). In terms of his Process Model, we cannot say that the felt sense is already alive, nor that the Focuser makes it alive. Rather, it is in the interaction that it becomes the kind of thing that can be alive. It is treated as alive, and thus it is alive... but not in a simply causative way.

Emotional Quality – "Its Mood" – and Situations

I discovered that for a Focuser who wasn't already sensing this "Living It," the most reliable way to bring it was to invite the Focuser to sense the emotion of the "it" as experienced at that moment. Emotion (the "I" empathically sensing "its" emotion) seemed to be the key that unlocked the door of deepening process.

An example: "I have a pressure in my chest... it gets stronger as I think about the project... something in me feels that project as a pressure... I'm acknowledging it... I'm sitting with it... I'm sensing how that pressure feels from its point of view... it's resentful... oh, I see... it's resentful that it doesn't get to follow its own timing... I'm letting it know I hear that... Ah, it's relaxing quite a lot..."

Another example: "There's a tightness in my chest... I'm acknowledging it... I'm sensing if 'tightness' is the right word... it's like there's a belt tied around my chest... I'm sitting with it... I'm sensing for its emotion... the belt is scared... I'm letting it know I can sense how scared it is... it's scared that something is going to get loose, go wild... I'm acknowledging that... yes, it's loosening a bit as it feels understood..."

(Notice, by the way, how easily this process can go wrong without the awareness that this "belt" is potentially alive. "I want to untie the belt" is common, but unfortunately totally unhelpful, since it is identification with another part rather than Presence with this one.)

In *A Process Model*, Gendlin defines a "situation" as something that can only be experienced by a human. Animals have "behavior contexts," but only humans, who live in a symboling world, have the external facts along with the internal meaning. (This is not meant to be interpreted as humans being "better" than animals, but simply to explain differences in how we process our lives.)

"People live and act in situations.... Situations are not the physically external facts, but the context of interactions with others, which also determines how these facts are defined. (A locked door is one thing if I am hiding from someone; if trying to get out, quite something else.)" p. 168.

When I read this recently, I realized something about why it can be so facilitative for a Focuser to sense *its* point of view, *its* mood. Point of view in this situational sense is something that a human can have, and inviting a sense of point of view is enlivening into the complexity of a human perspective. In the outer world, belts don't have moods. In the inner world, they do, or can... and do when treated as if they can.

Later Developments of Inner Relationship Focusing

Begun as a reliable way to show (most) people how to find Focusing, Inner Relationship work has developed further. I began to teach my "on-the-ground" guiding method to advanced students, and the handouts for these workshops became my *Guiding Manual* in 1990.

The concept of "disidentification" developed out of an understanding that people needed to *be with* what they were feeling, and couldn't do that if they were *identified* with the feeling. I coined the term "ittification" to refer to the process of forming a felt experience into an "it" that could be given company.

In 1992, I began to give workshops in "The Inner Relationship" to groups of Focusing people in Germany, the UK, Japan, and elsewhere. Recognizing what I was doing as something she too had already begun to work with, Barbara McGavin joined me in the development of IR Focusing, and we began to teach together.

Because the "I-it" relationship was so crucial to our work, IR Focusing led us to working with "parts" in a more specific and explicit way than Gendlin did in his six-step way of teaching Focusing – although as these two quotes from my favorite Gendlin paper show, he is no stranger to this perspective.

"Focusing is this very deliberate thing where an 'I' is attending to an 'it.'" ("The Small Steps...," p. 222.)

"The client and I, we are going to keep it, in there, company. As you would keep a scared child company. You would not push on it, or argue with it, or pick it up... If you will go there with your awareness and stay there or return there, that is all it needs; it will do all the rest for you" (p. 216).

The work with parts blossomed in 1994 as both Barbara and I realized that working with the difficult areas of our own lives required a conception of some parts being out of awareness – "exiled." The part that wanted to drink in an addiction to alcohol, the part that wanted to feel bad in depression, the part that didn't want to write in writer's block... these were clearly in dynamic tension with other parts, a tension so fierce it could even be called a war. In the midst of the impasse of these painful issues, we were identified with one part and dissociated from the other, yet both operated powerfully in us. Often the exiles, despite being out of awareness, seemed to have the most power!

Faced with this inner war, the importance of finding an "I" that was neither one side nor the other increased, and in 1998 we began calling this "Presence." Although Presence was first presented in a Treasure Maps to the Soul workshop, Barbara and I now teach it in our Level One Focusing workshops. Clearly, Treasure Maps to the Soul and Inner Relationship Focusing have been developing together, and are not sharply distinct.

Another development has been the method of inviting empathy for *its* "not wanting" and "wanting," which carries further the enlivening empathy of sensing its emotion. Again, this was developed first as part of Treasure Maps, and is now something we use in all our teaching. (See "Radical Gentleness" in this volume for an application of this method.)

A Subset of Focusing

There are many ways to do Focusing. Inner Relationship is only one way. And it isn't the best way for everyone. To go back to our analogy of crossing the little valley – some people need to leap, it doesn't work for them to go step by step. In developing a method that I could reliably use for most people, to give them successful Focusing experiences and avoid the negative consequences of going down unsuccessful avenues, I had to accept that I was doing something some people would not be helped by.

Not every successful Focusing session has a "Living It," nor does starting with being led into body awareness help everyone find Focusing. (See "Body? What Body?") For experienced Focusers there are many ways to do Focusing, but if we let new people play in that big a field, there are too many "wrong" things they may do — and pulling them back from those things sets up a negative set, where they feel like they are being told "no" too often. From a teaching perspective, it's more desirable if we can offer success, and keep saying "yes." That's what Inner Relationship Focusing is meant to do. But if anyone has trouble doing it, there is good news: Focusing is even bigger, and there are other possibilities.

I have already written of my uneasy history with the so-called "first step of Focusing," Clearing a Space. This article describes my evolution in relation to Finding Distance. Is Clearing a Space the same as Finding Distance? Not exactly.

Clearing a Space is a process of finding a relationship with a number of different issues or items without (or before) going into any of them. Traditionally (as taught in Gendlin's book *Focusing*), Clearing a Space is done by "setting out" the issues, for example on an imaginal shelf in front of one, or "setting down what one is carrying," as if on the ground. But Clearing a Space doesn't have to involve moving anything. It could be done by acknowledging, saying hello, to each thing one finds – like standing in a crowd of children and touching each one of them gently on the head, but not asking any of them to move. What I am about to say does not apply to this kind of Clearing a Space, which is one I still use and still teach. You could call it Clearing a Space by Acknowledging.

I went through the following stages with Clearing a Space (by Finding Distance):

(1) 1972-1979: No involvement at all. When I first learning Focusing, in 1972, there was no Clearing a Space, at least not as a regular part of the Focusing process, and I don't remember doing it or trying to do it.

(2) 1980-1982: Passionate advocate. When Gendlin's book *Focusing* was published and I was one of the people he asked to assist him in workshops, we spent a lot of time teaching people to do Clearing a Space. That period could be called the heyday of Clearing a Space. I remember people who passionately claimed that Clearing a Space was the essence of Focusing. Research done at that time to show the effect of Focusing often involved people being taught Clearing a Space alone, without the rest of the process.

(3) 1983-84: While still a passionate advocate, I started to notice how many difficulties people had with the Clearing a Space step. For the first workshop on guiding, I created a handout describing typical difficulties with Focusing and how to help with them. Well over 50% of them were difficulties with Clearing a Space.

(4) 1985-89: "Clearing a Space is still the first step of Focusing but it's

optional, and it's helpful for Too Close Process, not helpful for Too Distant Process." During these years I was in California teaching on my own, not yet ready to change the "six-step" model very much. I believed that people like me, who had difficulty feeling anything (a type of process that my teachers Elfie Hinterkopf and Les Brunswick called "Too Distant"), were not helped by Clearing a Space, but that the opposite type of process ("Too Close"), in which the person felt a lot and was easily overwhelmed, was helped by Clearing a Space. So I taught that it should be done "as needed."

(5) 1990-93: I came back from the weeklong Focusing retreat in Chicago in November 1989 ready to change my teaching. Inspired by a presentation by Reva Bernstein and Lakme Elior, I developed a model of "Steps and Skills." Clearing a Space was no longer a Step. Instead, Finding the Right Distance was a Skill; that is, an aspect of the process that might be needed at any time and/or all the time. Here's what I wrote about Finding the Right Distance in 1991:

> The skill of finding the right distance reflects the insight that people in Too Close process need the felt experience to be a little farther away, and people in Too Distant process need it to come a little closer. Once Focusing students understand the concept of finding the right distance, they have a skill that is helpful whether they are in Too Close or Too Distant process. If Focusing feels blocked, they can ask, "Am I at the right distance from this?" If the answer is "No," they can call on techniques for setting something out, or for bringing it closer.

This was the stage I was in when I wrote *The Focusing Student's Manual* and *The Focusing Guide's Manual*, during the period 1990-93. There, especially in the Guide's Manual, I enthusiastically described various methods for finding distance, noting that this move is especially helpful for people who are feeling overwhelmed by their emotional states.

After several years of this kind of teaching, I could sense an uneasiness growing in me. It became more and more evident to me that Clearing a Space was not the only alternative for people "feeling too much" ("Close Process"). Another kind of move, of a type I was calling Inner Relationship, was quite helpful to people in a state of overwhelm. Since both Distance techniques and Inner Relationship techniques helped with the same type of process, I wondered what the differences were. Why use one method rather than the other?

I realized that Relationship techniques could do everything that Distance techniques could, while avoiding some glaring problems. I began to drop Clearing a Space from my teaching. Inner Relationship techniques were easier to teach and use because, for one thing, they were helpful to both types of people and were used in the same order, with only one exception. Close Process people tended to benefit from the "Acknowledging" step, whereas

Distant Process people might find their felt senses too vague to be helped by Acknowledging, and needing simply to be described and stayed with.

Around this time, in 1995, Johannes Wiltschko and Klaus Renn invited me to give a presentation at the First International Conference for Focusing Therapy. I decided to use the opportunity to clarify my thoughts on the comparison between Finding Distance techniques and Inner Relationship techniques.

The title of the paper comes from my realization that Inner Relationship techniques accomplish the same purposes as do Finding Distance techniques, *and* they add the element of inner connection.

Perhaps the most controversial aspect of this paper is my suggestion that therapists and Focusing guides who use Finding Distance techniques with their clients are subtly reinforcing the client's "victim" position in relation to their emotional experience. I can imagine if I were a guide who used Finding Distance techniques with clients, and saw positive impacts for my clients, I might resent hearing an assertion like that.

I certainly did not intend to suggest that anyone using Finding Distance techniques has anything less than their clients' best interests at heart. I also understand now, perhaps more than when I wrote this paper, that giving help and support is not the same as reinforcing a "victim" position. I know that there are times in anyone's journey of emotional healing when it is necessary and right to lean on another person. Self-reliance is not the highest goal, even as an ideal.

Although I am aware that the situation is complex, I stand by the essence of what I wrote: That Inner Relationship techniques offer the same benefits as do Finding Distance techniques, and without the problems. For more about my alternative way of working with clients having overwhelming feelings, see "Facilitating Presence" in this volume.

Note: Because this article was written for a conference on therapy, the terms "therapist" and "client" are used where I might otherwise have written "guide" and "Focuser."

Relationship = Distance + Connection:
A Comparison of Inner Relationship Techniques to Finding Distance Techniques in Focusing

Presented as a workshop at the First Conference on Focusing Therapy, Lindau-Bodensee, Germany, August 1995

Summary

Clearing a Space and other Finding Distance techniques are often used to help a client find a comfortable relationship with overwhelming feelings. However, I have found that Finding Distance techniques are actually not the best way to accomplish this purpose. In this article I will explore Inner Relationship techniques, which include all the advantages of Finding Distance techniques and none of the disadvantages. The reason for this is that "relationship" includes "distance" and adds "connection."

Aspects of this presentation include: the four main disadvantages of Finding Distance techniques; the Inner Relationship techniques; implications for clients in Close Process (overwhelmed) and Distant Process (out of touch); implications for working with survivors of abuse, trauma, etc.; and implications for the relationship between the therapist and the client.

1. The four main disadvantages of Finding Distance techniques

Finding Distance is a Focusing move in which the client finds experiential "distance" from an issue or emotion by moving it away from him, or by stepping back from it. Clearing a Space is a special kind of Finding Distance technique in which the client finds distance from a number of issues/emotions before (or without) going into any of them. (But see below, where I describe a type of Clearing a Space which does not involve finding distance.)

Many therapists and guides use Finding Distance techniques with clients who are feeling overwhelmed (in "Too Close" process). Here is an example of a situation which would traditionally call for a Finding Distance technique:

Client: "There's a well of grief in my stomach. It's very intense."

Therapist: "There's an intense well of grief in your stomach."

Client: "It's scary. I don't like being near it."

Therapist: [Finding Distance technique] "Maybe you could see if you could move it away from you."

In using the Finding Distance technique, the therapist is responding to what may be seen as a request for help from the client. It is as if the client is saying, "This is too much for me. Please help me." The therapist then intervenes by helping the client move the "threatening" feeling to a farther distance. Later

I will comment further on the interactional implications of this situation.

Here I will list four disadvantages of Finding Distance techniques as a Focusing intervention when the client is feeling overwhelmed. In the next section, I will propose an alternative method, the use of Inner Relationship techniques, which does not share these disadvantages.

The first disadvantage is that, when this type of technique is used, the client tends to move into an increased victim relationship with the sense, with implicit agreement from the therapist. What I mean by a "victim relationship" is exemplified in the dialogue above when the client says, "It's scary. I don't like being near it." The client becomes a victim of her experience when she feels that she is at its mercy, that it is out of control and doing something to her. Other examples: "It's cutting off my breathing." "It's pushing in on me." "The sadness is drowning me." By bringing in a Finding Distance technique, it is as if the therapist is saying, implicitly, "I agree that this sense is too much for you." There may even be an implication that the therapist is a little scared of it, too.

The second disadvantage is that the client may be unable to follow the suggestion to move the sense, or may be able to follow it only with difficulty. In the early 1980s in Chicago, when we were working with Clearing a Space quite a lot, using it at the start of every session, we developed elaborate techniques for helping with all the difficulties that people had in moving the sense. The complexity of these techniques is evidence for the frequency with which Focusers could not easily move the sense. They often felt frustrated, and the Clearing a Space portion of the session became quite long. Barbara McGavin reports, "The belief that I had to do Clearing a Space every time meant that I stopped Focusing for two years, because it was too frustrating. Clearing a Space often took forty-five minutes, and left no time for Focusing."

The third disadvantage is that the felt sense itself may experience abandonment by being asked to move away, perhaps recapitulating earlier abandonment in the client's life. Focusing is an inner relationship, and the qualities of that inner relationship contribute essentially to the healing process. Even if the client does the "setting out" gently, the felt sense itself may feel it is being pushed away!

The fourth disadvantage is that the client may lose touch with the felt sense during the process of Finding Distance.

2. The Inner Relationship techniques

The reason that Inner Relationship techniques do not share the disadvantages of the Finding Distance techniques is that (as in the title of this presentation) relationship contains distance, with connection. If I am in a relationship with you, I am not you. That is the distance: experiencing "you" and

"I" as separate beings. Yet we are connected.

So if the Focuser experiences his *relationship with* the felt sense, that is, his separateness from it and his connection with it at the same time, this accomplishes what the Finding Distance techniques were intended to accomplish, yet without the disadvantages.

Let's see how the example given above would go differently with Inner Relationship techniques:

Client: "There's a well of grief in my stomach. It's very intense."

Therapist: "You're aware of an intense well of grief in your stomach."

Client: "It's scary."

Therapist: "See if it would be OK to acknowledge the part of you that's scared, and just be with that scared feeling."

Now the client can move into relationship with the scared feeling ("scard of the well of grief"), which automatically brings a kind of distance from the original sense, but without directly moving it away.

I have found myself coming more and more to trust that the felt sense comes in the way, in the place, and at the intensity that it most needs to be. If I can help the client come into relationship with the felt sense in the way that it is, without needing to change it, this is a very powerful act of acceptance.

Acknowledging. Acknowledging is the quintessential Inner Relationship technique. Often the easiest way to acknowledge is to say "Hello." The therapist would say, "Maybe you could say 'Hello' to the part of you that is so scared." Another way to say this is "I know you're there," as in, "You might say to that heavy feeling, 'Yes, I know you're there.'"

Over and over again I have seen this: the Focuser reports a scary or overwhelming feeling of increasing intensity; I invite her to say "Hello" to it; and then she reports with a look of surprise, "It lessened! It's almost as if it liked being acknowledged!" I would say that it *did* like being acknowledged. In fact, looking at Focusing as a process of inner relationship, we can say that it was as intense as it was as a way of getting attention; when it was acknowledged, it could relax, at least somewhat. It no longer needed to jump up and down and shout, because it knew it would be heard.

Whenever possible I like to try to see things from the felt sense's point of view. Why would *it* feel the need to be so overwhelming? I ask myself. It makes sense that in most cases it is overwhelming because it has been trying for a long time to get the Focuser's attention, and it feels it must resort to strong tactics in order to be heard. (See section 4 below for another reason "it" might need to be overwhelming.)

Clearing a Space by Acknowledging. Earlier I quoted Barbara

McGavin's frustration with Clearing a Space, that it often took forty-five minutes out of every Focusing session. Now that Barbara uses Inner Relationship techniques, she still does a version of Clearing a Space whenever she starts Focusing and finds that there is more than one thing wanting her attention. This could be called "Clearing a Space by Acknowledging," and does not involve Finding Distance. Instead, she says "Hello" to each thing that is there, and begins to form a relationship with it. This typically takes about five minutes altogether, even when there are many issues present.

Resonating. Resonating is checking whether a word, or other symbol, or a larger unit of meaning, fits how the felt sense feels. Resonating can itself be an Inner Relationship technique, because in order to do it, the Focuser must be in direct contact with the felt sense, with a neutral-observer (i.e., non-victim) perspective.

Client: "It feels tight."

Therapist: "And maybe take that word 'tight' and see if that feels like just the right word to describe that feeling."

Later in the session, it can be helpful to phrase the resonating suggestion from the point of view of whether "it" feels more understood now.

Client: "There's depression there and a little anger."

Therapist: "Maybe check that with the place and see if *it* feels more understood now, depression and anger."

Disidentification. Disidentification is the process by which the client disidentifies from felt experience ("A part of me feels sad") rather than being identified with felt experience ("I am sad"). Disidentification is often the first step toward establishing the Inner Relationship.

The essence of disidentification is to help the client move from "I *am* [this feeling]" to "I *have* [this feeling]." In most cases, disidentification can be facilitated simply with empathic listening or reflection, in which the therapist adds phrases like "a part of you" or "a place in you" or "something in you."

Disidentification often comes just before acknowledging, or is combined with it. It is difficult, even impossible, to acknowledge without disidentification.

Client: "I hate that fear."

Therapist: "So there's a part of you that hates that fear."

Client: "Yes."

Therapist: "You might see if you'd like to say 'Hello' to the part that hates the fear."

Or:

Client: "I hate that fear."

Therapist: "You might see if you'd like to say 'Hello' to the part of you that hates that fear."

"There must be some good reason…" When the client experiences the felt sense as oppressive or adversarial, I have found it very helpful to propose that *it* may have a good reason for being that way, at least from *its* point of view. Sometimes I add that this "good" reason may be an old reason; sometimes I say, "It may think it has a positive purpose for you." This is based on my philosophy, borne out my experience, that there are no enemies within the self. Margaret Warner, in her work with Dissociated Process (1998 and 2000), has pointed out that even aspects of the self that seem to be cruel and self-destructive, as in cases of self-mutilation, have been found to believe that they are serving a protective function.

Client: "It's cutting off my breathing."

Therapist: "And let's assume, just for a little while, that it may think it has a positive purpose for doing that."

Client: "It doesn't want me to feel so much," etc.

Sensing from its point of view. In addition to its "good reason" for being the way it is, other aspects of the felt sense may be sensed from *its* point of view. It is a powerful and empowering move when the client is able to shift from *her* point of view (which may be "overwhelmed" or "feeling a victim") to the felt sense's point of view. This brings in the possibility of empathy and compassion. The aspect of self which has the capacity for empathy and compassion is not a victim.

Client: "I'm afraid."

Therapist: "You might see if you'd like to ask the fear place what *it's* so scared of, from its point of view."

Having the Focuser become the felt sense's listener. When the felt sense begins to reveal its message, the Focuser can be guided to say to it, "I hear you," thus not becoming embroiled in any kind of argument with the felt sense, and encouraging it instead to say more.

Client: "It seems to be saying that it wants me to stay with it some more."

Therapist: "So let it know you hear that, that it wants you to stay with it some more."

See how the therapist follows the instruction to "let it know you hear that" with a quoted listening response, so that the client will find it as easy as possible to do the instruction. However, it doesn't have to be done that way:

Client: "That place is letting me know how hard it has been working."

Therapist: "So really let it know you hear that."

Including the Focuser in the listening response. In this technique, the listener includes in the reflection what the client is doing or experiencing right now, in saying those words. First say "you" to refer to the client, and then add a verb to describe his current experience. Typically this is something like "sensing," "realizing," "noticing," "are aware of," "feeling," etc.

Client: "There's a sadness in my heart area."

Therapist: "You're aware of a sadness in your heart area."

Client: "It's dark and heavy."

Therapist: "You're noticing that it's dark and heavy."

This kind of listening response is very powerful for helping the Client stay separate from and in relationship with her experience, instead of identifying with the experience.

Client: "There's a darkness that wants to pull me down."

Therapist: "You're sensing a darkness that wants to pull you down."

Now this client is aware, not only of the darkness, but of his own awareness of the darkness. This gives him a place to stand, to be with the darkness.

Including the focuser/client is an extremely powerful and helpful technique for several reasons. It helps the client feel more fully heard – because *all* her experience is being heard, not just her words but also her relationship to her words.

3. Implications for clients in Close Process (overwhelmed) and Distant Process (out of touch)

Based on teaching by Elfie Hinterkopf and Les Brunswick (Hinterkopf, 1983), we can describe a continuum of client process from Close Process (overwhelmed) to Distant Process (out of touch), with Middle Process, the ideal Focusing distance, in between. ("Close Process" describes the *client's* experience of being overwhelmed. It is not the same as cathartic process, as Kathy McGuire points out in her article "Cathartic Unfoldings are Not Too Close.")

Finding Distance techniques have quite different impacts on clients in Close Process and clients in Distant Process. For many years I recommended Finding Distance techniques for clients in Close Process. The model itself implies that if something is "too close," what is needed is distance. Finding Distance techniques are contraindicated for clients in Distant Process. We (I myself have characteristically Distant Process) find it frustratingly easy to lose the felt sense if it is set out, and why did we want to set it out at all?

But the Inner Relationship techniques are valuable for both types (and in fact all types) of process. When a client in Distant Process says "Hello" to a vague, elusive felt sense, it tends to become more distinct, more definitely there. When a client in Close Process says "Hello" to an overwhelming, intense felt sense, it tends to relax slightly, while remaining in awareness. What we can say about both cases is that when the felt sense is met, as it is, within a context of inner relationship, it responds by accommodating to the requirements of the communicational situation, by becoming either more definite or more relaxed, whichever is needed.

4. Implications for working with survivors of abuse and trauma

I have observed some cases in which having the client say "Hello" to an overwhelming felt sense (or using any of the other Inner Relationship techniques already described) has not resulted in an easing of the sense to the point where the client is able to be comfortable with it. Invariably these are people with a history of abuse or trauma from childhood. These clients are working with painful issues that change slowly, in which any moment of relief or fresh air should be celebrated.

These are not situations in which Finding Distance techniques work any better, usually, although from person to person there may be someone who gets a little inner breathing room from them, and it is good to have plenty of possibilities to try.

However, I would first try a slightly different version of the Inner Relationship techniques, which I will now describe. We are still trying to see things from the felt sense's point of view, and if "it" doesn't settle down to have a conversation after a "Hello," then it must have been overwhelming for some other reason than just to get the Focuser's attention. In survivors of abuse, my guess is usually that the felt sense has come in order to tell them about a situation of being overwhelmed in the past. It needs to be overwhelming because that is part of its message. Quite often, then, it will relax when *this* part of the message has also been heard.

Client: "This very intense feeling is coming toward me like an ocean wave. It just feels like it's too much."

Therapist: "Maybe you could say to it that you really see how *much* it is. Say to it, 'Yes, you're so big.'"

Client: "That's a little better, but it's still hard to stand."

Therapist: "Maybe what it has come to tell you about is a time when something was hard to stand, for you. You might just check with it, and see if that would fit, that it's about something that once felt 'too much,' like this."

5. Implications for the relationship between the therapist and the client

In section 1, I quoted an interaction between therapist and client in which the therapist brought in a Finding Distance technique:

Client: "It's scary. I don't like being near it."

Therapist: [Finding Distance technique] "Maybe you could see if you could move it away from you."

I said that in using a Finding Distance technique, it is as if the therapist is responding to a request for help from the client. At some level the client is saying, "This is too much for me. Please help me." When the therapist then intervenes by helping the client move the "threatening" feeling to a farther distance, it is almost as if the therapist is saying, implicitly, "I agree that this sense is too much for you."

Of course there is a rightness to this. If the client really needs help, then it is right for the therapist to help, and to bring in the tools she knows for doing this. Ideally the client will learn from this modeling to use these tools for himself.

However, we have to ask whether the help was really necessary. If the help was not really necessary, if there was a possibility that the client might have found his way through the session without the need for an intervention in which the therapist played the role of the savior, then surely this would be preferable.

I apologize for the ways in which this analysis oversimplifies the matter, but essentially it is as if the therapist using the Finding Distance technique says, "This emotional experience is too much for you to handle. You need help and I can help you," and the therapist using the Inner Relationship technique says, "You are capable of giving nurturing attention to yourself, just as you are."

The paradox is that although we sit with our clients in order to help them, we can often help them most by seeing and connecting with the parts of them that need no help. This is not to deny the parts in need of help, but simply to say, "…and there is more."

My work has become more and more centered on Inner Relationship because it embodies a deep trust in the body's process. This deep trust is something that we who do Focusing have every reason to hold. As we enable our clients and students to access the part of themselves that is able to be in a nurturing inner relationship, we are making a space which calls forth the already healed self, the one who is always there, all along.

Perhaps the most challenging area for Focusing teachers is how to help people find and invite a felt sense. Not surprising: after 33 years with Focusing, I feel as though I'm only just beginning to really understand what a felt sense is!

Just last night I did a session with someone who called me because Focusing wasn't working for her. She'd had a little training, and lots of reading in the books, and she had an issue that gave her ample incentive for Focusing. But she wasn't sure if she was getting felt senses.

It turned out she was having felt senses beautifully. Her doubt came from the fact that she didn't feel them, as she put it, "physically." She thought that the slight clenching in her stomach didn't count because it didn't feel "physical" enough.

I've heard this from many people over the years, and I've decided that the problem is with the word "body." We say that Focusing happens "in the body," and people make assumptions based on that phrase.

What people often don't realize, or we haven't yet succeeded in teaching, is that it is quite possible for something to be body-centered and yet not physically felt. Peter Afford writes about this in his fascinating 1994 article, "The Felt Sense Need Not Always Be Physically Felt":

> The bodily-felt quality is therefore one of a number of ways to explore inside, but it is not the *sine qua non* of Focusing. If it feels like this is Focusing but you don't have a physical referent, it doesn't matter. The Focuser can tell whether the process is body-centered and "real" or not, and the listener or guide can look out for signs of body-centeredness. These include: the eyes looking downward, pauses in the talking to check back inside, and that characteristic "feel" that the Focuser is connected to something inside and is not just wandering around in his or her head or outside the body. Such a "feel" is a felt sense itself, of course.

In other words, if we know how to have a felt sense, we can usually tell if someone else is having one! That still leaves us with the question of how to help someone have one, if they are understanding the word "body" in the usual way. This is the question I'm grappling with in this article.

When I showed this article to some people during the process of writing it, one person seemed surprised that I would dare to suggest a redefinition of the word "body." Don't words mean what they mean? Don't we simply have to accept that?

Actually, words are always being redefined, in the natural process of language use. The meanings of words expand and stretch as we find new areas we need to communicate about. Inventing new words is a rarity – much more often, people stretch the meanings of words that already exist. Over time, these new meanings become acceptable usage and find their way into the dictionaries. This process of meaning change, accompanied by equally natural processes of sound change, is how Latin became French, Spanish, Italian; how Old English became the English of today; how all languages constantly change.

Although I do at one point propose a redefinition of the word "body," the central point of this article is not what we should or might mean by "body," but what we actually do mean by that word, and how that meaning changes as we learn Focusing. (And what that implies for how we talk about and teach Focusing.)

One of the most powerful insights of modern linguistics is that words have their meanings within *frames* – regular and persistent contexts – and that we need to know the frame we're speaking in. If I'm talking about a "shot," you won't understand me until you know if I'm speaking within the frame of "hunting season" or of "flu season." Perhaps what this article is really about is how to give people the Focusing "frame."

Body? What Body?

Newly written for this book

Focusing is a body-based process. It happens, we say, *in* the body. And this statement gives rise to much trouble, because, in fact, we do not all mean the same thing by the word "body." What is even more problematic: People who know Focusing do not mean the same thing by "body" as non-Focusers do, because Focusers have had experiences that have transformed what "body" means to us. So we are communicating from two sides of a great divide, Focusers saying "Let your body show you...," and non-Focusers puzzled, confused, uncomprehending what we could possibly be talking about. This gap must be bridged, for it may be one of the primary reasons that Focusing has not become more widely known and used.

As my friend Rob Parker pointed out to me, the traditional view of the body is that it is just another object in a world of objects. This means that it is normally dead; one has to add something called "life" to it to make it alive – and it is separate from the world, as every object is separate from every other object. Gendlin's view of the body as interconnecting process is quite different from this. Our lungs imply air, our bones imply gravity, our stomachs imply food, our eyes imply sunlight, and so on. It is separation that is artificial; our bodies *are* ongoing living interaction with the environment.

With these two radically different views of the body, it isn't surprising that we Focusing teachers encounter some communication gaps as we try to invite Focusing experiences in those who are new to the process. In some examples of Focusing, it is obvious to everyone – beginner and experienced Focuser alike – that something is happening in the body – the "body" as we both understand it. But in other Focusing sessions, beginners are mystified: How is *this* the body?

In this article I would like to give three examples of Focusing sessions that are easily seen as Focusing by Focusers, yet which puzzle non-Focusers who are trying to comprehend how Focusing is "in the body." Then I will try to articulate the Focuser's definition of "body." I will proceed to delineate four positions from which people come to Focusing, and how each of these positions can be a place from which to find the Focuser's "body." And finally, I will give some examples of people for whom the word "body" does not facilitate learning Focusing, and what we can say instead.

Stan closes his eyes and settles down to do some Focusing on his longing for an intimate relationship. He waits, head lowered, and then he speaks. "Something holds back," he says slowly. "It's scared... no, not scared, exactly. Hesitant... yes, 'hesitant' is partly right. Cautious, that's it. Hesitant and cautious." He goes on to spend time with this "hesitant and cautious" part of him. By the end of the session he reports: "It's changed. There's a willingness now."

Laurel, a person new to Focusing, has a question after watching this session. "When was he sensing his body?" she asks. Yet an experienced Focuser, also watching, had no doubt that Stan was Focusing. Why?

Before we answer that question, let's ask Stan. Were you sensing in your body? "Oh, yes," Stan replies. "Absolutely. And I was describing what I found there, and checking back with it all through the session."

It turns out that Stan experienced himself as sensing in his body – he just didn't use any body *words* that would demonstrate to Laurel that he was doing so. He could have said, "I'm sensing something in my chest. It's holding back." But he didn't.

So how did the experienced Focuser know that Stan was Focusing? There were a number of clues, and although any one of them might have been missing, all of them together make up an unmistakable picture. Stan's head was lowered, making it likely that his attention was below his chin. He spoke slowly, searchingly. The words he used, though not specifically body words (like "chest" or "throat"), had a grounded, embodied quality. ("Holds back" rather than "resistant," for example.) And he was checking his words with something inside him that could tell if those words fit or not.

So now let's imagine this scenario a little differently. Everything is the same except that after the session, when Stan is asked if he was sensing in his body, he says, "I don't know. I'm not sure. Was I?"

And then the following dialogue might ensue:

Ann: So, Stan, it looked to me like you were sensing something that you could check with, so you could tell that the word "scared" wasn't quite right, and the word "hesitant" was partly right. Yes?

Stan: Yes, that's true. I was.

Ann: And it looked to me, maybe from the way you were holding your head, that you were sensing it somewhere *here.* (gestures in front of chest-belly area)

Stan: Well, yes. It was somewhere around here. That's right.

Ann: So when you say you're not sure it was in your body, I'm wondering if you could say more about what that means for you.

Stan: Well.... I guess because I wasn't exactly feeling anything in, you know, my *physical* body.

And there is that mysterious gap. People can have experiences that are undeniably Focusing, and yet, if they are inexperienced with Focusing, may be unsure whether their experiences are legitimate – because they are understanding something by the word "body" (or "physical body") that seems not to include the experiences they are having.

Let's take another example.

Della starts her Focusing session wanting to know more about a situation at work in which she has a hard time speaking up for herself. She brings awareness into her body, and soon finds a tightness in her jaw, especially on the left. She puts her hand there, in order to help give company and attention to *something* she can feel in her jaw. As she attends to it, she begins to speak: "It's tight. I'm checking that word with it... yes, it's tight, and it's worried. I'm letting it know I can sense how worried it is. There's like a pacing dog in there, pacing up and down, whining." As she says this, her hand begins to pull slowly away from touching her jaw, and stays about six inches away from her face.

"He's whining. He's really worried about something. I'm letting him know I see him, and I hear how worried he is. He's a wolf-like dog, shaggy, doesn't look like a pet. Is he a wolf? No... he's a wolf-like dog. I'm inviting him to let me know what he's worried about. Now he's going back to pacing. It's like he's guarding me, worried that something will happen to me...." And she goes on from there.

Della started with a body sensation, but as she stayed with it, it became a vivid, emotionally-alive image, a "someone" rather than a "something." Was she Focusing? Certainly we would say so, and for pretty much the same reasons we said that Stan was Focusing. She had something there she could check with, sense into, and stay with... and it even had a bodily location. That hand held six inches out from the face tells us that... although if she had dropped her hand, she could have been having the same inner experiences. But was her experience in her body, her "physical" body? That would depend on how you define "body," wouldn't it? When we say that Focusing happens in the body, *what body are we talking about?*

Let's give one more example. Barbara is Focusing. Her hand cradles the left side of her belly... "It feels like concrete in here," she says. "It's filled with fear. I'm sensing what it's afraid of... It's afraid of this part over here..." – she gestures to her right – "afraid it will get out of control."

Her gesture to the right is outside her physical body, seeming to indicate an area about two feet away from her right shoulder. Barbara continues to do Focusing with both parts, the one in her belly, and the one outside her right shoulder. Both parts have emotional content and interesting process to reveal in the rest of the session.

Can something be "in" the body and at the same time two feet away from it? We have a problem. We either have to say that this session wasn't Focusing – and it was – or that Focusing isn't body-based – but it is – or we have to re-think what we mean by the word "body." Since the other two choices aren't acceptable, we're going to go with the third. As Sherlock Holmes said, "When you have eliminated the impossible, whatever is left, however improbable, must be the case."

Experiences like these are not rare exceptions. They are part of the common coin of Focusing, and perhaps would even be more common if people weren't held back from them by a belief that "body" means "within the envelope of skin." Clearly, we can't use a conventional, physiological definition of "body" if we want to include experiences like these as legitimate Focusing experiences.

We either have to say that Focusing can happen outside the body, or we have to re-define "body" as being something larger than a set of physiological processes bordered by the skin. In fact Gendlin clearly intends the latter. The following quotes are from *A Process Model:*

"We are setting up a new conception of the living body..." (p. 19)

"The body is usually considered the stuff within the skin-envelope. ... What we call 'the body' is a vastly larger system. 'The body' is not only what is inside the skin-envelope." (p. 26)

"There is no body separate from process." (p. 27)

"Among the tasks of this work are: to re-conceptualize *the body* so that we could understand how focusing is possible, how we can feel complex situations, how the body can come up with an answer to a complex human living question we cannot figure out, how body and cognition are not just split apart. That obviously requires a different conception of the body than physiology currently offers." (p. 181, italics in original)

For Gendlin, there is an experiential space that is larger than the merely physiological body (and size is only one of the differences). This is the space where Focusing happens, while at the same time it is created by Focusing. ("And where does one look and let? That space too is new, and is generated. As one looks, so to speak, in the usual body-sentience, this looking finds itself carried forward by a change in a somewhat different space" p. 221).

Rather than defining Focusing as a bodily process, perhaps we'd do better to define the body by Focusing. Rather than saying that the body is where Focusing happens, we can turn the definition around, and say: Where Focusing happens, that is "the body."

How does someone who doesn't know Focusing learn to find the experience of this differently conceived body? Not having experienced Focusing, someone will only have the usual concept of body as known by our culture. Of course this isn't the same for everyone. A person who plays a sport regularly and vigorously has a different body experience from someone whose idea of exercise is opening the door of the refrigerator. A person who has studied anatomy and physiology has a more specific and elaborated body picture than someone who hasn't. But all of these people, before Focusing, have their culture's ordinary view of "body." In Western industrial society, this is generally body as matter, as "stuff," devoid of meaning, at best a finely detailed and complex machine.

In 750 years we haven't really gotten farther than St. Francis of Assisi's view of body as "Brother Ass." Our bodies are still beasts of burden that carry us about. We still think of who we really are as separate from body, a kind of non-material spirit that rides on body's shoulders.

It's a long way from this view to the body of Focusing: infused with life meaning, vital with purpose, situated in a interconnected web of relationship, wise beyond logic and reason, inseparable from our identity.

No wonder people are confused and suspicious when we tell them, "Your body is wise." Their bodies *aren't* wise. More precisely: they don't understand and experience their bodies in such a way that "wise" makes sense to say about those body experiences. And we can't make them *think* their way into that kind of body experience. No wonder Focusing has to be experienced in order to be understood!

The people who don't find Focusing easily are not all alike. Beyond their individual uniqueness, I would venture to say that they fall into four broad categories.

(1) Emoters. These people can find themselves in danger of being emotionally overwhelmed, and tend to experience their feelings "all over" and "everywhere."

(2) Thinkers. There are people who are used to relying on a rational or cognitive approach to issues. When invited to sense inwardly, they will say things like, "It must be..." or "I'm sure it's..." or "I think...."

(3) Visual imagers. There are people who find visual imagery easily, and who go there when invited to go into inner contact. Visual imagery isn't necessarily connected to a Focusing place.

(4) Physicalizers. Often trained in body awareness, these are people who can find elaborate detail in their bodies, tracing a tension across a deltoid and down a trapezius... but don't get what this has to do with emotional meaning in their lives.

(See my paper "The Full Felt Sense" in this volume, and its introduction, for more about images, thoughts, emotions, and body sensations as avenues of entry into Focusing.)

Let's explore these differences by encountering Camille, René, and Imogen, three (invented) people who don't know Focusing yet, and who have emotions easily (Camille), think easily (René), or get images easily (Imogen). I will describe how I would help each of them find Focusing, starting from where they are. Their conception of the body is not yet the Focusing conception, but they *are* helped to find Focusing by being invited into body awareness as they understand it. This fact – that some people are helped to find Focusing by sensing into their body as they understand it before learning Focusing – seems at first to be mysterious, now that we understand that the "body" of Focusing is different from the culture's general understanding of body.

But at second look, the fact that most people find Focusing through the body *as they understand it* (and, through doing so, then come to understand body in a different way) is not so mysterious after all, because Gendlin makes it clear that there is only one body. There isn't a physiological body *and* a Focusing body. We each have only one body, and it is in that one body that all these processes take place, or as we could put it, this one body *is* all of these processes: breathing, digesting, walking, cellular regeneration, ruminating, daydreaming, Focusing....

"[A felt sense] comes, something like the way an emotion comes, in the body, of its own accord, but in a somewhat different space than the literal space in the body. Indeed it is literally in the body... but it is also in its own new space" (*A Process Model*, p. 233).

As for the fourth category, "Physicalizers," we will come to that below, and we will discover an intriguing and surprising fact: that those with easiest access to their bodies may have the most difficulty learning this body-based skill of Focusing. What are the implications of that? We will see. But first: Emoters, Thinkers, and Imagers.

Camille sits down for her first Focusing session. She has sought out Focusing in the hope that it can help her handle a time of stress and crisis in her life. As she tells me a little about her life situation, she begins to cry, reaches for a kleenex, and apologizes for her tears. "Sometimes I wonder if it's all too much for me," she confesses.

If I only reflect what she is saying – and for a while that's what I do – she mostly tells me what she has already been feeling, what she is feeling now, and the repetitive thoughts that go with it. "I decided it's grief I'm feeling. I can't do without him and I can't have him in my life anymore. It's grief." More tears. Although this is an emotional process, it is not a Focusing process – and it isn't helping her much, no matter how sensitive a listener I might be.

I have two main choices for how to invite her awareness into a Focusing place. I can simply have her notice what she's feeling in her body as she's saying these things, or I can, with her permission, do a somewhat longer "Leading In" that will help her find some Presence in her body as well as the felt sense of her trouble. (See "Facilitating Presence" in this volume.) In either case, helping Camille get a felt sense is unlikely to be very difficult. Once her attention is invited to her body, she will almost certainly have a body feeling connected with what she is going through. She is so definitely aware already of the life connection and emotional content of her process that bringing awareness into her body will probably be all she needs to do to find Focusing – that, and a sensitive facilitation to help her stay in Presence with what she's feeling. Someone with Camille's type of process does tend to get identified with her emotions – but if she can be helped to stay in Presence, Focusing isn't hard for her to find.

René is a bit of a tougher job for a Focusing teacher. He is a thinker; sometimes he even identifies himself with his thoughts. He's come to learn Focusing because he'd like to make better decisions and not doubt himself so much. He tends to doubt and second-guess even the decisions he's already made. Having told me this much, he certainly isn't about to cry (unlike Camille), and an invitation to sense what he just said in his body will get me a puzzled look.

But if I take René through a "Leading In" that starts with his arms and hands, which he is likely to be able to feel, then his legs and feet, then any parts of his body that are in contact with something... that much he can do, and since it doesn't take any thinking, he is now already in a different state than usual, a state of greater receptivity than he might have expected. I then invite him to sense in the middle area of his body, the area that includes his throat... his chest... his stomach and belly... and to invite a sense of how he's feeling in there as he senses how his life is going.

Very likely René now feels something in his body, and even has a pretty good sense of what it's about. The sense may be vague and elusive, and he may wonder at times if he's making it up, but patient facilitation can keep bringing him back to it. He'll be helped greatly by being guided to describe what he's feeling and check the description back with his body. At times he will probably move into a mental process, since that's what he knows well, and say things like, "I think it's sad," or "It must be about ...," but all I have to do is listen for those telltale signs that he's slipped out of direct contact with something, and invite him back into contact again. ("So maybe you could check with *it*, if that's right, that it's feeling sad.")

Imogen gets images easily. Perhaps she's just naturally that way, or perhaps she's learned a method like Shamanic Journeying that has given her practice in forming and following images. (People can be slowed in learning a new method by having previously learned a somewhat different method.)

She has heard about Focusing from a friend and hopes it will help her get past some experienced blocks in her life. Whether I choose a general "Leading In," or whether I ask her what one of those blocks is and offer a "Leading In" tailored to that issue, she is quite likely to get images once she closes her eyes.

The relationship of those images to a Focusing process depends a lot on how they are treated. We need to recognize that images are not all alike. In a distinction shown to me many years ago by Dave Young, there are visual images and body-based images. Visual images appear in the visual field, in front of the eyes. They are easily changed by will ("I think I'll untie the rope") and tend to move quickly, either with a series of quick flashes or like a movie.

Body-based images are in the body. The person points to the chest and says, "There's a wall here." Body-based images are not easily changed by will. If I were to say, "Make it something else, not a wall," the person would rightly think I was nuts. It is a wall. Nor does it change quickly. If it changes, and it may, the change will come as a result of keeping it company as it is. In other words, this body-based image behaves very much like a felt sense – and that is what I am going to say it is.

But Imogen is not getting body-based images, she is getting visual images, and it is my job to help her find Focusing from there. What do I do?

It helps if I invite her awareness into her body, just as I did with Camille and René. This way we establish a "there," a place to sense into. If she is a persistent visual imager, here is what is likely to happen. After I say, "When you're aware of *something*, you might let me know" (see Leading-In, below), she says (for example), "I'm seeing a row of blackbirds on a wire." The phrase "I'm seeing" tells me that this is probably a visual image, but let me check and make sure: "You might notice where you're feeling that in your body, a row of blackbirds on a wire." If it's a visual image, Imogen will say, "It's not anywhere in my body."

Now my first thought is: I want to respect that image. It has come for *some good reason*. I don't want to give the message that it should go away, that body sensation is somehow better than imagery. At the same time, we need more than visual imagery, or we will not be doing Focusing.

There are a number of ways to go. I can invite her to form a relationship with what's in the image. In doing so, I avoid using the word "image," which is distancing. Instead I refer to the content directly: "You might want to acknowledge [or say hello to] those birds on a wire." From this acknowledging, she may move into emotion: "I feel sad as I look at them." After I reflect ("You're sensing something in you is sad, looking at them") we're almost certainly in Focusing territory. Or, after saying hello, she may sense that *they* are sad. Same result.

Or I can invite her to get a body sense *of* the image. "Maybe you could invite a whole body sense of those birds on a wire, what comes in your body as you see them there." If Imogen doesn't know Focusing yet, she may not get what this means, but it's worth a try – something may come.

Or we can go with the image, let it play out awhile, perhaps give some gentle Focusing invitations, and notice whether the process becomes Focusing-like. What does that mean? Let me give an example.

Imogen: "It's not anywhere in my body."

Ann: "And it's a row of birds on a wire."

Imogen: "That's right. They're huddled together, like there's a cold wind out there."

Ann: "They're huddled together. You're sensing maybe they're cold."

Imogen: "There's a cold wind."

Ann: "You're sensing there's a cold wind there."

Imogen: "Some of them are flying away, but some are just staying there."

Ann: "And you might want to acknowledge them, the birds that are flying away, and the birds that are staying there."

Imogen: "It's like they're resigned to the cold, the ones that are staying."

Ann: "You're sensing the ones that are staying, it's like they're resigned to the cold. See if it's OK to stay with them, continuing to sense them, how they are."

Imogen: "They're sad."

Ann: "Ah. You're sensing they're sad. M-hm."

Imogen: "Those are the ones that no other bird is near. They're on their own."

Ann: "And you're sensing they're on their own, no other bird is near, and they're sad."

Imogen: "There's especially one of them, huddled and cold and sad."

Ann: "Ah, you're sensing there's especially one of them. It's huddled... and cold... and sad..."

Imogen: "No, not exactly sad.... He's more... hard to put into words..."

And somewhere along the line, without an invitation to sense in her body, Imogen has started Focusing.

I hope it is clear from this fragment that what started out as a merely visual image has enriched into a more wholistic experience, infused with emotion and meaning, and undoubtedly connected to Imogen's whole life situation.

Imogen is now in the place where we found Stan, Della, and Barbara at the start of this paper: she is Focusing, yet without specific reference to a physical body. She is in contact with something within her that is rich and intricate, that has more to it than can be put into words, that can be checked with, and that, as she says with it, "makes steps" – evolves and shifts into its own next steps.

The fact that this is a Focusing session puzzles many people who get imagery easily and are trying to learn Focusing. To understand what is happening we need to remember that the body of Focusing is not merely the physical body; it includes that, and is more. By the time Imogen's experience of the birds on a wire has become rich enough to include her sensing that they are sad, this *is* in her body. It doesn't matter whether she would point to her chest, or use words like "throat" or "belly." She doesn't need to be asked to sense the sad birds in her body, because, in the Focusing sense of "body," they are already there.

There is a persistent spatial model that keeps coming to me as I work with these three types, and the fourth one we will discuss below. In it, the four process types or "starting places" for Focusing are placed as if on four points of a compass. In the center, between them, there is a space where these separate experiences are not so separate. Images are *in* the body. Emotions have a body location. Thoughts have emotions. At the center, there is something alive, something with eyes that can meet our gaze and that has its own point of view.

I see a person starting out at one of the compass points, in emotion or thought or image or body, and moving from there into the center, into contact with something that is all four... and more. That happens in Focusing all the time. I might start out with a tightness in my throat, but as I stay with it, I can sense its fear, at about the same time that I begin to get what in my life it points to, my relationship with M perhaps. If I am patient and compassionate, if I relate to it, It begins to relate back, as if it were alive, letting me know how It feels. By this time, calling it just a "tightness in the throat" or "fear" or "thinking about M" would be inaccurate, because I no longer experience it as any of those things separately. My awareness is very likely not even with my throat any more, but in a space which came into being because of this attention, where I can sense "It." Instead of starting with a tightness, I could have started out feeling afraid, or thinking about M, and then noticing the tightness in my throat. Wherever I started, I would move from there into that space (more "central" in the model I'm proposing) which is somehow all of that, and where I can sense the edge, the "more" that is not yet in words or symbols. Focusing happens there, and "there" is the body.

Physicalizers

If we thought that Focusing was about sensing in the physical body as already understood by our culture, then the people who ought to be best at it, and find it most easily, would be the people already familiar with sensing in the body: massage therapists, bodybuilders, practitioners and students of any of the many body-based physical practices, from Tai Chi to Feldenkrais to Authentic Movement.

In fact, as any Focusing teacher can tell you, familiarity with sensing the conventional physical body can actually interfere with finding Focusing. I remember Ray, a medical doctor and cranio-sacral trained bodyworker, who wasn't helped at all by the usual Focusing instructions to sense in his body. The word "stomach," for example, brought him a vivid anatomical image of where his physical stomach was and what it looked like.

I know I'm sitting with one of these people when their first description of something sensed has a great deal of expert detail ("It's along the left side of my diaphragm, just below my spleen"), and further descriptions keep coming from the physical dimension, instead of bridging into imagery, emotion, or life meaning: "It's got a kind of tension to it, like it's stretching. It's stretching more on the right, like it's elongated there. And there's a pressure, sort of underneath...."

If I have some reason to guess, before the session starts, that I'm dealing with this kind of person, I will try to offer a Leading-In that doesn't mention the physical body (see below). While I welcome physical awareness and physical descriptions as I welcome everything, I will gently and persistently invite such a person to sense "its emotion" and "its connection to your life." Just as sessions that don't include the physical body as narrowly defined may still be Focusing, sessions that include *only* the physical body may *not* be Focusing. Let us be clear: Focusing is not following physical sensations around in your body, and nothing more. Focusing is (as Gendlin said again recently, in a teleconference sponsored by the Focusing Institute) "paying attention to some unclear sense that you can feel in your body that is about, connects with, something in your life." He meant, of course, in your "body" as understood by Focusing.

When the Word "Body" Doesn't Help

In addition to Physicalizers, there are other people who are not helped by language that points them specifically to their bodies. Do we want to insist that they first learn to feel in their physical bodies, and then help them find Focusing? Or can we, knowing that the Focusing experience is not necessarily in the purely physical body, find a way to help them go directly to Focusing, without the interference of the word "body" as they understand it?

Brenda is having her first Focusing session. She was referred by her Focusing-oriented therapist, who felt that Focusing could really help her, but found that the usual invitations to sense in the body didn't seem to work for Brenda. My first impression of Brenda is of an intelligent and sensitive woman with a heightened awareness of language. Having been warned, I decide to try to help her find Focusing without mentioning her body.

As we're talking about what she wants from the session, Brenda tells me that she wants to be able to listen to herself and trust her own inner knowing about her life. I ask her if she's familiar with the experience of knowing that certain words *don't* fit, aren't right, to describe what is true for her. Brenda's eyes immediately tear up; she's deeply moved by my question. "Yes!" she says. "The right words are so important to me! And people think I'm strange for that!"

I have a feeling that Brenda already has Focusing-type experiences, and this sensitivity to words fitting accurately, or just right, points to these experiences for her. What *doesn't* point to these experiences is the word "body." When invited to sense how "the right words" feel in her body, she gets a puzzled expression on her face. What does that have to do with her body? We would do Brenda a disservice by expecting her to follow a conventional instruction like "Notice how that feels in your body." Instead, I spend the session making invitations like: "Notice if you have a *sense of rightness* for that." "Notice if that feels like it fits." Soon Brenda is gesturing toward her chest – although she's unaware that she's doing so, and it would distract her if I pointed this out. One time I forget, and suggest that she sense how a "sadness" feels in her body. A confused look comes across her face. "I don't know," she says. I apologize, and say it another way.

You might be wondering how I would categorize Brenda. Evidently she's not a Physicalizer or an Imager. Might she be a Thinker? Perhaps – but in her case I doubt that it matters. We have to face the fact that our four categories, helpful as they may be some of the time, don't always help us understand the process of the person sitting across from us. Categories are inherently limited, and are never as complex and subtle as the real person. This much we know: Brenda isn't helped to find Focusing by the word "body" – and we need to be ready to find other words that help her.

Ultimately, the journey of making the Focusing process one's own will be different for each person, and the privilege of facilitating that journey will remain a compelling one, calling on all our creativity, empathy, and improvisation.

As Focusing teachers we can't rest on any assumption, least of all that we comfortably know what the word "body" means to each person we say it to.

Felt sensing, brought to our awareness by Gendlin, is something never before described, and our languages are missing the concepts to describe it. It's not that we humans have never done it before – creative people at least have done it, as far back as art and invention have existed – but we've never seen it, we've never stepped back to understand what it was we were doing when we sensed the whole of a situation rather than following a given set of emotional responses.

The very process of using words to facilitate Focusing takes us to the edge that Focusing teaches us about: the border between what can be sensed and what can be said. If Focusing were easy to find – if the instruction to allow a felt sense to form were as easy to follow as, say, the instruction to boil water – this business of finding words for it wouldn't be so complex, but it also wouldn't be so interesting.

The purpose of this article has been to open up a dialogue about the concept of "body" in Focusing, and in our usual language. If I've opened a space for curiosity about what we mean when we say "body," I am satisfied.

General Leading In

So, take your time
to begin letting awareness come into your body.
Maybe first being aware of the outer area of your body—
your arms, and your hands.
[Noticing what your hands are touching, and how they feel.]...
Being aware also of your feet....
Noticing what your feet are touching, and how they feel....
Bringing awareness up through your legs, your lower legs, your upper legs...
Being aware of the contact of your body on the chair {couch, what you're sit-
ting on}... Letting it support you. Letting yourself rest into that support....
[Bringing your awareness up through your back, sensing your back... Sensing
your shoulders, your neck, your head on your neck... and letting movement
come there if it wants to... And being aware of your head, and your face...]

And then letting your awareness come inward, into the whole inner area of
your body, into the whole area that includes your throat, your chest, your
belly {stomach and abdomen} {stomach and below}.
And just be there.
Let your awareness rest gently in that whole middle area.
[And any part of your body may be calling for your awareness, and that's OK,
and we'll just start in this middle area, throat, and chest, and belly.]

And give yourself a gentle invitation in there, like you're saying,
"What wants my awareness now?"
or "What wants to come and be known?"
and then wait.

[and when you're aware of something, you might let me know.]

Leading In Tailored to an Issue

So, take your time
to begin letting awareness come into your body.
Maybe first being aware of the outer area of your body—
your arms, and your hands.
[Noticing what your hands are touching, and how they feel.]...
Being aware also of your feet....
Noticing what your feet are touching, and how they feel....
Bringing awareness up through your legs, your lower legs, your upper legs...
Being aware of the contact of your body on the chair {couch, what you're sit-
ting on}... Letting it support you. Letting yourself rest into that support....
[Bringing your awareness up through your back, sensing your back... Sensing
your shoulders, your neck, your head on your neck... and letting movement
come there if it wants to... And being aware of your head, and your face...]

And then letting your awareness come inward, into the whole inner area of
your body, into the whole area that includes your throat, your chest, your
belly {stomach and abdomen} {stomach and below}.
And just be there.
Let your awareness rest gently in that whole middle area.
[And any part of your body may be calling for your awareness, and that's OK,
and we'll just start in this middle area, throat, and chest, and belly.]

And remember that issue, [that whole issue about _____,]
[like you're inviting it to come into the room and sit down with you]
and invite your body to give you its feel of that whole issue right now
{and take some time to sense how your body feels with that whole issue right
now}
{Take some time to invite your body's sense of that whole thing about
_____.}

and then wait.

[and when you're aware of something, you might let me know.]

Leading In Without the Physical Body

So you might take your time
to just be aware of yourself right now, as you're sitting here...
and to begin slowing down...
and turning your awareness inward, in to your inner sense of yourself...
just as you are right now...
taking some time just to be aware of how you are,
how you're sensing yourself right now...
[and remembering that you have in you an inner knowing,
an inner sense of what feels right...
and maybe now could be a time to invite that inner sense of knowing to be
with you here...]
and invite or turn toward whatever in your awareness is wanting your attention right now

and then wait.

[and when you're aware of something, you might let me know.]

The idea that a Focusing session is a process in which an "it" comes alive is a very useful one, I think. It helps a great deal to see a Focusing session as a developmental process *for the felt sense.* What one meets at the start of a Focusing session is (usually) not yet a felt sense that can reveal itself, communicate, unfold, connect up to a million other strands. Or perhaps it is already all that, and our contact with it is what needs to develop. In either case, taking time for a series of steps of slowly increasing contact allows the felt sense, and/or the Focuser's contact with it, to develop to the point where the felt sense seems to have its own needs and wants. This is a good thing.

In *The Focusing Student's and Companion's Manual,* Barbara McGavin and I describe a series of steps that we recommend for this developmental process. They include: acknowledging, describing, sensing the kind of contact it would like, being with it, sensing how it feels from its point of view, etc. It also helps to remember to have the patience of a person encountering a shy animal in the woods. When one first encounters "something" inside, it is often vague, fuzzy, and unclear, and it often presents itself simply, as a body sensation or an image or a thought. Some people may get more than this relatively quickly. But others need support in moving from a one-sided awareness to a fuller one.

What doesn't work is to leap too quickly to a kind of contact that is appropriate at a later stage – like trying to kiss early on a first date! I have heard this kind of thing too often:

Focuser: "I'm sensing something vague and tight in my upper chest... I'm asking what it's all about... It's gone."

Obviously what would have helped this Focuser was to have some greater contact with this "something" before asking a question. (And perhaps in any case not asking it as a question at all: see "Questioning Questions" in this volume.) Let's try it another way:

Focuser: "I'm sensing something vague and tight in my upper chest... I'm just sensing it... it's tight and heavy... I'm checking those words... yes, heavy is right, like a pressure... I'm acknowledging it... it gets a little lighter when I do that... I'm sitting with it... I'm sensing it's sad... it's about Mary's leaving..."

The Focusing process is about staying with a *whole* sense of something, rather than getting caught up in one of its aspects. Having patience and going slowly help with this. So does methodically inviting more and more aspects, as you will see in the article that follows. The Full Felt Sense is like a tent with four poles that holds a space within for something not yet in words – the Living "It."

This piece of writing appeared as a chapter of my 1991 manual, *The Focusing Guide's Manual*. I'm no longer publishing that manual, because I no longer practice or recommend significant parts of it (notably Finding a Distance in cases where people feel overwhelmed by their emotional experience). Much of the material in that manual that I do still agree with has been incorporated into the 2002 manual I wrote with Barbara McGavin, *The Focusing Student's and Companion's Manual, Part Two*.

However, this piece of writing on the Full Felt Sense did not find itself into that new manual. It was omitted not because I disagree with it, but because Barbara and I were concentrating on the guiding skills that help with Focusing partnership. The model of the Full Felt Sense is most useful when guiding someone through Focusing for the first time. Someday I hope to do a whole manual on the skills of guiding someone new to Focusing, but until that day, I would like this piece to be out in the world again.

Others have pointed out the four aspects of experiencing, and I benefited from discussions with Rob Foxcroft, Peter Afford, Barbara McGavin, and Jay Shaffer as this model was developing.

Update: This article offers three ways to do "Inviting the story, or how this connects with the Focuser's life," including, "Would it feel right to ask it, 'What in your life brings this now?'" A few years later I discovered a much simpler way to invite life connection. Once there is emotion, e.g., "It's angry," one can make this suggestion: "You might sense what's getting it so angry." Or, a further development that came from Treasure Maps to the Soul: "You might sense what it is not wanting." Students of my (and Barbara's) work are familiar with these invitations. What they may not have realized is that they are also ways to bring in the life connection or story aspect.

Also, it can be noticed that several of these recommended invitations are in the form of questions. In 1991, I was not yet as clear as I am now on the problems with questions; see "Questioning Questions" in this volume for a listing of these problems as well as some handy ways to turn questions into suggestions.

See "Body? What Body?" in this volume for more about these four avenues as roads of entry into Focusing, and what this tells us about the "body" that Focusing gives us.

And see "The Origins of Inner Relationship Focusing" in this volume for more about "The Living It" and the developmental process of enlivening that happens in a Focusing session.

The Full Felt Sense

Excerpted from The Focusing Guide's Manual, *1991*

Sometimes you sense that the person is stuck, and it's not because they don't have anything – they have *something* – but because what they have seems somehow flat or incomplete. The "Full Felt Sense" is a model that can help you bring in what's missing. You would typically check for the presence of the Full Felt Sense after there is a physical description (handle) and before asking the focuser to "sense how *it* feels from *its* point of view."

Recently I have been picturing the Full Felt Sense as having four aspects: body sensation, emotional quality, imagery or symbolism, and life connection or story. I have observed that a person usually enters Focusing through one of these four avenues. Then, as the session progresses, the felt sense typically "fills out" so that more and more of these are present. The person may begin by telling a story about an issue in their life, then begin feeling an emotion, and then sense something in the body. Or the person may begin with a body sensation, then get an image for it, then sense its emotional tone, and then realize what it's about in their life.

From this we learn two things. First, it is legitimate to enter Focusing by any of these four roads. Body sensation is not the only way to begin. Second, if the session gets stuck, the guide might notice which of these four aspects is present, and if any are missing. The missing ones can be invited.

The four aspects of the Full Felt Sense are not all equal. Body sensation is most important; imagery is least important. Some Focusers come into the felt sense through imagery, but if imagery is not there for someone, I would not invite it except as a last resort. Imagery is just not a natural modality for everyone.

So first notice if the Focuser has body sensation yet. If not, invite it: "And maybe you could sense how all that is in your body."

If body sensation is there, but nothing else, try for emotional tone next. "You might also just wonder if it has some emotional quality, some way that it is feeling." (With a new Focuser, it's OK to guess, just to give them an idea of what we mean: "For example, it might be a scared pressure, or an angry pressure, or a hiding kind of pressure, or something else...")

Third, if it's not there already, you would ask for the story, or how this connects with the Focuser's life. You might say, "Do you have a feel for what this is about in your life?" Or, "Maybe ask this place what in your life brings this now?" This might be a good time to assure the Focuser that they do not have to tell you what it is, it just helps if they know themselves. So you might say, "Just notice if you have a general sense of what this connects to in your life, and you don't need to tell me."

Anything that comes in the process, including thoughts, may be helpful at this point. Let's say you ask the Focuser, "Do you have a sense of what that is about in your life?" After a moment the Focuser says, "I don't know, but I keep thinking about how hard my week has been." For this person, this may be the way the answer is coming. Try saying, "OK, check with that sense in your body, does it feel like it's about how hard your week has been?"

Suggestions for Inviting Missing Aspects

Inviting body sensation:
"Maybe you could sense how all that feels in your body."
"Would it be OK to notice how that sadness feels in your body?"
"See if you'd like to let your body give you a feel for that messy desk and what's in the way of organizing."

Inviting emotional tone:
"You might also just wonder if it has some emotional quality."
"Maybe you could notice if there is some way that it is feeling, from its point of view."

Inviting the story, or how this connects with the Focuser's life:
"Would it feel right to ask it, 'What in your life brings this now?'"
"Notice if you'd like to ask in there, 'What in your life feels this way?'"
"See if you have a sense that this is connected to your life somehow, even if you don't know how."

Inviting imagery or symbolism:
"You might want to notice if there's an image connected with that."

Thoughts or images that might be distracting if the person were already with something definite can actually be ways the body uses to supply what's missing.

The person may not know exactly what the sense is connected to, and that's all right. What we are looking for is a feeling that it's about *something*. Your question helps the person feel the "aboutness" of the sense, which makes the rest of the session much fuller and richer – even if that "aboutness" cannot be explained. Without this connectedness to the life, the session can be reduced to merely following sensations that have no meaning. If you start to feel that this is happening, that is definitely a flag that you should ask about the life.

When the "it" comes alive

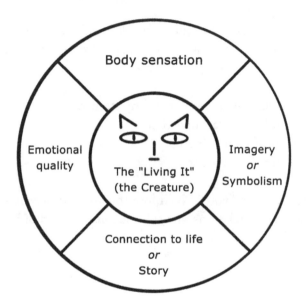

At the center of the circle is a creature I call the "Living It." This is part-ly humorous representation of the fact that in a Focusing session that really flows, there is a time when the felt sense seems to come alive, when it has wants and needs and its own point of view. When this happens, it's wonder-ful, because the Focusing process is no longer stuck. The relationship with the Living It contains everything the Focuser needs in order to focus successfully with what is there – because the It will say what it needs.

The Living It is at the center of the Full Felt Sense circle because it embodies all four aspects of the felt sense. It is in the body, it has emotional tone, it has symbolic quality (it often feels like a child, or an animal, etc.), and it has a rich life-connectedness.

The It may come alive at any point in the session. I remember one session where a man had a feeling in his left chest that was like a claw. He didn't know what it was about, he didn't sense any emotional tone, and it just wasn't going to open up no matter how long he sat with it. Finally, just to try something, I asked him if he could move it out. He reported, "It doesn't want to move." How exciting! That was the turning point in the session. I asked him if he'd like to sense what it did want instead, and we were off and running.

When guiding or even Listening, be alert for the coming of the Living It, because so much more can flow when it is welcomed. Notice how this listener ignored the It:

Focuser: "I'm sensing a darkness in my stomach."
Listener: "You have a darkness there."
Focuser: "It's scared of something."
Listener: "You're feeling scared."

Don't turn "it" into "you"! You'll lose the lovely differentiation that will help the Focuser have a relationship with the sense instead of being identified with it.

During the brief time (1981-83) when I was practicing psychotherapy, under the aegis of the Chicago Counseling Center, I was profoundly influenced by the works of Swiss psychologist Alice Miller, especially *The Drama of the Gifted Child*, in which she shows how selective parental praise can be a form of neglect, and *For Your Own Good*, a chilling three-part portrait of a heroin addict, a child murderer, and a despotic mass murderer, showing how their behavior as adults mirrored the deprivations and abuses of their childhoods. After reading *For Your Own Good*, I felt I was seeing the whole world differently, in a more connected, meaningful way. As I say in the article, "No pain is ever really buried in childhood. Your whole present life embodies the pain, expresses it like a dream symbol waiting to be understood."

We cannot reason forward from trauma and abuse. Two people can have similar experiences but process them differently, and make different meanings out of them for their lives. No one can predict what impact a traumatic event or abusive childhood will have on adulthood for the one who survives it. But we *can* look at present-day difficulties, life circumstances and symptoms, and understand them as mirrors for past events that are still working their way to resolution.

Miller offered hope: in her view, being allowed to give expression to what one had suffered – and being heard – was the key to healing.

> Theoretically a child beaten by his father could afterwards cry his heart out in the arms of a kind aunt and tell her what happened; she would not try to minimize the child's pain or justify the father's actions but would give the whole experience its due weight (*For Your Own Good*, p. 116).

That fit well for me. Having been trained as a client-centered therapist and a Focusing guide, I was well aware of the power of empathy. But for the first time I began to have a conceptual frame in which to understand that empathy for what happened back then, how it felt and what meaning was made of it, has healing and transformative power.

When this article was written, I was in the process of working out an approach to Focusing that would later be called Inner Relationship. Miller's view of the power of simply hearing what had happened would form one of the foundation stones of that approach. Miller hints at the possibility that a person healing from childhood trauma might become able to give inner empathy, empathy to the child within who went through the pain.

> ...she is alone with her suffering, not only within her family but also within her self. And because she cannot share her pain with anyone, she is also unable to create a place in her own soul where she could "cry her heart out" (p. 117).

This hint was enough for me, along with other understandings that were coming in from other sources, to build up a picture of an inner listener, an inner "kind aunt," to use Miller's phrase, who would stand beside the child who suffered and be willing to simply hear how it was. It is absolutely clear that "minimizing" and "justifying" betray the process. The inner listener must not say, "He didn't mean to hurt you" or "She was doing her best." Perhaps later such understandings will arise, but during the time when the pain is being expressed and heard, they stop the process, as surely as handing someone a kleenex will often stop the crying. Someone must hear how it was, as bad as it was, in order for the process of carrying forward to happen. And that carrying forward *will* happen, *does* happen, when the empathy is there.

Focusing on Childhood

Appeared in The Focusing Connection, *July 1987*

My client sits across from me, feeling a tight, pushing sensation in her chest. She's been working with it for fifty minutes now, acknowledging it, listening to it, letting it be there. It speaks to her in a harsh, critical voice, telling her she has to be completely different in every way. "It seems to want to wipe me out completely," she tells me.

I, too, have been patient with the tight, harsh place, for fifty minutes now. I have kept quiet about my suspicions about where that voice comes from. But now I feel I must speak, because if my guess is right, the chances of it leading to healing are very high. I tell her I'd like to make a guess, and have her check and see if it feels right. She agrees.

"When people are born," I say, "they deserve to be welcomed with delight. But often that doesn't happen. Because the people who should have welcomed you had their own pain, they couldn't see you or delight in you as you deserved. You didn't understand why you weren't loved and welcomed. You probably felt there must be something wrong with you. You might have said to yourself, 'If only I were a completely different person, they would love me then.'"

By now I know my guess is at least partly right, by the tears streaming down my client's face. "I don't remember anything like that," she says. "But when you said those words, 'If only I were a completely different person,' something in me really responded."

Those of us who work with the gentle process of Focusing often hesitate to make guesses about the sources of pain in our clients' lives. We do not want to intrude, or push, or rush the process. But there are very good reasons to help direct people's attention to sources of pain in their early childhood.

"I don't have any memory of something like that," says my client.

"You probably wouldn't have any conscious memory," I tell her, "because something that feels this total probably happened before you had language. But your tears show that some part of you remembers."

Often the very person who needs to learn Focusing gives little credence to emotional memory, as opposed to memories of logical, understandable events that occurred after they could speak. It comes as a surprise to them that they can work, in a Focusing way, with very old experiences. This is one reason why I mention my guesses about childhood pain: I'm showing the person a door they often didn't know existed. They can then open it at their own pace.

"I feel very hopeful," says my client. "I can tell this really gets to a deep place. But I'm also asking myself, 'How can something *this* big ever change?'"

"This is the place where the change starts," I assure her. "Next you just look at it and acknowledge how big it is."

The primary reason I direct attention to childhood is that I have seen, over and over again, that the deepest, biggest pain comes from there. The child casts a big shadow on the adult. And at the same time, working directly with the source of pain brings more healing, more relief, more hope. Working on the present only heals the present – often slowly. But working on the past heals the present *and* the past.

My guesses about people's childhoods have become more accurate and more helpful since I read the work of Swiss psychiatrist Alice Miller, especially her first two books, *The Drama of the Gifted Child* (also called *Prisoners of Childhood*), and *For Your Own Good: Hidden Cruelty in Child-Rearing and the Roots of Violence.*

After reading those books, I felt that windows had been opened into my own childhood and the childhoods of the people I worked with. Once I saw how understandably people react to what happens in childhood, I began to trust my *feelings* about my childhood, rather than my conscious memories or my family's stories.

The essence of Miller's insight is that a child needs most of all to be seen and known as a unique, special being. The yearning for this kind of "seeing" is very powerful, and it is a legitimate, perfectly understandable need. But when you are born to parents who have unhealed emotional pain, they often cannot really see you. Instead, they see only themselves, reflected in you. They are reminded of their own failures, lacks, and losses as a child, and this brings up feelings in them which they have never acknowledged or learned to accept. They deny, criticize, or reject the child, who reminds them too much of their own hurt selves.

When this denial/rejection is blatant, it becomes physical or verbal abuse. But when it is more subtle, it is still profoundly painful. Sometimes the parents deal with their own childhood pain by setting up an image of an Ideal Child, and casting you to play the part. They praise you and "see" you when you are "good," ignore you at other times. They love your high grades in school, but don't seem to notice the less clean-cut, more complicated parts of you. It's possible to remember only praise and kind treatment from your parents, and still have been deeply hurt by them.

There are many cruel parents (most child abusers had at least one), but there are also many who are well-meaning, who want only to treat their children well and be good parents. Unfortunately, the very intensity of their wish to be good parents may blind them to their mistakes. They may be unable to notice when the child has needs unmet by them.

My client says, "I don't have the memories of being hurt by my parents. My parents were very affectionate to me." But later she says, "Even now I can't talk about feelings to my parents. They always change the subject." So they were affectionate to her – but not to her feelings! Now it is even more understandable that she wants to wipe herself out. Part of her *was* wiped out.

The clearest window into childhood is this: that we repeat what happened to us. If you want to know what your childhood was like, look at your present life. You are probably repeating the key, painful aspects of your childhood right now. If you have no friends who really listen to you, if your primary relationship is cold or unequal or abusive, if you're always taking care of other people and never getting taken care of yourself, those are surely aspects of your childhood that you can touch with Focusing and start to heal. No pain is ever really buried in childhood. Your whole present life embodies the pain, expresses it like a dream symbol waiting to be understood.

Another client was plagued by feelings that all good things are temporary, that something wonderful was always going to be snatched away. He felt a pervasive anxiety, afraid that he could make a simple, seemingly innocuous mistake, and blow his happiness forever. As I listened to him, a guess about his childhood began to form. I sensed how he might feel this way if he had "off and on" experiences with an early caregiver, where that person was there strongly with love, and then suddenly gone, then back again, then gone again. He might then assume that *he* had caused the going, that whatever he had done last had been the mistake that caused the catastrophe. When I shared this guess with him, he began to cry. Once again, he didn't have memories, but it felt right – though part of him still doubted. Over time, he was able to confirm that this particular pattern of early pain had affected many parts of his present life, and begin to heal it.

Alice Miller says that childhood pain repeats itself in your present life because it is yearning to be known, and it will repeat, like someone knocking at your door, until you finally hear it and let it in. Pain stays stuck, and repeats, as long as it is cut off and excluded from your sense of who you really are. So the essence of healing is to acknowledge that pain. Often I will suggest to people that they imagine holding the pain in their arms, cradling it like a child. "Imagine that you can walk around all day with that pain, being tender to it, taking care of it. No matter what else you do, that can be there too."

It helps me to image myself as a child, to see the child inside me, feeling the pain it wasn't possible to feel when the hurt happened. If she lets me, I comfort her. Sometimes she is angry or shy, and I can only stand near her, not touching, just letting her know I'm there and I can be patient. As children we often were not allowed to feel pain or anger, especially toward our parents. That pain and anger is still there, waiting to be acknowledged through Focusing and to be seen at last – by us.

The pain of not having been seen as a child is big, deep pain. It's linked to the fear of death, because to the child, if the parents don't see you, they won't take care of you and you will die. When we understand this, we realize part of why that earliest pain is so terrifying that many people will do anything rather than feel it: stay stuck, suffer addiction, hurt others. But with Focusing there is hope, because Focusing is an excellent method for dealing with pain that seems overwhelming. Focusing lets you touch the pain a little at a time; if the pain is the whole ocean, Focusing lets you stand on the shore.

Here is another specific technique for using Focusing to heal childhood pain (with thanks to Bonnie Davenport). It is similar to the "How would it have been if it had all been OK?" Focusing question. After you get in touch with how your parents were that was so difficult for you, you can ask, "How would it have been if my parents had been all healed?" Image that and stay with the sense that comes. If you have trouble imagining your parents healed, go back to what you know of *their* childhoods, and imagine their parents (your grandparents) having been more supportive. (Working on your grandparents can be nearly as productive as working on your parents. Some packages of pain get handed down wrapped through the generations.) Or, alternatively, you might send your adult self, your best self, back into your childhood, and be the parent to yourself that you needed.

I have found that acknowledging deep pain never feels complete, never heals as deeply as it could, unless I'm acknowledging not only my present pain but also its links to my childhood. Sometimes I'll spend fifty minutes on some present difficulty, and only ten touching on how it reminds me of my dealings with my parents. But that can be enough to deepen the healing remarkably.

As my client gets up to go, she shakes her head a little sheepishly. "It's kind of hard to believe…it seems so trite…" I know what she means. It was great-great-grandfather Freud who taught us to look into childhood for sources of present pain. That's so "old-hat"! But if it's true, if it works…then it works! Even great-great-grandfathers have something to teach us, after all.

The Last
Word

There is always more to say... and yet, as I like to say at the end of a Focusing session, we need to find a comfortable stopping place for now. Perhaps an appropriate last word is this article about whether Focusing is as well-known as it could be – and why not. Like all good endings, this also points us toward the future. Surely Focusing has not yet fulfilled its destiny as a supportive method for our lives and society as we move through changing times, even radical ones. There is more....

It was 1996, and we met in a simple room with wide windows open to the beautiful view, the lush Bavarian fields in their deep colors of August green. The participants were mostly German, but one man was from Switzerland, and he always sat to my right. He would arrive promptly and set out his materials as the class was starting: a large unlined notebook and a rainbow of colored pens. Once after I'd been speaking for a while, he showed us what he had done – taking notes in graphic form, with shapes morphing into other shapes, circles, arrows, all in the bright colors. Kuma, he called himself, because he'd lived in Japan and was a big fan of all things Japanese. Kuma for "bear."

Probably it was Kuma who asked me, "Why isn't Focusing better known?" When I said "There are four reasons!" no one was more amazed than me, because up till that point I hadn't given much thought to the reasons, but there they were, ready and numbered. Certainly he is the one who asked, "And what are they?" with an irrepressible twinkle in his eye, and his colored pens poised.

Since then, Daniel Bärlocher has become a certified Focusing Trainer, well known in the Focusing community for his quirky humor (at the 2003 Focusing International Conference, his presentation "Why Sex Hurts" was a multimedia show crossing Focusing with country music) and his groundbreaking work with Focusing and migraine headaches.

Yes, there are five reasons (the article explains where and how the fifth one got added) and although Focusing is better known than it was in 1996, we are still a long way from being a household word, and I believe for the most part the reasons still hold.

However, two updates. At the time I wrote the article, my third reason was that "Focusing teaching froze in 1978." I didn't understand at the time what has become obvious to me since, that Focusing teaching is *not* frozen. There are many hundreds of Focusing teachers, and almost all of them teach somewhat differently from the way they were taught. This glorious diversity is encouraged by the Focusing Institute, and I may modestly say that I perhaps had a role in it as well. (One woman wrote to me, "I heard you changing Gene's six steps, and I realized I could do that too!")

So to substitute for that third reason I have a new one, which came to me as I was writing the article "Body? What Body?" for this volume. Focusing is a body-based, body-oriented process, and yet what is meant by the word "body" changes once one does Focusing. No wonder Focusing is hard to talk about – when you learn Focusing, your language changes, and it becomes really hard to talk to the people who haven't learned it yet! My hope is, of course, that having become conscious of this issue, we can now address it.

Focusing does need to become better known, because it opens up for us who we truly are: complex, multi-faceted beings living in an intricately inter-connected universe. It's one of the essential "ways of being" that we need in order to meet the challenges of the times we live in with empathy and compassion as well as intelligence and vision. Solving the problems of the community of life on this planet will need us to include all the voices and all the parts. Focusing is a key resource for this – pass it on.

Five Reasons Why
Focusing Is Not Better Known (Yet)

Appeared in The Focusing Connection, *November 1996*

Whenever people become enthusiastic about Focusing, or contemplate going home from a workshop to present it to their friends and colleagues, the question inevitably comes up: "Why isn't Focusing better known?" Or, as I heard it at a talk I gave in New York recently: "Why haven't I heard of this before?"

When this question arose at a workshop I gave in Germany this August, I found myself answering, "Well, there are at least five reasons..." These are the five reasons which came.

The first reason why Focusing is not better known (yet) is that it isn't very dramatic or flashy to watch and to experience. A therapist or practitioner who uses Focusing doesn't get to look impressive. We don't seem to be experts, wielding magic. We look like we aren't doing much (and that's true!). So practitioners who need an ego-boost are not attracted to Focusing.

Some popular methods are very dramatic. People spend a weekend lying on their backs, breathing and sobbing. They feel that such work is very "deep." (Cathartic methods, in which crying and rage are experienced, are often felt by the client as "deep.") Have they really changed? Perhaps not – but after all that crying, they feel they must have changed! Or perhaps the practitioner orchestrates the drama, talking to the person's "parts," moving them to different chairs, having them talk back. Not only the client but also the observers are very impressed. Something really happened! Focusing, by contrast, usually looks and feels very subtle. Watching a Focusing session, especially if you don't know what to look for, can be like watching the grass grow. Even the people who stay with it are unlikely to run home and tell all their friends.

The second reason why Focusing is not better known (yet) is that Focusing is so general in its purposes that it is hard to understand, and hard to sell. In the early days of European settlement in America, people in a travelling "medicine show" would sell an elixir which was hailed as a cure for "anything that ails you." This magical medicine was supposed to cure anything, from broken legs to menstrual cramps. When analyzed, it was found to be primarily alcohol and water.

In modern times, people are confused when a method is brought forward which is useful for so many purposes, from improving therapy to decision-making to grounding spirituality to healing childhod sexual abuse. It would probably be easier for them to grasp a tool with one purpose. In our discussion last August, the therapists in the room, practicing mainly in Germany, Switzerland, and Austria, recalled that insurance forms ask for the specific purpose of any process or technique used.

We know that describing Focusing is difficult anyway. New people, hearing about Focusing, want to know "What is it for?" and when we can't tell them, their eyes glaze over. People tend to connect with methods that will help with something that's hurting or bothering them right *now*. Even if Focusing *would* help, they don't recognize it as what they need when they hear that its purpose is something vague and general like "getting in touch with yourself." So I feel frustrated when I give an introductory talk to a large audience. I know that some people need to hear how Focusing helps release blocks to action, others need to hear how Focusing will help their therapy get moving, others need to hear how Focusing will help them deal with overwheming emotions. I can't give an individually tailored talk to each person! (When I think that most people have found Focusing by chance and Divine guidance, it amazes me that Focusing is as well known as it is!)

Compare EMDR (Eye Movement Desensitization and Reprocessing), which has become quite well-known in just a few years. EMDR clearly has the purpose of recovering and processing traumatic memories. The simplicity of its purpose surely has something to do with its popularity.

The third reason why Focusing is not better known (yet) is that the steps of Focusing teaching froze in 1978 when Gendlin's book *Focusing* was published, and at that time the first step of Focusing was Clearing a Space. Most Focusing teachers still teach Clearing a Space as the first step of Focusing, and this is a problem for a number of reasons:

(a) Clearing a Space is not part of the essence of Focusing. It is simply *not* a very Focusing-like thing to do. Focusing is spending time with something unclear, allowing it to be as it is and sensing how it is. Clearing a Space (in its classic form) moves things out. So it *isn't* spending time with things, and it *isn't* allowing them to be as they are. The fact that Clearing a Space isn't a very Focusing-like thing to do means that when people learn Clearing a Space as the first step of Focusing, they tend to be confused about what Focusing is.

(b) Not everyone can do Clearing a Space. So when people learn that Clearing a Space is the first step of Focusing, and they can't do it, they either give up on Focusing, or they do Focusing but they feel so sheepish about it ("I'm not doing this right because I'm just spending time with what I feel instead of moving it out") that they don't tell anyone else what they're doing.

(c) Not everyone *should* do Clearing a Space. If their feelings are subtle, hard to find and easily lost, they shouldn't set them out. So, once again, they either don't do Focusing or they don't tell others about it.

Focusing is hard to describe anyway, and the fact that Focusing teaching froze in 1978 has meant that, when teachers are asked, "What is Focusing?" the answer has too often been, "Focusing has six steps." Having six steps is *not* what Focusing *is*. This is led to unnecessary confusion when people hear about Focusing and attempt to tell others about it.

I'd like to make it very clear that my objection is not to the process of Clearing a Space, which many people find useful, but to *teaching Clearing a Space as the first step of Focusing*. This makes it sound as if one *must* do Clearing a Space in order to do Focusing, which I don't think anyone would claim.

The fourth reason why Focusing is not better known (yet) is that it is radical. It goes counter to the mainstream trends and themes of our society. We live in a world which emphasizes rationality, speed, and clarity. Focusing brings in a way of knowing which is holistic and intuitive rather than purely rational and logical. It honors what is fuzzy and not-yet-clear, and it is not instantaneous.

Many years ago, when a friend and I were planning to teach Focusing in a business setting, we were told that business people would never stand for Focusing "because it isn't fast." Whether or not this was actually true, we were sufficiently discouraged to drop our plans. The perception is that the mainstream requires speed.

Similarly, Focusing is not goal- and results-oriented. I remember once doing a Focusing demonstration in front of a naive audience. The focuser was a fellow teacher, and he announced that he would use the session to work on a decision. He brought awareness into his body and sensed into the decision. He found a part of him that didn't want to make the decision yet. As he spent time with this part, it opened up into a deep feeling about many parts of his life. It was a great session. After he opened his eyes and we asked for questions, a woman raised her hand and said, "But when does he make the decision?"

Many people are attracted to Focusing because they recognize that it will support them in changing their lives in profound ways. I suspect that as many people avoid it, when they hear about it, because they recognize that if they listen to the voice of their own truth within, they will have to change their lives. "If I listened to my deeper wisdom, I would have to leave that job, or leave that relationship, or quit that addictive behavior. And I don't want to!" Society supports the slumber of the true self. "Have another drink, another cigarette, another pain pill," it says. When we open up to our inner guide, we don't only *risk* losing society's comfortable supports, we *will* lose them. Our friendships will change. We will awaken. This isn't so easy. And yet there is something inside us – I like to call it *the soul* – which will not rest until this happens.

The fifth reason why Focusing is not better known (yet) is best expressed as the answer which was given at the talk in New York. Janet van Berger, the host of the talk, knew little about Focusing but much about speaking to audiences. When a wide-eyed woman in the first row asked "Why haven't I heard of this before?" and I was about to launch into my reasons, Janet smiled at her and said, "You haven't heard of this *before*, because *now* is the time." For each person who has found Focusing, and any other life-changing way of being, there is a right time. Perhaps we are now verging on the right time for Focusing and the world. May it be so.

Focusing Resources

Focusing Resources works with people wanting to become free of repetitive emotions, self-criticism, and inner war, helping them to be proactive in their own emotional healing and personal growth.

People who seek our services may be struggling with one or more of the following: action blocks, addictions, self-criticism, frustration, longing, dissatisfaction, difficulty with decisions, overwhelming emotion or an inner sense of deadness, life being incomplete, "something" being missing. They may have an inner sense that there is "more" to life, that they are living in a more limited, constricted way than they really need to – but they don't know how to change.

We work with people who want to have a more grounded and open relationship with their own emotional lives, who seek to have a sense of clarity and perspective about the issues in their lives, to trust that what they know is true, to feel confident in the rightness of the next steps they take.

Focusing Resources offers full support to people learning and using the Focusing process in every part of their lives, including people working with particular issues and people who want to learn Focusing to support themselves more generally in their lives, as well as professionals who want the Focusing process to support their work with clients. We offer one-to-one sessions (in Berkeley and on the phone), in-person workshops, phone seminars and classes, books, manuals, CDs and videos, and print and email newsletters.

We also offer support and training to teachers of Focusing, including certification as "Focusing trainer."

We make the full four levels of the Focusing Training Program available in phone seminars or in-person weekend workshops. There are also workshops and classes in releasing blocks to action, decisions, good boundaries, and transforming the inner critic with gentleness. Call for our latest schedule of workshops or consult our website.

Ann Weiser Cornell PhD
    Focusing Resources
    2336 Bonar Street
    Berkeley CA 94702-2019
    510-666-9948
    annweisercornell@mac.com
    www.focusingresources.com

The Bath Focusing Centre

The Bath Focusing Centre helps people who wish to take responsibility for their own inner wellbeing and the further development of their lives. Those who feel constrained, unfulfilled, and confused about where to go next can experience increasing flow and a deepening sense of inner richness, satisfaction, and clarity. Those who are experiencing conflict or stress find that it can become an opportunity for greater self-awareness and development of inner resources. People struggling with self-criticism learn how it can be transformed into a source of strength and support. Those who feel out of touch with their feelings and bodies can learn how to access the power and wisdom held within themselves. Those who feel overwhelmed by their feelings learn how to hear what is trapped in those emotions, safely releasing the vitality held within them. Those whose creativity feels blocked, stifled, off-track learn how to deepen their own unique creative processes, feeling freer and more confident as their creative flow returns. Those who experience difficulty connecting with others learn to express themselves with increasing authenticity and aliveness, becoming more and more able to connect with others from the heart while staying in touch with their own experiencing and needs.

Whether someone has a particular issue that they wish to concentrate on, or if they want to learn Focusing to support themselves more generally in their lives or to enhance their professional abilities, the Bath Focusing Centre offers a complete range of individual sessions and group workshops for beginners through to professional training as a Focusing practitioner or teacher recognized by The British Focusing Teachers Association and/or The Focusing Institute. We also offer specialized workshops focusing on creativity, dreams, action blocks, and self-criticism.

We help people to create an optimal inner environment for holistic, natural change in any area of their lives that needs attention. People have often expressed how surprised they are by how gentle and yet very deep and powerful this work is. The changes that occur spontaneously and naturally come from deep within the person themselves and are always in the direction of greater aliveness.

Barbara McGavin – Director
The Bath Focusing Centre
    46 Chilton Road
    Bath, BA1 6DR
    England
    +44 (0)1225 311062
    bath.focusingcentre@ntlworld.com
    www.focusing.uk.com

The Focusing Institute

The primary resource for Focusers all over the world is The Focusing Institute, the nonprofit organization founded by Eugene Gendlin. The Institute is a supportive matrix whose purpose is to help the human community integrate Focusing into its many ways of living and working and to see to the continued thriving and evolution of Focusing and Focusing teaching.

"We organize what has already been done so that people have access to it, and we make links between people who need to know about each other. We support a thriving philosophical community centered around the Philosophy of the Implicit. We generate continued Focusing research."

Joining as a member is a way to support their work, which includes reaching out on many levels: publicity; archiving resources; and bringing Focusing into schools, medicine, churches, businesses, and other areas. Members receive a quarterly newsletter, *Staying in Focus,* as well as the scholarly journal of Focusing, *The Focusing Folio* (published occasionally). There is a lively annual conference hosted each year by a different international center.

The Focusing Institute is the best source of information about the work of Eugene Gendlin and access to his writings. His rare workshops are offered through The Focusing Institute.

Professional Members, Trainers-in-Training, Trainers, and Coordinators are listed in the annual directory. The Focusing Institute is a nonprofit organization, and all contributions are tax-deductible.

The Focusing Institute
    34 East Lane
    Spring Valley NY 10929
    845-362-5222
    www.focusing.org

Treasure Maps to the Soul

Treasure Maps to the Soul is a process developed out of our own struggle with addictions, depression, self-criticism, action blocks, and unfulfilled desire. It's designed to help people who feel blocked, trapped in an inner struggle that can feel like a war inside, leaving them feeling helpless, frustrated, even despairing about the whole thing. They often think that the problem is that there is something wrong with them – they're too lazy, not good enough, too pushy, self-sabotaging...

People who feel that they have some part of them that they would just like to cut out and get rid of can find, with Treasure Maps to the Soul, that those are the very parts that hold the key to unlocking their unique potential, leading to a resurgence of life flowing within and a greater sense of wholeness.

Treasure Maps to the Soul is a powerful way of transforming any stuck area of life, any inner struggle, any place where energy is bound up in fear, shame, self-criticism, hopelessness, despair. More than just techniques, Treasure Maps to the Soul embodies a philosophy of the radical importance of every part, how even the most critical "critics" and rebellious "rebels" hold vitally important aspects of a person's essence. Our models have helped hundreds of people find their ways through the mazes of their inner world, with a renewed, lighter spirit and deeper sense of self.

We offer three intensive six-day retreats each year, in beautiful parts of the world, for people wishing to experience this process. More than just theory, the workshops give people the opportunity to build the practical skills we call the Powers. People are deeply changed, both by the workshop itself and by the resources they take home. We also offer Treasure Maps to the Soul phone seminars and individual consultations. The best way to find out more is to join our email newsletter at www.focusingresources.com.

Barbara McGavin &
Ann Weiser Cornell
    Treasure Maps to the Soul
    www.focusingresources.com
    www.focusing.uk.com

References

Afford, Peter. 1994. "The Felt Sense Need Not Always Be Physically Felt," *The Focusing Connection*, XI, 1.

Batt, Jane. 1986. "The Fearsome Critic is a Panicking Child," *The Focusing Connection*, III, 3.

Brenner, Helene. 2003. *I Know I'm in There Somewhere*. New York: Gotham Books.

Cornell, Ann Weiser. 1991. "Teaching Focusing with Five Steps and Four Skills," presented at the Second International Conference on Client-Centered and Experiential Psychotherapy, University of Stirling, Scotland. In *Beyond Carl Rogers*, ed. David Brazier. London: Constable & Robinson, 1993.

Cornell, Ann Weiser and Barbara McGavin. 2002. *The Focusing Student's and Companion's Manual, Parts One and Two*. Berkeley, CA: Calluna Press.

Feuerstein, Heinz-Joachim, Dieter Müller, Ann Weiser Cornell, eds. 2000. *Focusing im Prozess, Ein Lesebuch*. Köln, GwG-Verlag.

Flanagan, Kevin. 1998. *Everyday Genius: Focusing on Your Emotional Intelligence*. Dublin: Marino Books.

Friedman, Neil. 2000. *Focusing: Selected Essays, 1974-1999*. Xlibris Corporation. www.xlibris.com

Gendlin, E.T., J. Beebe, J. Cassens, M. Klein & M. Oberlander. 1968. "Focusing ability in psychotherapy, personality and creativity." In J.M. Shlien ed., *Research in psychotherapy*. Vol. III, pp. 217-241. Washington, D.C.: APA.

Gendlin, Eugene. 1984. "The Client's Client," in *Client-Centered Therapy and the Person-Centered Approach*, eds. Levant and Shlien. New York: Praeger.

Gendlin, Eugene. 1986. *Let Your Body Interpret Your Dreams*. Wilmette, IL: Chiron Publications.

Gendlin, Eugene. 1990. "The Small Steps of the Therapy Process: How They Come and How to Help Them Come." In *Client-Centered and Experiential Psychotherapy in the Nineties*, G. Lietaer, J. Rombauts, R. van Balen. Leuven (eds), Belgium: Leuven University Press.

Gendlin, Eugene. No date. *Experiential Psychotherapy*. Draft, distributed by The Focusing Institute.

Gendlin, Eugene. 1996. *Focusing-Oriented Psychotherapy.* New York: The Guilford Press.

Gendlin, Eugene. 1997. *A Process Model.* Distributed by The Focusing Institute. www.focusing.org.

Hart, Judy. 1996. "'It Stinks, Doesn't It?': Ways to Connect without Fixing," *The Focusing Connection,* XIII, 1.

Hinterkopf, Elfie. 1983. "Experiential Focusing: A three-stage training program," *Journal of Humanistic Psychology,* 23.

Kirschner, Ellen. 2003. "When a Friend is Diagnosed with Cancer," *The Focusing Connection,* XX, 2.

Levy, Phil. 1989. "Is the So-Called Critic a Hidden Door to Our Experience?" *The Focusing Connection,* VI, 3.

Lowell, Jane. 1985. "The Critic: A Despairing, Unattended Felt Sense," *The Focusing Connection,* II, 2.

Marten, Shirley. 1987. "And Then the Pain Went Away," *The Focusing Connection,* IV, 5.

McGavin, Barbara. 1995. "Some Thoughts About Why Disidentification in Focusing Does Not Encourage Dissociation." *Focusing News,* III, 4.

McGavin, Barbara. 1996. "Disarming the Critic," *The Focusing Connection,* XIII, 1.

McGavin, Barbara. 1997. "Focusing with Small Physical Ailments," *The Focusing Connection,* XIV, 5.

McGavin, Barbara. 1999. "The Sentient Body: Focusing on the Physical," *The Focusing Folio.*

McGuire, Kathy. 1991. "Cathartic Unfoldings are Not Too Close," *The Focusing Connection,* VIII, 6.

McMahon, Edwin M. and Peter A. Campbell. 1991. *The Focusing Steps.* Kansas City, Missouri: Sheed & Ward.

Miller, Alice. 1981. *The Drama of the Gifted Child (Prisoners of Childhood).* New York: Basic Books.

Miller, Alice. 1983. *For Your Own Good: Hidden Cruelty in Child-rearing and the Roots of Violence.* New York: Farrar, Straus, Giroux.

Müller, Dieter. 1994. "The Critic as Signpost: Changing the Focus from Criticizer to Criticized," *The Focusing Connection,* XI, 6.

Purdy, Ray. 1994. "Does the Critic Exist?" *The Focusing Connection,* XI, 5.

Rogers, Carl. 1980. *A Way of Being.* Boston: Houghton Mifflin.

Rogers, Carl. 1986a. "A Client-Centered/Person-Centered Approach to Therapy," in *Psychotherapist's Casebook: Theory and Technique in Practice,* eds. Kutash and Wolf. Reprinted in *The Carl Rogers Reader.* Boston: Houghton Mifflin, 1989.

Rogers, Carl. 1986b. "Reflection of Feelings," *Person-Centered Review,* vol. 1, no. 4. Reprinted in *The Carl Rogers Reader.* Boston: Houghton Mifflin, 1989.

Rosenberg, Marshall. 2003. *Nonviolent Communication: A Language of Life.* Encinitas, California: Puddledancer Press.

Schwartz, Richard C. 1995. *Internal Family Systems Therapy.* New York: Guilford Press.

Stevenson, Bev. 1998. "A Remarkable Focusing Session with Pain from Severe Physical Damage," *The Focusing Connection,* XV, 3.

Tein, Joseph. 1986. "Focusing with Pain," *The Focusing Connection,* III, 5.

Warner, Margaret. 1991. "Fragile Process." In L. Fusek, ed. *New Directions in Client-Centered Therapy: Practice with Difficult Client Populations* (Monograph Series 1). Chicago: Chicago Counseling and Psychotherapy Center. Available at www.focusingresources.com.

Warner, Margaret. 1998. "A Client-Centered Approach to Therapeutic Work with Dissociated and Fragile Process." In *Foundations of Experiential Theory and Practice: Differential Treatment Approaches,* L. Greenberg, J. Watson, and G. Lietaer (eds). New York: Guilford Press.

Warner, Margaret. 2000. "Client-Centered Therapy at the Difficult Edge: Work with Fragile and Dissociated Process." In *Person-Centered Therapy Today: New Frontiers in Theory and Practice,* Dave Mearns and Brian Thorne, eds. Thousand Oaks, California: Sage.

Welwood, John. 1996. "Reflection and Presence: The Dialectic of Self-Knowledge." In *The Journal of Transpersonal Psychology,* Vol. 28, No. 2. Reprinted in *Toward a Psychology of Awakening,* Boston: Shambala, 2002, page number cited from this edition.

Wiltschko, Johannes. 1995. "Focusing Therapy: Some Basic Statements," *The Focusing Folio,* 14, 3. Available at www.focusing.org.

Back issues of The Focusing Connection *may be ordered at www.focusingresources.com/materials/tfcbackissues.html.*

ANN WEISER CORNELL learned Focusing in 1972 from Eugene Gendlin, the originator of the process, and has been teaching it since 1980. In 1972 she was also a graduate student in Linguistics at the University of Chicago on a Woodrow Wilson Fellowship from the National Science Foundation. She earned her Ph.D. in Linguistics there in 1975, and taught Linguistics at Purdue University from 1975 to 1977. She taught Focusing with Eugene Gendlin from 1980 to 1983, and went on to become the first fulltime Focusing teacher.

Today she is internationally known as one of the leading theoreticians, teachers, and innovators of Focusing, as well as the primary person combining linguistics and Focusing. Her previous book, *The Power of Focusing* (New Harbinger, 1996), has been translated into Japanese, Spanish, Dutch, Hebrew, German, Dari, and Italian. Ann has taught Focusing and advanced Focusing topics in eighteen countries on five continents.

Ann Weiser Cornell and BARBARA McGAVIN are the co-creators of Treasure Maps to the Soul, a process for using Focusing with areas of difficult inner conflict, as well as of Inner Relationship Focusing. They are the co-authors of *The Focusing Student's and Companion's Manual, Parts One and Two.* They are also very good friends.

www.focusingresources.com